THE POWER OF TANTRA

Hugh B. Urban is Professor of Comparative Studies at Ohio State University. One of the leading Western scholars of Tantric religion, Professor Urban is the author of several books which include *Magia Sexualis: Sex, Magic and Liberation in Modern Western Esotericism* (2006), *Tantra: Sex, Secrecy, Politics and Power in the Study of Religion* (2003), and *Songs of Ecstasy: Tantric and Devotional Songs from Bengal* (2001).

"*The Power of Tantra* is a major scholarly treatment of a much misconstrued esoteric tradition and a well-written and illustrated guide to a dimension of Hinduism that deserves the careful research Hugh B. Urban has given it. An impressive achievement."

– Paul B. Courtright, Professor of Religion and Asian Studies, Emory University

"Building on his extraordinary knowledge of the Sanskrit, Bangla, and Assamese sources, Hugh B. Urban flies straight into the heart of the raging controversy over the sex and violence of Tantra: Is this an Orientalist fantasy, or a Hindu nightmare, or a profound religious phenomenon? Drawing richly upon previously untapped texts and new fieldwork, Urban boldly and creatively takes the arguments about Tantra in an entirely new direction, revealing aspects of the worship of the goddess that have deep meaning for Hindus and great potential power even for the heirs of Orientalism."

– Wendy Doniger, Mircea Eliade Distinguished Service Professor of the History of Religions, University of Chicago

"Once again, Hugh B. Urban has given us a sophisticated, reflexive, mind-bending study of a specific set of Tantric traditions. In the process, we are taken down what he aptly calls "a path of desire and power" whose paradoxical energies center on the goddess, flow through the human body and its fluids, the social order, and the body politic (all at once), are unleashed through esoteric ritual practices, experienced as a source of supernatural powers, and put in the service of kingship, political rule, even ultra-modern forms of a new embodied spirituality. Writing against and beyond all the old East–West dualisms, tired anti-intellectualisms, and easy idealizations, Urban has become one of our most able, artful, and careful guides."

– Jeffrey J. Kripal, J. Newton Rayzor Professor of Religious Studies, Rice University

LIBRARY OF MODERN RELIGION

Series ISBN: 978 1 84885 244 0

See www.ibtauris.com/LMR for a full list of titles

1. *Returning to Religion: Why a Secular Age is Haunted by Faith*
Jonathan Benthall
978 1 84511 718 4

2. *Knowing the Unknowable: Science and Religions on God and the Universe*
John Bowker (ed.)
978 1 84511 757 3

3. *Sufism Today: Heritage and Tradition in the Global Community*
Catharina Raudvere and Leif Stenberg (eds)
978 1 84511 762 7

4. *Apocalyptic Islam and Iranian Shi'ism*
Abbas Amanat
978 1 84511 124 3

5. *Global Pentecostatism: Encounters with Other Religious Traditions*
David Westerlund (ed.)
978 1 84511 877 8

6. *Dying for Faith: Religiously Motivated Violence in the Contemporary World*
Madawi Al-Rasheed and Marat Shterin (eds)
978 1 84511 686 6

7. *The Hindu Erotic: Exploring Hinduism and Sexuality*
David Smith
978 1 84511 361 2

8. *The Power of Tantra: Religion, Sexuality and the Politics of South Asian Studies*
Hugh B. Urban
978 1 84511 873 0

9. *Jewish Identities in Iran: Resistance and Conversion to Islam and the Eaha'i Faith*
Mehrdad Amanat
978 1 84511 891 4

10. *Islamic Reform and Conservatism: Al-Azhar and the Evolution of Modern Sunni Islam*
Indira Falk Gesink
978 1 84511 936 2

11. *Muslim Women's Rituals: Authority and Gender in the Islamic World*
Catharina Raudvere and Margaret Rausch
978 1 84511 643 9

12. *Lonesome: The Spiritual Meanings of American Solitude*
Kevin Lewis
978 1 84885 075 0

13. *A Short History of Atheism*
Gavin Hyman
978 1 84885 136 8

THE POWER OF TANTRA

Religion, Sexuality, and the Politics of South Asian Studies

HUGH B. URBAN

I.B.TAURIS
LONDON · NEW YORK

Published in 2010 by I.B.Tauris & Co Ltd
6 Salem Road, London W2 4BU
175 Fifth Avenue, New York NY 10010
www.ibtauris.com

Library of Modern Religion, Vol. 8

ISBN: 978 1 84511 873 0 (HB)
ISBN: 978 1 84511 874 7 (PB)

A full CIP record for this book is available from the British Library
A full CIP record is available from the Library of Congress

Library of Congress Catalog Card Number: available

Typeset in Plantin Light by Aptara Inc., New Delhi

For Nancy

CONTENTS

List of Illustrations		ix
Acknowledgments		xi
Introduction	Tantra and the Politics of South Asian Studies	1
Chapter One	Matrix of Power: The Śākta Pīṭhas and the Sacred Landscape of Tantra	31
Chapter Two	Blood for the Goddess: Animal Sacrifice and Divine Menstruation	51
Chapter Three	Goddess of Power: Tantra, Kingship, and Sacrifice in South Asian History	73
Chapter Four	The Sacrifice of Desire: Sexual Rites and the Secret Sacrifice	99
Chapter Five	What About the Woman? Gender Politics and the Interpretation of Women in Tantra	125
Chapter Six	The Power of God in a Dark Valley: Reform, Colonialism, and the Decline of Tantra in South Asia	147
Chapter Seven	The Power of the Goddess in a Postcolonial Age: Transformations of Tantra in the twentieth and twenty-first Centuries	165

LIST OF ILLUSTRATIONS

Plates between pages 116 and 117

1. Kāmākhyā temple today
2. Possible Yoginī, Kāmākhyā temple grounds, ca. twelfth century
3. Bala Bhairavī, ruins behind the Bhairavī temple, ca. twelfth century
4. Siddha with female consort or disciple, Assam State Museum, twelfth to fourteenth centuries
5. Contemporary popular poster of Kāmākhyā
6. Kāmeśvarī, Kāmākhyā temple
7. Cāmuṇḍā, Kāmākhyā temple ruins, ca. twelfth century
8. Female figure with severed head, Sixty-Four Yoginī temple, Hirapur, Orissa
9. Menstruating figure, Kāmākhyā temple outer wall
10. Śākta Tantric guru, Kāmākhyā temple
11. Bhairava, Deopahar ruins, central Assam, tenth to eleventh centuries
12. Sacrificial post for goats, pigeons, and fish, Kāmākhyā temple
13. Sacrificial post for buffaloes, Kāmākhyā temple
14. Mahiṣamardinī with severed head, Kalipahara, Guwahati, tenth to eleventh centuries

15. Buffalo skull, Ugratārā temple, Guwahati

16. Severed buffalo head, Kāmākhyā temple

17. Mask worn by sacrificial victims, Jaintia Durgā temple

18. Śākta priest ladling offerings into the fire, Tārāpīṭh, West Bengal

19. Couple in *viparīta-rati*, Madana Kāmadeva temple, Assam, tenth to twelfth centuries

20. Female Śākta, Kāmākhyā temple

21. Female Śaivite, Kāmākhyā temple

22. Cover image for Kāmākhyā Tantrasāra

23. Shree Maa of Kāmākhyā

24. The "White Sadhu" and Shree Maa

Map

The four early Śākta Pīṭhas *and other major goddess temples in South Asia* 33

ACKNOWLEDGMENTS

Research for this book was conducted in Assam, Bengal, Orissa, Tripura, and Meghalaya between 2000 and 2008 based on generous funding from the Fulbright Foundation, the National Endowment for the Humanities and the American Academy of Religion. The many individuals and groups who deserve thanks here include: Maitreyee Bora, Paul Courtright, Patricia Dold, Wendy Doniger, Susan Huntington, Padma Kaimal, the Kāmākhyā Temple Trust Board, Jeffrey Kripal, Bruce Lincoln, Rob Linrothe, Rajiv Malhotra, Kimberly Masteller, Prem Saran, Shree Maa of Kāmākhyā, Swami Satyananda Saraswati, David Gordon White, and Alex Wright.

INTRODUCTION: TANTRA AND THE POLITICS OF SOUTH ASIAN STUDIES

> She is supreme, the primordial power whose nature is eternal, incomparable bliss, the source of all that moves or is motionless...
>
> —Puṇyānandanātha, *Kāmakalāvilāsa* (KKV 2)

> The omnipresence of power... Power is everywhere; not because it embraces everything, but because it comes from everywhere.
>
> —Michel Foucault, *The History of Sexuality*[1]

Surely no aspect of South Asian religion has generated more confusion, controversy, or misunderstanding than the complex body of texts and traditions known as Tantra. Since their first encounter with Indian religions, Western audiences have been at once fascinated and horrified, by turns shocked and titillated by this seemingly most exotic of all aspects of the exotic Orient. For European colonizers, Orientalist scholars, and Christian missionaries of the Victorian era, Tantra was generally seen as the worst, most degenerate and depraved example of all the worst tendencies in the "Indian mind," a pathological mixture of religion and sensuality that had led to the decline of modern Hinduism. Yet for most contemporary New Age and popular writers, conversely, Tantra is now celebrated as a much-needed affirmation of physical pleasure and sexuality, as a "yoga of sex" or "cult of ecstasy" that might counteract the hypocritical prudery of the Christian West.[2]

In the last decade, Tantra has also come to the center of a much larger debate over the politics of scholarship and the interpretation of South Asian traditions. Indeed, a number of authors—and particularly

American scholars such as Jeffrey Kripal, David Gordon White, and Sarah Caldwell—have received fierce criticism from some Hindu readers for their allegedly hypersexual and neo-Orientalist interpretation of Hinduism in general and Tantra in particular. Wendy Doniger had an egg thrown at her head during a public lecture, while Paul Courtright received death threats for his interpretation of Hindu traditions, which some interpreted as a new form of American-style cultural imperialism.[3] In 2007, a group of Indian critics published a 500-page volume entitled *Invading the Sacred*, which argues that Western (especially American) scholars have perpetuated a form of neo-Orientalism that continues to exoticize and eroticize Tantra for a Western consumer audience.[4] In this sense, the study of Tantra raises some of the most profound ethical and political questions at the heart of all cross-cultural understanding, above all, in our increasingly violent and contested global context.

In my previous book, *Tantra: Sex, Secrecy, Politics and Power in the Study of Religion*, I examined the representations and misrepresentations of this complex tradition in both European and Indian discourse over the last several hundred years, from British colonial authorities and Hindu nationalists down to contemporary New Age enthusiasts.[5] The modern imagining of Tantra, I argued, has been a key part of the larger imagining of India and the "exotic Orient" as a whole, which has been conceived as an irrational, erotic, and feminized opposite of the rational, scientific, progressive, and masculine "West." In place of this exoticized phantasm of Tantra, I argued that we need to re-imagine Tantra as an embodied and historical category, that is, as a category that is the mutual construction of *both* Asian and Western imaginations, and one that is very much rooted in material circumstance, social context, political conflict, and historical change.

The Power of Tantra undertakes this more "embodied" and historical approach to Tantra by focusing on one of the oldest, most important, and yet little-studied Tantric traditions: namely, the goddess Kāmākhyā and the worship at her temple in Assam, northeast India. Since at least the eighth century, Kāmākhyā temple has been revered as one of the oldest "seats of power" (*śākta pīṭhas*) or sites of Tantric worship in South Asia, as the "birthplace," "principal center," or "headquarters" Tantra,[6] and indeed as the locus of the goddess' own *yoni* or sexual organ. As the goddess of desire (*kāma*), Kāmākhyā herself is believed to menstruate once a year, the occasion of her most important festival, which is said to give life to the earth and power to her devotees. It is in this sense that Kāmākhyā can be called the "matrix of power," as the generative mother or womb (Sanskrit *mātṛ*, etymologically related to Latin *mater* and *matrix*) that gives birth to the universe and the divine energy that flows through all its elements (*mātras*). Kāmākhyā temple has for centuries been infamous as a center of Tantric practice in its most extreme forms, including both the regular offering of animal (and, allegedly, human) sacrifice and esoteric sexual rites.

So the question that the case of Kāmākhyā presents is the following: if we have deconstructed the idea that Tantra is primarily an exotic tradition of sex and violence, what do we do with a tradition that *does* seem to contain many erotic and violent themes, such as divine menstruation, sexual rites, and blood sacrifice? What do we do with a tradition that is considered "exotic" even by many Indian audiences? How do we engage in a sophisticated encounter with these traditions in a way that does not simply continue a kind of neo-Orientalist fascination with the exotic Other or promote a new form of cultural imperialism?

Far from a source of postcolonial angst or neo-imperial despair, I argue, a serious encounter with the Tantric traditions of Assam can help transform the way we understand both the rich history of South Asia and our own ambivalent position in the twenty-first-century global order. Borrowing some theoretical insights from Gilles Deleuze and Michel Foucault, I hope to reframe our understanding of Tantra by rethinking basic Tantric concepts such as desire (*kāma*) and power (*śakti*). More important, however, I will also use Indian concepts like *kāma* and *śakti* to *critique and reframe our own taken-for-granted understandings of desire and power.* Most modern literature on Tantra, both popular and scholarly, continues to define and discuss Tantra primarily in terms of sex. What I will argue, however, is that the Indian concept of *kāma* contains a vast range of meanings that include, but far exceed, the level of sexual desire that has so long preoccupied modern observers. So too, the concept of *śakti* contains yet far transcends mere political power, also embracing the vital energy that pervades the cosmos, social order, and human body alike.

Rather than an exotic cult of ecstasy, Tantra thus turns out to be a far more complex, dynamic—and more interesting—tradition that has played very different roles in different periods of Indian history. This book traces the complex history of one particular tradition, Śākta Tantra in Assam, as a microcosmic lens through which to view the changing role of Tantra in South Asia. As a "path of power," centered on the divine *śakti* of the goddess, Tantra has in some historical periods been closely tied to kingship, blood sacrifice, and war. Yet as a path of desire, Tantra has also in other cases involved transgressive rites such as the consumption of male and female sexual fluids as a source of esoteric power. And in still other periods, Tantra was attacked by Hindu reformers and Christian missionaries alike as a dangerous path of black magic for the fulfillment of worldly desires. Finally, in the twenty-first century, the power of the goddess has been globalized for a new age of Tantra. Indeed, we now see internationally famous gurus like Shree Maa of Kāmākhyā who have spread the worship of the goddess from Assam to California, while transforming this once-esoteric tradition into a devotional path for a global audience of spiritual consumers.

In sum, the "power of Tantra" is hardly either singular or static, but has in fact been reconfigured in different periods in response to a wide range of shifting historical forces and social-political influences. And it continues to challenge us today, forcing us to rethink the very nature of cross-cultural understanding and our own role in these complex "matrices of power."

Beyond the "extreme Orient": Tantra and imperialism, old and new

As most modern scholars agree, the term Tantra (or "Tantrism" or "Tantricism") does not refer to a singular, monolithic, or neatly defined category. Rather, this is an extremely messy and ambiguous term used to refer to a "bewilderingly diverse array of esoteric precepts and practices attested across much of South, Inner and East Asia from the sixth century down to the present day."[7] Indeed, it covers a huge range of diverse texts, traditions, and ritual practices that spread throughout the Hindu, Buddhist, and Jain communities of India, China, Japan Tibet, Pakistan, Mongolia, and parts of Southeast Asia; and it is reflected in a wide variety of different sects and schools, such as the Pāñcarātra, Sahajiyā, Pāśupata, Kāpālika, Kaula, Krama, Trika, Śākta, Nātha Siddha, Śrīvidyā and Paścimāmnāya. As André Padoux and others have argued, the abstract category of "Tantrism"—as singular, unified "ism"—is itself a relatively recent invention, and in large part the creation of Orientalist scholars and Hindu reformers writing in the nineteenth century:

> Tantrism is a protean phenomenon, so complex and elusive that it is practically impossible to define it... Tantrism is, to a large extent, a "category of discourse in the West," and not, strictly speaking, an Indian one. As a category, Tantrism is not... an entity in the minds of those inside. It is a category in the minds of observers from outside... The term Tantrism was coined by Western Indologists of the latter part of the nineteenth century whose knowledge of India was limited... Neither in traditional India nor in Sanskrit texts is there a term for Tantrism; no description or definition of such a category is to be found anywhere.[8]

Derived from the root *tan,* "to spread" or "to stretch," the term *tantra* has been used since Vedic times in a huge variety of different ways, signifying everything from a loom or weaving machine, to a system of philosophy, to a drug or remedy.[9] For example, in texts like the *Kālikā Purāṇa*—the most important Assamese text from the tenth to the eleventh centuries that I will use extensively in this book—*tantra* has a very mundane meaning: typically it means any rite or form of worship of a particular deity, such as the worship of the goddess Kāmākhyā or Vaiṣṇavī (*kāmākhyā tantra, vaiṣṇavī tantra,* and so on).[10] Most commonly *tantra* simply means a kind of text—but one that may or may not contain the sort of tantalizing and titillating things we normally associate with "Tantra" today.

In the course of my own research in northeast India between 2000 and 2008, I interviewed hundreds of priests, devotees, gurus, and holy men and received more or less as many different answers to the question "what is Tantra?" For example, at Kāmākhyā temple in 2004, I interviewed two priests and asked for their definitions of "Tantra." The first priest laughed and tried to explain how difficult it is to define such a complex term, but then said: "Tantra is essentially *mantra*—the power of sound and vibration that we use to worship the goddess." Immediately, however, the second priest interrupted, saying, "No, no. That's not Tantra. Tantra comes from *tan* and *man*; *tan* means the 'body' and *man* means the 'mind'. So Tantra is mind and body together, the whole human being in spiritual practice." Finally, overhearing our conversation, another (non-Tantric) *sādhu* from Tripura came over and decided to offer his opinion on the subject. Like many non-Tantric *sādhus*, he had a very low opinion of Tantra, which he dismissed as a very bad, unclean (*khārāp, aśuddha*) thing, mostly associated with phony magic tricks to dupe the ignorant. To illustrate his point, he pulled something out of his bag that looked like dried grass. He placed a few blades of the stuff in his mouth and said, "I'll show you 'Tantra.' " Once the blades were wet from his saliva, they began to wave and wiggle around. He smiled and laughed gleefully "*This* is your 'Tantra,'" he snickered, meaning that Tantra is little more than silly mumbo-jumbo and trickery.[11] In sum, the meanings of Tantra, even at a single site like Kāmākhyā, are not only remarkably varied but often contradictory and reflective of a complex series of historical transformations.

In twenty-first-century America and Europe, however, the meaning of Tantra is usually much more straightforward. If we browse the shelves of any major book store or search through the thousands of offerings on Amazon.com, we find that Tantra in popular culture is defined by one thing alone: really, really good sex. Thus we now find thousands of books, DVDs, and videos with titles such as *Tantra between the Sheets: the Easy and Fun Guide to Mind-Blowing Sex* or *Tantra for Erotic Empowerment*; *The Key to Enriching your Sexual Life*, all of which define Tantra primarily as the means to fabulous sex, extended orgasms, and more fulfilling relationships. Indeed, the more erotically challenged among us may even consult the *Complete Idiot's Guide to Tantric Sex*, which promises to teach the reader to "make sex juicy with magic and play" and "please your partner as never before." The *Idiot's* version of Tantra is explicitly advertised as a uniquely "American" spiritual practice, perfectly suited to our highly individualistic, materialistic, and quick-fix lifestyle.

> Although Tantric practices were developed in the Eastern part of the world, they are particularly applicable and appealing to the Western world today . . . Tantric sex promises simple steps and instant results, which are appealing to Westerners who are conditioned to "instant" lifestyles (instant coffee, fast food, instant gratification) . . . Tantric sex starts with individual practice . . . This is consistent with the individualism that is the basis of Western society . . . Tantric sex encourages heightening the senses through beautiful clothing, attractive surroundings and stimulation of all the senses, which is consistent with Western obsessions with worldly pleasures.[12]

But how exactly did this complex and heterogeneous body of South Asian traditions come to be reduced to the singular goal of enhanced sexual pleasure?

Orientalist views of Tantra and the politics of empire

If "Tantra" in its original usage had a wide array of different meanings, it was primarily during the nineteenth century that it began to be congealed into a sort of homogenous, unified "ism"—and one primarily identified with sex. However, the "ism" of Tantrism was by no means simply a kind of Orientalist fabrication. Rather, it was the far more complex product of real South Asian traditions that were interpreted, reinterpreted, and misinterpreted by Orientalist scholars, Christian missionaries, and Hindu reformers alike. As such, the modern imagining of Tantra was closely tied to both the politics of empire and the politics of emergent Hindu nationalism in the nineteenth century.[13]

As Ronald Inden has shown, Orientalist discourse on India was closely linked to the larger British imperial project. Throughout nineteenth and early twentieth-century Orientalist literature, the "Indian mind" was consistently described as "feminine," dream-like, irrational, and disorderly, and so "an inferior substitute for the West's masculine, world-ordering rationality." Though "weak" and effete, this exotic tradition was also imagined as dangerous and beguiling to European rationality: "Hinduism is a *female* presence, who is able, through her very amorphousness and absorptive powers, to boggle and perhaps even threaten Western rationality . . . European reason penetrates the womb of Indian unreason, but always at the risk of being engulfed by her."[14] In sum, India was imagined as the quintessential "other" or "shadow" of Europe, a primitive, uncivilized, irrational, and effeminate realm set in contrast to the modern, civilized, rational, and masculine West.[15]

And Tantra, above all, was repeatedly and consistently singled out as the epitome of this effeminate, irrational, and dangerous world, as the "extreme Orient" or "India's darkest heart." Throughout nineteenth-century Orientalist literature, Tantra was described in the most vivid language as "nonsensical extravagance and crude gesticulation" (H.H. Wilson), "Hinduism arrived at its last and worst stage of medieval development" (Sir Monier-Williams) and "black art of the crudest and filthiest kind" in which a "veritable devil's mass is purveyed in various forms" (D.L Barnett).[16] Imagined as the darkest, most debauched aspect of the irrational Indian mind itself, Tantra thus offered perhaps the clearest evidence of the need for rational, orderly imperial rule.[17]

The womb of Tantra: Assam as the original heartland of Tantra

As the eastern-most corner of India, Assam was frequently identified as both the most exotic, dangerous, effeminate region of the subcontinent and as the original homeland of the perverse rites of Tantra. A mountainous, heavily forested region with tremendous diversity of wildlife and among the heaviest rainfall in Asia, Assam has long been imagined as the most extreme aspect of the "extreme Orient" itself. The people of the region are no less diverse, representing a complex mixture of ethnic and linguistic groups that include Mon-Khmer, Tibeto-Burman, Indo-Aryan, and Tai-Shan. Today, the state of Assam alone contains twenty-three recognized tribal groups, including the Bodo Kacharis, Rabhas, Lalungs, Mikirs, Khasis, Jaintias, Garos, and Nagas, each with their own unique cultures, dialects, and religious histories.[18]

The identification of Assam as the heartland of Tantra long predated European Orientalist discourse. Throughout Indian, Tibetan, and Muslim accounts alike, Assam was long quite infamous as a land of black magic, tribal superstition, and human sacrifice. According to a Tibetan author of the seventeenth century, "there are so many witches (*ḍākinīs*) and various kinds of demons and devils there that even a person who has fully mastered the Tantras can hardly stay there."[19] In medieval Muslim literature, too, Assam was said to be "notorious for magic and sorcery," for human sacrifice and sexual rites.[20] This association of Assam with the most extreme forms of magic and above all sexual rites continues in the Indian imagination to this day. For example, the popular Bengali novelist, Samaresh Basu, published a widely read and highly imaginative account of a secret sexual rite that he allegedly witnessed in Assam in 1981. As he described the intense love-play of the devotees, he had never seen anything so shocking and had no idea that sex could be quite so exciting: "The whole thing seemed to me so incredible that I experienced none of the normal reactions that an individual would feel when he or she saw anyone making love, though they were masters of the myriads of techniques of lovemaking."[21]

But if Indian authors saw Assam as an exotic and strange land, British colonial authors and missionaries saw this region as nothing less than the most remote, dangerous, and extreme corner of the extreme Orient itself. As Sir Charles Eliot put it in 1921, these are lands of "barbarous and immoral worship," whose "outward signs are repulsive" and "inner meaning strange."[22] Likewise, as Sir Edward

Albert Gait wrote in his classic account of Assam, "the whole country is famed . . . as a land of magic and witchcraft"[23] and its people characterized by their femininity, sensuality, and "tendency towards physical and moral deterioration. Any race that had been long resident there . . . would gradually become soft and luxurious."[24] Finally, Christian missionaries such as J.H. Lorain concluded that the religion of Assam is not just a form of sensual worship with blood sacrifice and liquor, but nothing less than "a revelation from the Evil One."[25]

But above all, Assam has long been regarded by both Indian and European authors as the original home of Tantra. As the locus of the goddess' sexual organ, as the very "embodiment of desire" (Kāmarūpa), and as the home of the supreme "goddess of desire" (Kāmākhyā), Assam has been frequently cited as "the principal centre" and even the "birthplace" of Tantra.[26] As H.H. Wilson put it in 1840, Assam is "the source from which the Tantric corruption of the religion of the Vedas and Purāṇas proceeded."[27] As we will see below, such a land of strange sexual rites, human sacrifice, and tribal religion seemed to present the clearest evidence (and most convenient excuse) for the need for strong imperial rule in the subcontinent.[28]

In fact, despite these disparaging and often outlandish Orientalist views, Assam *does* appear to have been one of the oldest and most important early sites for the development of Tantra in South Asia. Known in ancient times as Prāgjyotiṣapura ("the city of eastern lights") and Kāmarūpa ("the form of desire"), Assam was widely regarded as one of the oldest seats of power and the site at which some of the earliest and most influential Tantric texts were revealed. As D.C. Sircar notes, "the Kāmarūpa Pīṭha became unrivalled as a center of Tantric culture by absorbing the popularity of the other Yoni *tīrthas* of ancient India at a fairly early date."[29] In sum, as the twentieth century's greatest historian of religion, Mircea Eliade, put it, "Assam (= Kāmarūpa) was the tantric country *par excellence*."[30]

Yet remarkably, despite its obvious importance for the early development of Tantra and goddess worship in South Asia, there is very little scholarship on Kāmākhyā or Śākta Tantra in Assam.[31] There are a few notable exceptions, such as Loriliai Biernacki's *Renowned Goddess of Desire*, which, however, focuses on a small number of late medieval texts from northeast India and does not examine either the ancient or the contemporary forms of Tantra in Assam.[32]

For the most part, both Indian and Western scholarship has frequently dismissed the Assamese tradition as a kind of thin veneer of

Hinduism pasted clumsily over a deeper substratum of tribal superstition and magic.[33] And it is true that the form of Tantra that we find in Assam is very different from the elite, highly philosophical, and *brāhmaṇic* Tantra of traditions like Kashmir Śaivism or South Indian Śrīvidyā. In contrast to the sophisticated philosophical discourses of Abhinavagupta or Bhaskararāya, the Assamese Tantric tradition is heavily infused with non-Hindu and often highly un-Vedic elements drawn from the many indigenous religions of the northeast. And yet, as we will see in the chapters that follow, the Assamese tradition is by no means a simple veneer of Hinduism slapped onto a deeper tribal substratum. Instead, it is the result of a far more complex *negotiation* between the many indigenous traditions of the northeast and the Sanskritic, *brāhmaṇic* traditions coming from north India that resulted in what is among the oldest and most powerful forms of Tantra in South Asia.

In my attempt to engage in a more embodied, historical, and culturally contextualized study of Tantra, I will use a wide range of textual, archeological, and ethnographic materials from roughly the eighth century to the present. These include: sculptural and architectural evidence from ancient Assam; Sanskrit texts from Assam and Cooch Behar ranging from the *Kālikā Purāṇa* and *Kaulajñāna Nirṇaya* (tenth to eleventh centuries) to the *Kāmākhyā Tantra, Yoni Tantra,* and *Yoginī Tantra* (sixteenth to seventeenth centuries); historical texts (*burañjīs*) from medieval Assam; modern popular literature in Assamese and Bangla; British colonial and American missionary writings; and interviews with contemporary Śākta gurus and devotees.[34] Finally, I will also include a serious reflection on contemporary theoretical approaches to desire and power, such as the widely influential work of Deleuze and Foucault. Here I will suggest that a reflection on Tantric concepts of *kāma* and *śakti* can not only help us rethink current understandings of desire and power, but also help imagine a kind of embodied spirituality, an approach to religion that is rooted very much "in the flesh."

From Pax Britannica to Pax Americana: Empire, American style?

If much of the nineteenth-century literature on Tantra was often closely tied to the project of British imperialism, we might well ask what sorts of political implications twenty-first-century literature on Tantra might have? After all, the clear successor to the British as the world's dominant power is the USA, with economic, cultural, and military might that far surpasses its imperial predecessors. As Niall Ferguson asks in *Colossus: The Price of America's Empire*, "If the British Empire was America's precursor as the global hegemon, might not the United States be Britain's successor as an Anglophone empire?"[35] A decade ago, Charles Maier notes, the very concept of American empire aroused "righteous indignation" because the USA was "an empire that dared not speak its name. But these days . . . the bashfulness has ended."[36] Today, both liberal and conservative commentators alike acknowledge that "not since Rome claimed both imperial and spiritual precedence has a single political entity managed to achieve such a double preeminence."[37]

Until relatively recently, the USA has not been a direct or explicit sort of imperial power, in the sense that Great Britain had been, but rather an "indirect" or "informal" empire, working more through tremendous cultural and economic influence than direct military intervention. As Anne McClintock comments in *Imperial Leather*,

> Since the 1940s, the U.S.' imperialism-without-colonies has taken a number of distinct forms (military, political, economic and cultural). Some concealed, some half-concealed. The power of U.S. finance capital and huge multinational corporations to command the flows of capital, research, consumer goods and media information around the world can exert a coercive power as great as any colonial gunboat.[38]

With the preemptive invasion of Iraq in 2003, however, the USA seems to have opted for the more old-fashioned, direct sort of imperial conquest and aggressive pursuit of valued resources.[39]

So if America is today the world's dominant empire (even if indirectly), one might justifiably wonder: If nineteenth-century Orientalist scholarship on Tantra went hand in hand with the expansion of British imperial power, what are the political implications of contemporary American scholarship on Tantra? What is its relation to the current imperial formation? As Sheldon Pollock asks,

> A history of Indology, extracolonial no less than colonial, that finds it to be enmeshed in power from its beginnings, and an analysis of the object of Indology . . . as an indigenous form of knowledge production equally saturated with domination, have important implications. We

are forced to ask ourselves whether the Indology we ourselves practice continues its past role?[40]

Invading the sacred? Critiques of American representations of Tantra

Over the last decade, a number of Indian critics have leveled precisely this charge against American scholarship on South Asia. The best-known case is Jeffrey J. Kripal's groundbreaking but controversial book *Kālī's Child* (1995), a study of the life and mystical experiences of the Indian saint and national hero, Shri Ramakrishna. Kripal's two most controversial arguments were (a) that Ramakrishna is best understood not as a spokesman of abstract, monist, Vedānta philosophy, as the later tradition had portrayed him, but rather as a *tāntrika* whose worldview is profoundly shaped by Śākta Tantra; and (b) that Ramakrishna's life and mystical experiences reveal homoerotic tendencies that neither the saint nor the tradition could accept and therefore concealed.[41]

Not surprisingly, many Indian readers (and many who had never read the book but simply heard about its scandalous contents) took issue with Kripal's arguments. And many asked whether this was not a new form of cultural imperialism or "colonialism updated," yet another example of foreign scholars pillaging the traditions of India's sacred heritage in order to titillate an audience of Western consumers.[42] As Narasingha Sil put it, this is but the latest example of American authors "McDonaldizing" the values of other cultures, an agenda that is "parallel to the political and economic evangelization of the world in the 'mantra' of free market and democracy."[43]

Among the most outspoken critics is Rajiv Malhotra, an entrepreneur and activist living in New Jersey, who founded an organization called the Infinity Foundation. According to its mission statement, the Foundation is dedicated to "upgrade the quality of understanding of Indian civilization in the American media and educational system."[44] In Malhotra's eyes, Kripal's book is only one symptom of a much larger disorder in the American academic system and the study of India—what he calls the "Wendy's Child Syndrome," meaning a disorder that has been transmitted by Indologists like Wendy Doniger through her many students now situated throughout the academy. Smitten by this syndrome, American scholars have continued an imperialist agenda by portraying Indian religions as sexual, exotic, and extreme: "Under

Western control, Hinduism Studies has produced ridiculous caricatures that could easily be turned into a Bollywood movie." In Malhotra's opinion, Western scholars have transformed great saints like Ramakrishna into "child molesters," while the Hindu goddess is imagined to be "a sex maniac with a variety of pathological conditions," and essentially "the entire Hindu society needs to be psychoanalyzed in terms of sexual deviance."[45] As Malhotra explained to me in an interview in 2008, all of this is evidence that colonial images from the British era still linger on in American representations. India is still seen as a wild, dangerous frontier, and Hindus are seen as either "noble savages" when they fit Western stereotypes or "dangerous savages" when they challenge those representations.[46]

Malhotra and others are particularly critical of the American study of Tantra, which, in their opinion, has been consistently reduced to its sexual aspects with little regard for its deeper spiritual content. Some of Malhotra's most intense critiques have been directed at another of "Wendy's children," David Gordon White, and his 2003 book, *Kiss of the Yoginī*. Among other things, White argues that the earliest forms of Tantra centered on the oral consumption of sexual fluids, and it was only later that this "hard core" form of Tantra was sublimated and transformed into the more elite philosophical traditions such as the Kashmir Śaivite school. In the eyes of Malhotra, however, White has simply missed the deeper religious significance of Hindu Tantra and reduced the tradition to mere "decadent sexuality, without spiritual purpose."[47]

Malhotra's critique generated something of a firestorm, not only among academics but in the larger Hindu diasporic community. In 2007, a group of Indian writers compiled the volume *Invading the Sacred*, which argues that American scholarship on Hinduism is in fact "the hallmark of a new imperial structure."[48] American scholarship, they argue, denies Indians any standing in the representation of their own culture and produces "fast-food like publications" that portray Indian culture as a "series of abuses, such as caste, sati, dowry, murders, religious conflicts, instability, immorality, grotesque desires, etc."[49] And American studies of Tantra, by focusing "exclusively on the sexual meaning"[50] of the tradition, are seen as the epitome of this neo-imperialist trend.

While the critiques leveled by Malhotra and others have been generally civil, even if heated, the debate has also spilled over into more violent confrontations. Not only did Doniger have an egg thrown at her head during a lecture, but Paul Courtright received a variety of personal threats for suggesting that one could do a Freudian interpretation of the god Ganeśa. According to one critic, Courtright "should be tortured alive and burned to ashes."[51] James Laine's book, *Shivaji: Hindu King in Islamic India* was not only banned in India, but one of his collaborators was assaulted by Hindu extremists, and the library in Pune where he did research was seriously vandalized.[52] Clearly, these "academic" debates strike at much deeper tensions at the very heart of religious and national identity in the postcolonial context. Indeed, they raise central questions about the very nature of cross-cultural understanding amidst an increasingly contested, often violent global order.

A "recovering Orientalist's" approach to Tantra

Not surprisingly, American scholars have responded with forceful and intelligent critiques of their own. Kripal, for example, has written extensively and quite thoughtfully in response to his critics. While he acknowledges the injustices of colonialism and its legacy in the postcolonial context, he argues that his critics have seriously misread and distorted his genuine attempt to reveal the complex religious life and Tantric world of Ramakrishna. At the same time, they threaten to impose a kind of "ideological censorship" that is both fundamentally at odds with the spirit of academic inquiry and a suppression of India's rich religious history.[53] Similarly, Paul Courtright has noted that it is not just American scholars but also their critics who have political interests—in many cases, the interests of "well-financed and organized groups on the political and religious right [who] want to control the memory of India's past in ways that suit their own ideological agendas," while attacking those like himself who "challenge those constructions."[54] But he also suggests that these incidents can open the more hopeful possibility for more respectful dialogue and mutual understanding between members of the Hindu community and those who study them.[55]

One of the most thoughtful responses to these criticisms has come from the "mother" of American Hinduism studies herself, Wendy Doniger. After long and deep reflection on the "Wendy's Child" debate, Doniger has described herself as a kind of "recovering Orientalist." As she explained in an interview with me in 2007, she herself comes from Orientalist background and still finds much to admire in early British scholarship on India. But she can now also appreciate the political dimensions of scholarship, both past and present:

> By temperament and training I am still an Orientalist . . . I am still interested mainly in literature, in stories, in Sanskrit texts. But now I think I have a better balance: I have acknowledged the political dimension of the work and of my own scholarship. I still greatly value British scholarship on India, even though it was in the service of an evil empire, but now I read that scholarship differently.[56]

Doniger acknowledges that Orientalist scholarship was historically complicit in the imperial project and that India today continues to be subject to a new, American-style form of economic domination: "For many years Europeans wrote anything they wanted and took anything they wanted from India . . . Even now much of Indian culture is influenced by American political and economic domination. And India is quite right to object to that."[57] She also notes that Malhotra and others have pointed to real and important issues in the modern study of South Asian religions. But they had, she said, "messed up the solutions," by mounting a wholesale and unproductive attack that has only further alienated contemporary scholars from their critics.[58]

As a "Wendy's child" myself—but also one trained in the midst of postcolonial theory and subaltern studies—I find myself both sympathetic to and critical of both sides of this divide.[59] In general, I am not unsympathetic to many of Malhotra's criticisms and have made similar criticisms in my own work—though I am not sympathetic to his tone or argumentative style. While it would surely be absurd to link contemporary American scholars directly to the policies of the current US government, it would also be naive to pretend that they are not part of a larger social, cultural, and political context that both shapes and is shaped by their work. As Richard King argues in *Orientalism and Religion*, we cannot "divorce academics from the wider cultural context in which they work and from the network of power relations that locates the scholar as an institutionally inscribed 'expert' "; instead, he suggests, we need to "criticize the power dynamic implied in the use of taken-for-granted categories (such as 'religion,' 'Hinduism' and 'mysticism')."[60] Here I would add "Tantra" or "Tantrism" to his list of taken-for-granted categories.

The USA, it seems to me, is a new kind of imperial power—though an indirect and informal one—and it does exert a form of cultural colonialism on much of the world. And American literature on Tantra, both popular and academic, has focused disproportionately on the exotic and sexual aspects of this tradition, often to the neglect of its less titillating aspects. As N.N. Bhattacharyya long ago pointed out, "Most of the modern writers on this subject insist solely on its sexual elements, minimal though they are compared to the vastness of the subject... Thus the historical study of Tantrism has been handicapped, complicated and conditioned by the preoccupations of those working in the field."[61] This equation of Tantra with sex has continued in even the finest recent scholarship, which continues to define Tantra as a path surrounded by "strangeness, seediness and sex,"[62] with sexual union as the "distinguishing feature of the most esoteric and advanced class" of Tantra.[63] As David Gordon White's otherwise excellent book defines it, the "hard core" form of Tantric practice, "which gives Tantra its specificity," centers on "sexual interactions between male practitioners and their female counterparts."[64]

It seems to me that the problem with the approach of Malhotra and the authors of *Invading the Sacred* is not that their criticisms of Western scholarship are groundless. On the contrary, as Vijay Prashad observes, "Much of what [Malhotra] said is correct (there is an insensitivity toward the Hindu tradition and a disregard for the real living Indians), and it had been the basis for a long-standing debate around the institutions."[65] Rather, the problem with their criticisms is threefold.

First, many of the critiques of American scholarship rest on a simplistic and now quite outdated binary view of the world—a world still seen as divided into an "East" and a "West," where a domineering Occidental empire exploits an innocent Orient. While this narrative may have been partially true of Orientalist discourse of the nineteenth century, it no longer makes much sense in the increasingly interconnected, globalized world of the twenty-first century, where the centers of power and wealth are as much in New Delhi, Mumbai, Tokyo, and Abu Dhabi as in London or New York. Indeed, today the centers of global poverty are as much in New Orleans as in Kolkata. The USA may well be the dominant force in the current form of imperialism, but it is hardly the sole or central power. Hence, it is perhaps more accurate to speak of a form of "market imperialism," the imperialism of multinational corporations and global capital,[66] which is hardly limited to the "West" and in which many Indians are as implicated as any Americans. Malhotra, for example, lives in New Jersey and describes himself as a former "senior executive in several multinational companies, as a management consultant, and as a private entrepreneur, spanning the computer, software, telecom, and media industries."[67] It is difficult to see him as a voiceless subaltern colonized by an imperial American regime.

Moreover, if one can ask whether American scholarship is implicated in a new kind of imperial politics, so too, one can ask whether the writings of Hindu critics are not also implicated in larger political agendas. If discourse and power are always interrelated, as Said suggests, then is the discourse of *Invading the Sacred* interrelated with the politics of Hindu nationalism? Today all of us—defenders of Hinduism no less than American scholars—are enmeshed in complex matrices of power that far transcend the simplistic binaries of "East" and "West."

Second, the criticisms aimed at American scholarship can easily devolve into a very unproductive form of identity politics. As Lily Shapiro notes, they often assume that persons of Hindu background "possess an innate understanding of Hindu categories of thought which can never be reached by someone not indigenous to the tradition."[68] They also seem to assume that theoretical models generated in Europe have nothing useful to contribute to the understanding of non-European cultures. Both of these assumptions, it seems to me, are fundamentally opposed to the larger goal of cross-cultural understanding. If we can say nothing about another group with which members of that group might disagree, and if we can in turn hear nothing from others that challenges our own beliefs, then the idea of cross-cultural dialogue is a hollow charade. The key, I think, is to *allow the critique to work in both directions*, that is, to also allow the encounter with other cultures to challenge our own biases and assumptions. A genuine encounter with another tradition is not simply a matter of applying some European theoretical model and running it through the theory-mill; rather, it should also force us to rethink our theoretical models, to incorporate non-European concepts, and to generate new, more complex models in their place.

Finally, in the case of Tantra, many of the critiques of American scholarship also strike me as an attempt to sanitize or deodorize Indian history, to censor evidence of anything that today might appear embarrassing or extreme. As Peter van der Veer comments, this is a common strategy of many Hindus living in the USA and Europe, who hope to present a "respectable" image of Hinduism, downplaying the messier and more complex aspects of the tradition. Ironically, however, this is often only the inverse image of the Orientalist stereotype of Hinduism:

> The construction of a unified Hindu identity is of utmost importance for Hindus who live outside India. They need a Hinduism that can be explained to outsiders as a respectable religion, that can be taught to their children in religious education . . . In an ironic twist of history, Orientalism is now brought by Indians to Indians living in the West.[69]

As Prashad suggests, Malhotra's goal is to "rebrand India" by imposing the idea that there is just "one Indic thought"—and one that happens to conform with the conservative vision of the Hindu nationalists. In reality, of course, the complex traditions we now call Hinduism are an incredibly rich and diverse body of texts, rituals, and sects that have evolved over the last 3500 years. Our task should therefore not be to promote a singular version of Hinduism that makes modern India look good on the global stage, but rather to appreciate the complex plurality of traditions that comprise its rich religious history: "we [are] not invested simply in making India look good: we wanted to ensure that the diversity of India's history and its struggles be represented . . . The solution is not to brown-wash the textbooks on ancient Indian history, but to write more honest books about the contradictions of all civilizations."[70]

In sum, as King points out, we should not allow ourselves to be blackmailed into thinking that there are only two alternatives in the study of things Indian, namely, "western colonialism or Hindu nationalism—and that to repudiate the former is to align with the latter." Rather, we can reflect critically on both sides of the binary, and thereby open "a space for alternative models to emerge in a post-nationalism world" that resist both the logic of Orientalist imperialism and reactionary appeals to some kind of imagined, pristine Hinduism.[71]

As I will show in the chapters that follow, there are in fact many aspects of Tantra that appear quite extreme, not just to Western readers, but to most Hindus as well. And this is clear from *the very first mention* of texts called *tantras* in Indian literature—Bāṇabhaṭṭa's *Kādambarī* (seventh century), which satirically describes a crazy old holy man who had a collection of *tantras*. This negative perception of Tantric traditions continued throughout later Indian literature, from Sanskrit plays that mock the perverse practices of the Kāpālikas to devotional literature that attacks the bloody rites of Śākta *tāntrikas*.[72] However, the "otherness" of Tantra in my view has less to do with *sex* than with other sorts of practices, such as ritual transgression, the use of impure substances, animal sacrifices, and elements drawn from non-Hindu indigenous traditions. The otherness of Tantra, I will suggest, is less about sexual pleasure than about unleashing the tremendous energy of the goddess that flows through the cosmos and the human body.

The path of desire and power: Re-imagining Tantra for a post-imperial era

So how, then, do we best go about re-imagining Tantra in a more productive way today, in a "recovering Orientalist's" sense? While there are many, many ways of defining Tantra, each of which reflects its own particular historical and cultural biases,[73] I find it most useful to define Tantra in terms of the key Indian concepts of *kāma* and *śakti*, roughly translated as desire and power. Here I find Madeleine Biardeau's definition of Tantra particularly helpful. Tantra, she suggests, is primarily concerned with *kāma* or desire in the very broadest sense of the term. Indeed, Tantra could be defined as a means of "harnessing *kāma*—desire (in every sense of the word)—and all of its related values to the service of deliverance."[74] Whereas most South Asian traditions see *kāma* as the primary obstacle in the religious life, the sensual attachment that binds us to this temporal world, Tantra is the path that seeks to harness, transform, and redirect desire toward the aims of both this-worldly power and spiritual liberation:

> Rather than placing desire and liberation in opposition to each other, and rather than denying the one to benefit the other, the theory holds, quite to the contrary, that desire is the hallmark of each and every individual's initiation into the path of salvation. It is the seal of the divine in man, so long as he is schooled in the proper techniques for its transformation. It is therefore no longer one's acts, ritual or otherwise, that are valorized as such; rather it is desire itself which is actually positively re-evaluated.[75]

Much of the Western misunderstanding of Tantra over the last 200 years, I would argue, has been borne of a fundamental misunderstanding of the concept of *kāma*. From missionaries and Orientalists like

Ward and Monier-Wilson down to American neo-Tantric gurus and even many contemporary scholars, Western authors have consistently defined *kāma* primarily as sexual desire—whether cast in the Victorian horror of sexual promiscuity or the modern American celebration of sexual freedom and sensual pleasure.

And yet, if we look more carefully at the meanings of *kāma* in Sanskrit literature, we find that the valences of this term go well beyond mere sexual desire. According to Monier-Williams' Sanskrit dictionary, its meanings include wish, desire, longing, love, affection, object of desire, pleasure, enjoyment, love, sexual love, sensuality, Love or Desire personified, and so on.[76] In sum, sexual desire is but one and not necessarily the most important manifestation of *kāma*. As Doniger suggests in her introduction to the world's great manual of desire, the *Kāma Sūtra*, *kāma* is thus better rendered in a plural manner as "desire/love/pleasure/sex," for it includes the full range of sensual experience: "*kāma* represents pleasure and desire (what the Germans call *Lust and Wollust*), not merely sexual but broadly sensual—music, good food, perfume and so forth."[77] Moreover, *kāma* is not an isolated goal in itself but is closely tied to the other primary aims of life, namely *artha*—power and wealth—and *dharma*—religious and social duty. Indeed, these three ends of life—desire, power, and religion—are intimately and inseparably intertwined.[78]

The Tantric traditions for the most part accept this basic definition of *kāma*, but they also interpret and use desire somewhat differently. As Gavin Flood points out, Tantra attempts to use desire to go beyond desire, to alchemically transform *kāma* from a source of bondage into a means of liberation: "*kāma* is not an end in itself but a means to an end; desire is used to transcend itself as a thorn can be removed by a thorn."[79] Not primarily a means to pleasure alone, *kama* is rather a means to awaken and channel the tremendous energy that lies within the body and the cosmos.

If we look at key Śākta texts from Assam such as the *Kālikā Purāṇa* (tenth to eleventh centuries), we find that *kāma* encompasses but far exceeds mere sexual desire. In fact, even within a single brief description of the goddess, *kāma* assumes a wide range of meanings, from the sensual pleasures of enjoyment and eros to the cosmic powers of creation and destruction. It is, in sum, the fluid energy of the goddess that circulates through every level of the cosmos. As Lord Śiva declares,

> Because the goddess has come to this great mountain Nīlakūṭa to make love [*kāma*] to me, she is called Kāmākhyā, who dwells there secretly. Because she gives pleasure [*kāmadā*], is a loving woman [*kāminī*], is desire [*kāmā*], and is desirable [*kāntā*], because she restores the limbs of [the god] Kāma and also destroys the limbs of Kāma, she is called Kāmākhyā. Now hear of the great glory of Kāmākhyā who, as Primordial Nature, sets the entire world in motion.[80]

As we see in another remarkable passage from the *Kālikā Purāṇa, kāma* is said to pervade everything, to flow through everything—indeed, it *is* everything. Thus, worship of the goddess is about desire in every sense of the word: "*kāmasthaṃ kāmamadhyasthaṃ kāmadevapuṭīkṛtam, kāmena kāmayet kāmī kāmaṃ kāme niyojayet.*" Taken literally, this translates as something like: "Engaged in desire, established in the midst of desire, enveloped by the god of desire, the desirous one should desire with desire and join desire in desire."[81] In sum, desire is the cause of everything, the end of everything, and the flowing energy by which everything is sustained.

In this sense, desire is also power (*śakti*), a concept to which it is intimately related in Tantric practice. Indeed, if Tantra can be defined as a "path of desire," it can equally be defined as a "path of power," or a spiritual discipline that harnesses the tremendous power of desire in order to attain both this-worldly and ultimate liberation. As Charles Orzech argues in his work on Chinese esoteric Buddhism, power is simultaneously a religious and political phenomenon, as much tied to matters of kingship and state formation as to spiritual realization.[82] Yet surprisingly few authors have thought seriously about what *śakti* means as a theoretical, religious, and political category. Indeed, the term "*Śakti* cannot be adequately translated by a single word," since it combines the many complex concepts of power, potentiality, and sovereign authority.[83] The Sanskrit noun *śakti* comes form the root *śak*, "to be able" or "to do," and means "capability," "power," "energy," or "strength" on all levels of the universe. *Śakti* is the divine energy of the goddess, the power of both life and death, creation and destruction, which flows through the cosmos, the social order, and the human body alike: "Śakti is the root of every finite existence. The worlds are her manifestation. She supports them, and one day they will be reabsorbed into her."[84] As Padoux suggests, the Tantric path can thus be defined as "the quest for liberation and the acquisition of supernatural powers result from a tapping, a manipulating of this ubiquitous power."[85]

Theorizing Tantra: Using and challenging contemporary models of desire and power

In this sense, the Indian concepts of *kāma* and *śakti* present important challenge to most contemporary understandings of desire and power. As a productive, creative yet violent energy that flows through all levels of social, cosmic, and physical existence, *śakti* is a kind of power that cannot be neatly divided into religious, political, or sexual categories. As Sarah Caldwell notes, "This organic, feminized conception of power appears to be at odds with European-language concepts. The latter split power into political, ritual and psycho-erotic components, which are not necessarily seen as related."[86] Śakti here is not simply material or political power, and not even simply what David Chidester calls "religio-political power."[87] Rather, in the case of Śākta Tantra, this is really a kind of *sexo-religio-political power*, in which desire, gender, spiritual authority, and political legitimacy are inextricably intertwined. Here I would like to borrow but also critically modify some insights from modern theorists such as Gilles Deleuze and Michel Foucault and their influential work on desire and power. Deleuze, I think, is particularly useful for understanding the concept of desire in ways that go beyond the usual Western, sexo-centric, and psychoanalytic views of desire. Modern discourse, and particularly psychoanalytic discourse, Deleuze argues, consistently "reduces sexuality to sex." That is, it limits the complex diversity of desire, "as a historically variable and determinable desiring-assemblage," to the singular aspect of genital sex.[88] In contrast to Freud, Deleuze sees desire not as a kind of lack or longing for some lost object, and not as simply a matter of genital sexuality or the Oedipal conflict; rather, desire is fundamentally *generative*, a source of *power and potentiality* that far exceeds the narrow confines of genital orgasm:

> psychoanalysis was shutting sexuality up in a bizarre sort of box painted with bourgeois motifs, in a kind of rather repugnant artificial triangle, thereby stifling the whole of sexuality as production of desire so as to recast it along entirely different lines, making of it a "dirty

little secret", the dirty little family secret, a private theater rather than the fantastic factory of Nature and Production.[89]

Desire in this sense is less a dirty little secret than a pervasive force that is fundamentally positive and productive in nature. As a kind of "productive plenitude of its own energy which propels it to seek ever new connections and instantiations," desire is better understood as a "free-flowing" and "incessant flux." As such, desire has perhaps its closest analogue in Friedrich Nietzsche's "will to power."[90] And the human body itself is a kind of "desiring machine," overflowing with powerful productive energies, from menstrual blood to feces:

> Desire causes the current to flow, itself flows in turn, and breaks the flows. "I love everything that flows, even the menstrual flow that carries away the seed unfecund." Amniotic fluid spilling out of the sac of kidney stones; flowing hair; a flow of spittle, a flow of sperm, shit or urine . . . [91]

However, while I find Deleuze's post-Freudian concept of desire extremely useful for understanding the Tantric concept of *kāma*, I think it also leaves some unanswered problems that need to be critically rethought. As a number of critics have pointed out, there is a fundamental tension in Deleuze's concept of desire. On the one hand, he wants to look historically at the ways in which desire has been repressed, controlled, and "territorialized" in different periods and political regimes—above all, in the context of modern capitalism. Yet on the other hand, he seems to assume an essentialized concept of desire that transcends history and social context, almost as a kind of monist metaphysical ideal.[92] As Judith Butler observes, Deleuze tends to slip into a universalizing view that makes desire "the privileged locus of human ontology" and a kind of "precultural eros" that somehow precedes social structure and history.[93] This universal, precultural view of desire seems to stand in serious tension with Deleuze's historical critique of desire in modern capitalist society.

Following the lead of Foucault, Butler suggests that it is more useful to think of desire, not as a universal ontological truth or "natural given," but rather as a culturally constructed phenomenon, one that has very different meanings in different social, historical, and political contexts. In short, desire and sexuality are inherently tied to relations of power, formed through complex and historically specific "matrices of power."[94]

Contrary to most earlier analyses of power, which begin from the top down, viewing power primarily as an oppressive and dominating force wielded by the few, Foucault approaches power from the "bottom up," as it were. Rather than viewing power on the macro-political level of nations and states, Foucault turns instead to the micro-politics of power, that is, the ways in which power operates in the lives of all members of the social order, in the most mundane details of daily life such as dress, bodily comportment, diet, etc. Power in this sense is not something possessed by a small group at the top of the social hierarchy, but rather, a more diffuse, decentralized, "capillary" phenomenon: "[I]t is produced from one moment to the next, at every point... Power is everywhere; not because it embraces everything, but because it comes from everywhere."[95] Power in this sense is not a static entity, but a fluid series of relations that "circulates" through a net-like organization among all individuals in a social formation: "Power must be analyzed as something which circulates... Power is employed and exercised through a net-like organization. And not only do individuals circulate between its threads; they are always in the position of simultaneously undergoing and exercising this power."[96]

Above all, Foucault is interested in a specifically *embodied* kind of power that is exercised upon and through individual human bodies: "Historical forces act upon and through the human body. As the center of the struggle for domination, the body is both shaped and reshaped by the different warring forces acting upon it."[97] As a capillary, circulating phenomenon, "power seeps into the very grain of individuals, reaches right into their bodies, permeates their gestures, their posture, what they say, how they learn to live and work with other people."[98] One of the most crucial fields for the operation of power, for example, is sexuality. As the key "linchpin" between the individual body and the larger social body, sexuality lies at the crucial nexus between the production of the physical self and the reproduction of the social organism.[99]

It would be difficult to find a closer analogue to the Tantric concept of *śakti* than this notion of power as an omnipresent, productive, circulating, and embodied phenomenon. As we will see throughout the chapters that follow, *śakti* is very much a "capillary" sort of power, flowing throughout both the human body and the body politic, and symbolized above all by the circulation of blood as the fluid vehicle of this pervasive energy. Just as the Tantric concept of desire includes yet far exceeds the modern understanding of sexual desire, so too, the Tantric concept of power includes but far exceeds the limits of merely political power, also including the productive energy that flows through the human body, the social order, and the cosmos.

However, if contemporary Western theories of desire and power may be extremely helpful for understanding concepts like *kāma* and *śakti*, they are also quite limited in certain ways and need to be critiqued and countertheorized by way of a reflection on South Asian traditions. Perhaps most important, as many feminist critics have pointed out, both Foucault and Deleuze are surprisingly "gender blind," that is, while they have very sophisticated analyses of desire and sexuality, they pay little attention to the question of gender, to the different constructions of male and female sexuality, or to the shifting balances of power between the sexes. As Grace Jantzen observes, Foucault's analysis fails to examine the extent to which "the structures of power and knowledge have operated unequally upon women and men." For in the analysis of any major concept—whether it is sexuality or mysticism or religion itself—it is critical that we be aware of the inevitable ways in which "gender and power are interlocked."[100]

As we will see in the case of Tantra, the concept of power is very clearly "gendered." On one hand, as the divine feminine energy that generates the universe, "*śakti* is essentially a female power, engendering both life and death in its temporal unfolding."[101] Yet on the other hand, this is also a power that can be harnessed and channeled for the "masculine" ends of priesthood, kingship, and war. Tantric ritual, I will argue, involves a complex "alchemy of gender and power," which transforms the female energy of the goddess into the masculine energy of the king and priest; but it also opens the possibility for women to assume new kinds of authority, to take power in a more active way as gurus and embodiments of *śakti* in their own right.

The threefold power of Tantra

As such, the "power of Tantra" in this book has a threefold meaning, with three major implications for our current discussions of religion, sexuality, and the politics of South Asian studies. First, as a "path of power" in the broadest sense of the term, Tantra forces us to rethink our own modern concepts of power and, above all, the complex relations between the religious, sexual, and political dimensions power. *Śakti* here is a profoundly *embodied* phenomenon, focused on "the body as a structured receptacle of power and animated by that power,"[102] but also embodied in the messy world of social change, political struggle, and gender relations.

Second, much of the unique power of Tantra lies in its ability to tap into the liminal, transgressive, and impure elements in the social and physical universe—the *power at the margins*. Above all in the case of Assamese Tantra, this power at the margins lay in the offering of normally impure animal sacrifices, the consumption of impure polluting substances, and the incorporation of non-Hindu and indigenous rites from the various tribal peoples of the northeast hills. For, as David Shulman aptly observes, "Power is . . . derived from forces that are contaminating; these forces belong to the violent substratum of chaos out of which the world emerged."[103] At least in the northeast tradition, I will argue, the power of Tantra has less to do with sex than it does with the transgressive power of blood sacrifice and rites drawn from non-Hindu indigenous traditions.

Finally and perhaps most important, however, Tantra is also a striking example of the fact that our encounters with other cultures and traditions are *also tied to real relations of power*—to the historical relations of imperialism and nationalism, to postcolonial struggles, and late capitalist appropriations of other cultures. As such, perhaps the greatest power of Tantra today is to challenge us to rethink our own biases and assumptions in the contemporary global order. Above all, I will argue, it can help lead beyond the Orientalist fascination with the exotic Other and toward a more embodied approach to religion—an approach that sees both ourselves and those whom we study as deeply embedded in the messy realities of history, social change, and political struggle. As Kripal aptly put it, "We too are historical beings. We too think and speak within and as bodies that . . . have been deeply 'entextualized' by the terms, languages and doctrines of our cultures."[104]

Structure and outline of the book: A history of Tantra, in the flesh

The chapters that follow attempt to put this embodied approach to Tantra into effect, by focusing on one particular Tantric tradition and its complex place in South Asian history, culture, and politics. The chapters follow a roughly historical progression, beginning with the oldest known texts describing the major Tantric centers of power and working forward to the role of Tantra in the twenty-first century, amidst the new forces of globalization, diaspora, and transnational capitalism.

Chapter 1, "Matrix of Power," begins by examining the mythic and historical role of Kāmākhyā temple among the *śākta pīṭhas* or "seats of power" that dot the sacred landscape of South Asia. In mythic terms, Kāmākhyā temple is said to have been created after the goddess Satī committed ritual suicide, was dismembered, and left various pieces of her body at various sacred spots on the subcontinent. The goddess' sexual organ is believed to lie inside Kāmākhyā temple, making it literally the "mother of all places of power." In historical terms, Kāmākhyā lies at a complex intersection between mainstream Hindu traditions coming from north India and the many indigenous religions of the northeast hills. Her unique form of worship is largely the result of a long negotiation between Hindu and indigenous traditions that evolved over several hundred years.

Chapter 2, "Blood for the Goddess," focuses on the major public rituals at Kāmākhya temple. These include the large summer festival celebrating the goddess' annual menstruation, which is believed to give life to the earth and power to her devotees through Kāmākhyā's blood, and the public performance of sacrifices that return this power to her through the blood of the goats, birds, and buffaloes offered to her each day. It is here that we see most clearly the mixture of Hindu and tribal practices, for example, in the offering of animals that are normally considered highly impure by Hindu standards (such as buffaloes) and in a manner that is also considered quite impure (bloody beheading). But such intentionally impure offerings are considered appropriate to a goddess who embodies the power that can handle and dispel dangerous impurity.

In Chapter 3, "Goddess of Power," I then look at Tantra's role in Assamese politics and kingship from mythical narratives down to medieval historical texts. As a goddess of power, closely tied to the land, Kāmākhyā was long patronized by Assam's kings who hoped to draw upon her tremendous *śakti* in defense of the kingdom and conquest of enemies. From the mythical king Naraka down to Assam's historical dynasties like the Pālas, Koches, and Ahoms, Kāmākhyā has been closely tied to royal power. Like the menstruating goddess, the king is described as an ambivalent figure, at once the embodiment of power and yet also inevitably tied to the impurity of violence and war. According to the *Kālikā Purāṇa*, the king's power, again, centers largely on the circulation of blood—the blood of animal and human victims offered for protection of the kingdom and the blood of enemies slain in the "sacrifice of battle."

In Chapter 4, "The Sacrifice of Desire," I examine the esoteric side of Kāmākhyā's worship and her secret rites, which became increasingly popular in the later medieval period. Again, these rites center primarily on the literal and symbolic significance of blood as the bearer of divine power. According to a wide range of texts from the tenth to the eighteenth centuries, these rites involve sexual union and the oral consumption of sexual fluids, above all menstrual blood, as a sacramental meal. As I will argue, however, these rites are hardly a matter of "nookie nirvana" or optimal sexual pleasure; rather, they represent the esoteric counterpart to the sacrificial rite and, again, incorporate both Vedic and tribal elements in a ritual that embodies the circulating, capillary power of the goddess in the physical form of blood.

Chapter 5, "What about the Woman?" looks specifically at the complex and much-debated question of women's roles in Tantric practice. Much of the modern scholarship on Tantra has fallen into one of two, rather simplistic, binary positions: either Tantric ritual is seen as a kind of exploitation of the female body for the spiritual benefit of the male practitioner, or it is seen as a form of liberation and empowerment of women. Instead, I argue for a more complex view of agency in Tantric ritual, which involves a complex negotiation between the limitations imposed by structures of power and the available spaces for subversion and transformation. In the case of Kāmākhyā, the female is often represented in the most hetero-normative and "essentialist" form imaginable, as the very embodiment of the *yoni* or female sexual organ. And yet, because women are seen as the embodiments of the goddess' divine creative power, at least some women have been able to appropriate that power in more concrete ways, for example, to become respected gurus and spiritual authorities in living Tantric lineages.

Chapter 6, "The Power of God in a Dark Valley," examines the decline of Hindu Tantra in the face of two powerful rival forces. First, from the sixteenth century onward, Assam witnessed a popular revival of Hindu devotional worship, which was fiercely critical of Kāmākhyā's transgressive Tantric rites. Second, by the end of the eighteenth century, British colonial rule had spread to Assam, bringing the formal end of independent kingship in the region. Even more so than the Hindu reformers, the colonial authorities and Christian missionaries were horrified by the Tantric worship of Kāmākhyā, which they decried as bloody idolatry and disgusting debauchery. By the nineteenth century, Kāmākhyā had ceased to function as the religio-political center of the region, while the more extreme forms of Tantra were forced further underground and to the margins of Assam.

In Chapter 7, "The Power of the Goddess in a Postcolonial Age," I examine the role of the Kāmākhyā temple and Tantric practice in contemporary Assam, in the aftermath of colonialism and independence. Here I argue that the centralized political power of the goddess may have been dismantled in the wake of the Hindu reforms and British colonial critiques, but it still survives as a pervasive force throughout Assamese society to this day. Although it is now decentralized, the power of the goddess remains a vital spiritual and cultural resource, which has now been sort of "exotericized," "sweetened," and "softened" for a broad audience of devotees who make their way to her temple as a popular devotional site. Perhaps most interestingly, the power of the goddess has also now been globalized and transnationalized through popular saints like Shree Maa of Kāmākhyā, who have transformed this once esoteric Tantric tradition into a more accessible devotional path for a Western audience of spiritual seekers.

Finally, the Conclusion returns to the original starting point of the book to argue that the particular case of Assam strikes to the heart of much larger theoretical, ethical, and political questions in the study of South Asian religions. Above all, it forces us to recognize that both we and those whom we study are very much embedded in the larger matrices of power that comprise the contemporary geo-political order. This need not, however, be a cause solely of neo-imperial guilt. Rather, it can also be a cause of *hope* and open the way to a more embodied, corporeal approach that can transform the way we think about both religion and politics in the twenty-first century.

Chapter One

MATRIX OF POWER: THE ŚĀKTA PĪṬHAS AND THE SACRED LANDSCAPE OF TANTRA

Of all *pīṭhas,* the supreme *pīṭha* is Kāmarūpa. It bears great fruit, even if worship is done there only once . . . That *pīṭha* is the secret mouth of *Brahman,* which brings happiness, where Mahiṣamardinī [the goddess as slayer of the buffalo demon] dwells with her millions of *śaktis.* Since the gods, goddesses and sages are of this [*Brahman*] nature, they are all present here. Therefore, this place is kept secret by the great *kula* adepts.

—*Kulacūḍāmaṇi Tantra* (KCT 5.36–40)

Sexuality is always situated within matrices of power . . . it is always produced or constructed within specific historical practices.

—Judith Butler, *Gender Trouble* (1990)[1]

As a living, embodied, and historical tradition, Hindu Tantra spread throughout South Asia in a network of holy sites or epicenters of divine feminine energy known as the *śākta pīṭhas* or "seats of power." Extending from Kāmākhyā in the northeast to Pūrṇagiri in the south and Uḍḍiyāna in the northwest, the *śākta pīṭhas* embody a complex, capillary network or matrix of power, comprising many veins and nodes that reflect the vast, flowing system of energy that is the goddess as Śakti, embodied and embedded in the physical world. This matrix of power is from its origin born from bloodshed and sacrifice—the death and dismemberment of the goddess Satī, whose various body parts make up the *śākta pīṭhas.* But it is also intimately tied to the creative power of sexual union—the union of Śiva and Śakti who lie joined in secret love play on Kāmākhyā hill, giving life and vitality to the entire universe.[2]

In this chapter, I offer a brief overview of the history and context of South Asian Tantra, with particular focus on Kāmākhyā as one of the oldest and most enduring seats of power (Fig. 1). Today, it is impossible to say exactly when or where the complex body of traditions we now call "Tantra" originated. Various authors have suggested that Tantra's origins lie outside of India (China, Tibet, the Middle East) or in non-Hindu indigenous groups (the hill tribes of northeast India) or in the mountains of northwest India (Uḍḍiyāna or the Kashmir Valley). There is no clear evidence of actual texts called *tantras* until the ninth century,[3] though many believe their origins lie in Hindu Śākta or goddess-centered traditions going back to at least the fifth century.[4]

Yet virtually all the early sources agree that Kāmarūpa (the "form" or "body of desire") is one of the oldest and most revered of the early seats of goddess worship and Tantric practice, dating back to at least the eighth century.[5] The *śākta pīṭhas* in general and Kāmākhyā in particular, I will argue, represent a complex interaction or negotiation between mainstream Vedic or *brāhmaṇic* traditions and indigenous elements from the pre-Hindu areas of India. Particularly in the case of Assam, Tantra draws much of its power from the tremendous, dangerous, and potentially impure "power at the margins," the power associated with non-Aryan traditions and with the dangerous forces at the edges of the Hindu social-political order.

The concept of *śakti* and the network of the *śākta pīṭhas*, I will suggest, also reveal both the usefulness and the limitations of contemporary models of power such as Foucault's widely influential work. In many ways, the Foucaultian view of power as a shifting, capillary, and productive network of relations is quite helpful for understanding *śakti* as a pervasive, creative energy that flows through every aspect of the physical universe and the social order. Yet at the same time, as a "female power, engendering both life and death in its temporal unfolding,"[6] *śakti* also reveals the inherent gender-blindness of the Foucaultian model; indeed, it forces us to grapple very directly with the gendered dynamics of power as it is played out in lived history, social relations, and political struggles. Finally, as we will see in the subsequent chapters, the Tantric view of *śakti* also highlights the fact that power is not simply an abstract theoretical concept but an inherently *performative* phenomenon. It is a kind of power that is continuously reenacted

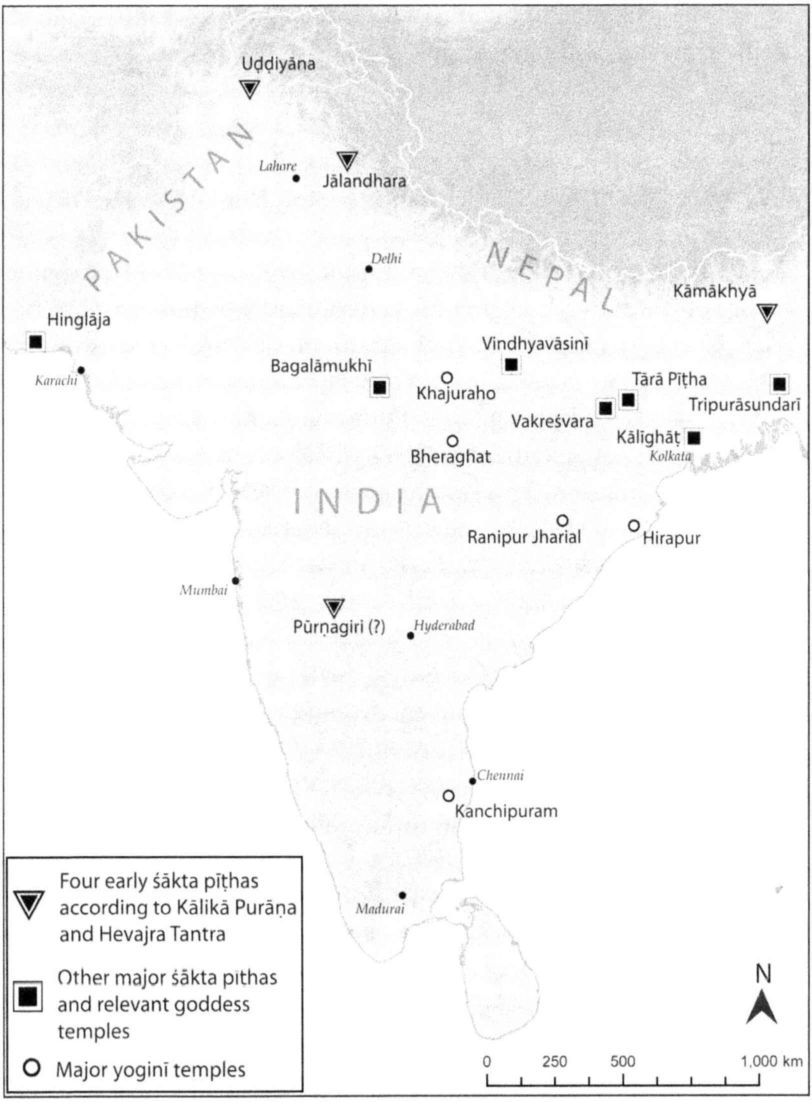

The four early Śākta Pīṭhas and other major goddess temples in South Asia

through the recitation of myth and the ongoing performance of ritual, sacrifice, festival, and pilgrimage.

Divine sacrifice and the origins of the śākta pīṭhas

The mythic narratives about the origins of the *śākta pīṭhas* tie together three key themes that later become central elements throughout South Asian Śākta and Tantric traditions: the themes of sacrifice, desire, and power. According to a well-known story found in various retellings in the Brāhmaṇas, the Epics, and the Purāṇas,[7] Lord Śiva was married to the goddess Satī, the daughter of Dakṣa. However, Dakṣa very much disliked his son-in-law, Śiva, who is a fierce, frightening, outsider sort of god; so when Dakṣa arranged for a large sacrificial ritual, he intentionally did not invite Śiva. This disinvitation was such a profound insult that Satī committed suicide by throwing herself onto the sacrificial fire. In his rage, Śiva became "Mahārudra, the god of destruction," as "millions of ghosts and demons came out of his beauty and began a wild dance . . . The *yajña* was postponed and then became a wholesale massacre."[8] Having destroyed the entire sacrifice, Śiva beheaded his father-in-law, Dakṣa, and replaced his head with that of a goat—the original sacrificial victim—thus making him the ironic victim at his own sacrifice.[9]

In sum, what we have in this myth is the story of a sacrifice gone awry, an interrupted ritual that turns into a dangerous, inverted sacrifice spun out of control. After destroying the sacrifice and beheading Dakṣa, the distraught Śiva then carried off the body of his dead wife upon his shoulders. So terrible was Śiva's rage that it threatened to destroy the entire universe; so, in order to defuse the situation, the gods entered into Satī's body and dismembered it. The various parts of Satī's body then fell in various sacred places in India, the *śākta pīṭhas* or "seats of power," which are intimately joined to Śiva in the form of his liṅgam. The oldest and most powerful of these seats are usually said to be Kāmarūpa in the northeast, Uḍḍiyāna in the north (probably in the Swat Valley of modern Pakistan), Pūrṇagiri in the south (real location undecided[10]), and Jālandhara (near Kangra, Himachal Pradesh). The *Kālikā Purāṇa's* version of the story also adds two additional *pīṭhas* in Kāmarūpa and one in Devīkūṭa (in the Dinajpur district of Bengal):

> The gods entered the corpse of Satī in order to tear it to pieces so that various [holy] places could arise on the earth where these pieces fell. First the feet fell to earth in Devīkūṭa. The thighs fell in Uḍḍiyāna for the good of the world. The *yoni* region fell in Kāmarūpa on Kāma hill. And to the east of that, the navel fell to the earth. The breasts, adorned with golden necklaces, fell in Jālandhara. The neck fell in Pūrṇagiri, and the head again fell in Kāmarūpa. Out of his love for Satī, bound in infatuation, Śiva himself remained in the form of a phallus wherever these pieces fell.[11]

The self-sacrifice of the goddess Satī and the creation of the *śākta pīṭhas* is thus an ironic inversion of a normal sacrifice. Indeed, it is a kind of twisted mirror of the original creative sacrifice described in the Vedas, the sacrifice of the Primordial Person (Puruṣa) recounted in the famous creation myth of the *Ṛg Veda*. In the Vedic narrative, Puruṣa is ritually dismembered by the gods in a primordial, creative sacrifice "in which everything is offered," a sacrifice that generates all the various parts of the cosmos and the social order from the pieces of his severed body.[12] In the Satī narrative, conversely, the sacrifice of the goddess is a *destructive and nearly apocalyptic act*—a sacrifice that threatens to destroy the entire universe because of its divine but dangerous power. And it infuses the earth, not with the abstract male principle of Puruṣa, but with the vital, creative but also destructive energy of the goddess.

As the seat of the goddess' *yoni* or sexual organ, Kāmākhyā is widely regarded as the most powerful of the *pīṭhas* and, indeed, literally the "mother of all places of power." According to the *Kālikā Purāṇa*, it is here that the goddess dwells in the form of a reddish stone, the physical embodiment of her *yoni*, which grants all desires; and it is here on the blue mountain (Nīlācala or Nīlakūṭa) that the goddess and lord Śiva lie in secret union, their *yoni* and *liṅgam* joined in lovers' play beneath the mask of stone:

> And in this most sacred *pīṭha*, which is known as the *pīṭha* of Kubjikā on mount Nīlakūṭa, the goddess is secretly joined with me [Śiva]. Satī's sexual organ, which was severed and fell there, became a stone; and there Kāmākhyā is present.[13]

> Kāmarūpa, the great *pīṭha*, is more secret than secret. There Śaṅkara [Śiva] always resides with Parvatī [the goddess].[14]

In sum, the Satī story combines the themes of sacrifice, dismemberment, and sensual desire, centering all of these powerful forces on the mountain on Kāmākhyā hill where the goddess and her lover lie in secret union. As Nihar Ranjan Mishra observes, "This narrative makes Nīlācala both a graveyard and a place of Śiva-Parvatī's amorous pastime."[15] This fusion of the creative energy of desire and the destructive violence of sacrifice, we will see, lies at the core of Śākta Tantra and at the heart of the goddess' power.

Later Hindu traditions would add a great variety of other *śākta pīṭhas* or centers of the Devī and her dismembered body parts, whose number varies in different lists, ranging from 3 to 108, though it is usually fixed at 51. Historically the oldest *pīṭhas* seem to be centered on two regions on the northern Himalayan range: Kāmarūpa in the northeast, which is mentioned in all the earliest lists of *pīṭhas*, and the Tantric centers of the northwest regions like Kashmir and the Swat valley. With the coming of Islam, the northwestern *pīṭhas* largely declined, and there appears to have been a proliferation of new *pīṭhas* emerging in northeast India, especially in Bengal.[16] Today, the major living *śākta pīṭhas* include a wide array of vibrant goddess temples, such as Kāmākhyā in Assam, Kālīghāṭ in Kolkata, Hiṅglāja in Baluchistan, Bagalāmukhī in Datia, and Tārāpīṭha in Bengal. Together, the *pīṭhas* comprise a vast, interconnected, sacred landscape suffused with the goddess' vital energy. As Sarah Caldwell observes in her study of Śākta Tantra in South India, "Throughout India, the earth is regarded as a sacred, living entity having a female nature. From the temple of Bhārat Māta in Banaras to Kāmarūpa in Assam . . . the land of India is infused with *śakti*, female creative power."[17]

Sociologically, the *pīṭhas* also played a key role in the culture of South Asia's many traditions of *siddhas* (perfected beings), *sādhus* (holy men), *yogis*, and *yoginīs*. As Davidson notes, "Modern Indian *sādhus* congregate and encounter one another at sites of mythic importance, and it might be expected that such was formerly the case as well."[18] As we will see below, there is much evidence that Kāmākhyā was a central pilgrimage site for *sādhus* and *siddhas* from an early date, and today, one can find hundreds of holy men and women camped around the precincts of the temple. Along with Rishikesh, Haridwar, and Varanasi, it remains one of the most popular destinations for *sādhus* of every sectarian persuasion, but above all for the red-clad Śāktas who fill the temple grounds.

Finally, throughout Tantric literature, the geographic *pīṭhas* are also mapped onto the physical body and the sacred landscape of the individual self.[19] As we will see in Chapter 4, the *pīṭhas* are typically identified with specific power centers within the individual human body, the microcosmic reflection of the divine cosmic body. And Kāmarūpa, the place of desire, is identified with the most hidden, most sacred place within the human body in which Śiva and Śakti unite in secret love: it is at once the *yoni pīṭha* or sexual organ of the female body and the secret center between the genitals and anus within the male body.[20]

The power of the goddess, in short, suffuses the macrocosm, the socio-cosm, and the microcosm alike, at once the geographic landscape of the *śākta pīṭhas,* the social landscape of South Asian religious life and physical landscape of the individual body. The entire universe itself is born from the creative interplay of desire and power, the love play of Śiva and Śakti, which generates and pervades every aspect of being. According to another tenth- to eleventh-century text, the *Kulacūḍāmaṇi Tanta,* "Whatever exists in this world is of the nature of Śiva and Śakti. Therefore, O Great Lord, you are everywhere and I am everyone. You are everything, O Lord, and I am everything, O Eternal One."[21]

The body of desire: The historical origins of Kāmarūpa and Śākta Tantra

If the mythic origins of Kāmākhyā are well known, the historical origins of Tantra in Assam (and in South Asia as whole) are much more difficult to trace. From the textual, sculptural, and archeological evidence, there appears to have been a major goddess temple here from at least the eighth century, if not long before. As D.C. Sircar notes in his study of the *śākta pīṭhas,* the region of Kāmarūpa seems to have been identified as an unrivaled center of Tantric culture and the seat of the goddess' *yoni* from an early date, mentioned as early as the fourth century in the Allahabad pillar inscription of Samudragupta.[22] Many art historians believe there is archeological evidence on Kāmākhyā hill and in the lower strata of the temple that indicates the existence of an older structure dating back perhaps as early as the fifth to seventh centuries.[23] However, the earliest textual reference to Kāmarūpa as a *pīṭha* comes from the *Hevajra Tantra,* one of the oldest Buddhist *tantras* composed in probably the eighth century. Here Kāmarūpa is mentioned together with Jālandhara, Oḍḍiyāna (Uḍḍiyāna), and Paurṇagiri (Pūrṇagiri) as one of the four great seats of power.[24]

The existence of a major goddess temple in Kāmarūpa at this time does seem to be supported by at least one of the royal land grant plates from the Varman dynasty. According to a copper plate of King Vanamāla from the ninth century, the great river Lauhitya (the modern Brahmaputra) flows "over the slopes of the mountain Kāmakūṭa at the top of which there is the residence of the illustrious god Kāmeśvara and the goddess Mahāgaurī."[25] Since the *Kālikā Purāṇa* explicitly refers to Śiva and Kāmākhyā as Kāmeśvara and Mahāgaurī and to Nīlācala hill as Kāmatagiri or Kāmakūṭa, most scholars take this to be an early reference to Kāmākhyā temple as a major seat of Śākta Hinduism in the northeast.[26]

The height of the temple's early flourishing, however, appears to have been during Kāmarūpa's Pāla dynasty (tenth to twelfth centuries), the Assamese counterpart to the Pāla dynasty of Bengal–Bihar, which was a great patron of Tantric Buddhism. With its seat of power in the Guwahati/Kāmākhyā area, the Pāla dynasty gave birth to the greatest flourishing of sculpture and architecture in ancient Assam.[27] Other scholars and I have discovered a vast number of fragments scattered all over the present Kāmākhyā temple complex and hillside, including a number of quite beautiful female *yoginī* and other goddess figures, most of which are far older than the present temple and have been dated by art historians to the late Pāla era (Figs. 2–3).[28] As we will see below, the presence of these female *yoginī* figures may also indicate the possible existence of an actual *yoginī* temple here, or at least the worship of *yoginīs* as part of the original Kāmākhyā complex.[29]

The Pāla era is also believed to be the period in which Assam's oldest and most important Śākta text—the *Kālikā Purāṇa* (tenth to eleventh century)—was composed, probably under the reign of King Ratnapāla (920–60) or more likely King Dharmapāla (1035–60). According to copper plate inscriptions from the region, Dharmapāla was praised as a ferocious warrior in battle: "In the battlefield, decorated with flower-like petals, struck from the heads of elephants, killed by the blows of his sword, that king alone remained victorious."[30] Yet, he was also renowned as a supporter of religion and learning, a generous patron of priests, sacrifices, and sacred texts: "With Dharmapāla's ascension the kingdom regained her lost prestige. Being peaceful at home and warlike abroad, Dharmapāla not only established a reign of virtue within the kingdom but he extended the bounds of Kāmarūpa by conquering the lost possessions in north Bengal."[31]

Indeed, much of the *Kālikā Purāṇa* centers on the greatness of the goddess Kāmākhyā as supreme goddess of power, the wonders of the kingdom of Kāmarūpa as the abode of the goddess, and the benefits to kings who offer their patronage to the goddess:

> Just as Viṣṇu and Lakṣmī are the greatest of all [deities], so too worship of the goddess in Kāmarūpa, the abode of the gods [is the greatest of all worship]. Kāmarūpa is known as the land of the goddess. There is nowhere else equal to it. Elsewhere the goddess is rare, but in Kāmarūpa, she dwells in every household .... One who performs worship of the goddess of Great Illusion at Kāmākhyā attains all his desires here on earth and assumes Śiva's form in the afterlife. He has no equal, and for him there is nothing left to be done. Having had his desires fulfilled here on earth he lives a long life. His movement is like the wind, unobstructed by others. He becomes invincible in battle and in debate on the scriptures.[32]

This link between kingship and the powerful goddess of the *śākta pīṭha* reflects a much broader trend in the rise of Hindu and Buddhist Tantra in South Asia during these centuries. With the collapse of the great Gupta empire in the sixth century, much of South Asia was divided into a multitude of smaller, shifting centers of political power, many of them ruled by low-class or non-Hindu kings who were seeking divine authority for their new-found power. As White observes, these medieval kings often sought the authority offered by Tantra and the worship of fierce, protective, and destructive goddesses: "In order to legitimate their power, these newly arisen rulers called on a variety of religious specialists to ritually consecrate them with tantric mantras, transforming them into divine kings."[33] As we will see in the following chapters, this linkage between kings in search of power and the goddess as divine power is one that recurs throughout the history of Assamese Tantra, from the Pāla dynasty down to the coming of British colonial rule.

The homeland of Tantra: The siddhas and the Yoginī Kaula tradition

One of the primary reasons that Kāmākhyā is often said to be the original heartland or homeland of Tantra is that it is so closely tied to the origin of one of the oldest and most quintessentially Tantric traditions: the Yoginī Kaula school founded by the great *siddha* (perfected being or sage) Matsyendranātha, who probably lived around

900 CE.[34] Perhaps the most important figure for the early development of both Hindu and Buddhist Tantra in South Asia, Matsyendra is said to have received his esoteric knowledge in Kāmarūpa while living among the many powerful female *yoginīs* who dwell there. As P.C. Bagchi notes, "Matsyendra was the founder of a new sect of the *Kaula* school, called *Yoginī-kaula*, and its chief seat was Kāmarūpa."[35] The term *yoginī* here has multiple meanings, ranging from human female practitioners of *yoga* to powerful and frightening female deities who are worshipped with blood, meat, and wine in secret Tantric ritual.[36] In any case, it was from these powerful *yoginīs* that Matsyendra learned the secret Kaula (from *kula*, "clan" or "family") doctrine, which then spread throughout South Asian Tantra. Two of the earliest works ascribed to Matsyendra both cite Kāmarūpa as his original inspiration. Thus the *Akulavīra Tantra* tells us that the sage was granted this secret teaching by the grace of the female *yoginīs* of Kāmarūpa.[37] Likewise, the key early Tantric text, the *Kaulajñāna Nirṇaya* (tenth to eleventh centuries), suggests that this secret practice was known in every one of the *yoginīs'* homes in the land before being revealed to Matsyendra:

> Female *sādhus*, adept at yoga, dwell at Kāmākhyā *pīṭha*. If one joins with one, he attains *yoginī siddhi* [the supernatural power of the *yoginīs*].[38]

> The [work known] by the name of the "Bringing Forth of the [Kaula] Gnosis" was one million five hundred thousand [verses in length]. This [teaching] is the essence, O Lord, extracted upward from the midst of that. This teaching [is found] in every one of the Yoginī's lodges in Kāmākhyā. Through their pure knowledge of this [teaching], O Goddess, the Yoginīs confer "seizure" and "release," supernatural power and union with themselves.[39]

As we will see in Chapter 4, the reference to Kāmākhyā or Kāmarūpa here can also be a purely metaphorical reference to the "place of desire," which is usually identified with the female sexual organ as the central object of Tantric worship. But whether it is a symbolic or literal geographic locale, Kāmākhyā holds a central place in the narrative of early Tantra in South Asia.

The first temple here is said to have been built by Lord Kāma and the divine architect Viśvakarman, who constructed a temple dedicated to the goddess surrounded by images of the 64 *yoginīs*.[40] And the *yoni* itself was encircled by the eight primary *yoginīs*: "On that *yoni*, the loving goddess in her five forms eternally amuses herself . . . There the eight eternal *yoginīs*, namely Śailaputrā and the rest, are always seated around the goddess in their primary forms."[41] The worship of the *yoginīs* spread throughout India from about the eighth to tenth centuries and gave rise to many key Tantric temples dedicated to the 64 (or 81) *yoginīs* at sites such as Hirapur, Bheraghat, and Khajuraho. Although there is today no solid evidence of a *yoginī* temple in Assam comparable to Hirapur or Khajuraho, Kāmākhyā is still credited by many as the original homeland of the *yoginī* tradition. As art historian Vidya Dehejia comments,

> [I]t seems undeniable that the cult was once prominent in these regions. The Kāmākhyā temple in Assam is one of the few Devī shrines where, to this day, the daily worship of Devī Kāmākhyā includes the invocation of the 64 Yoginīs, who are named one by one in the pūjā . . . The Yoginī cult was obviously of importance at Kāmākhyā . . . The *Kālikā Purāṇa*, which contains material pertinent to the Yoginīs, including two varying lists of 64 names . . . contains an entire chapter describing Kāmarūpa . . . with its rivers and mountains.[42]

In fact, scattered around the grounds of the present Kāmākhyā temple are a number of much older and finer images of female figures, most dating from the tenth to twelfth centuries. Perhaps the most beautiful of these is the Bala Bhairavī that now lies just behind the Bhairavī temple below the main Kāmākhyā temple, which probably dates to the twelfth century.[43] I have identified at least six other very similar fragments scattered around the complex, including two Cāmuṇḍās, which appear to be part of a set from a single workshop. According to several art historians who specialize in *yoginī* temples and images, including Kimberly Masteller and Padma Kaimal, it is likely that these figures are *yoginīs* and possibly part of a larger temple complex.[44] Are these the remains of the eight *yoginīs* that were said to have been installed at the original Kāmākhyā temple surrounding the *yoni-pīṭha*? Or were they even part of a larger *yoginī* temple that once existed on the hill? It is perhaps impossible to say today, but at least some authors have taken these to be remnants of *yoginīs* and Bhairavas from the original Tantric complex. Pranav Deka has even argued that there was in fact a 64-*yoginī* temple on the hill that was demolished sometime after the Pāla dynasty came to an end in the twelfth century:

> [The] Causaṣṭi Yoginī is totally ruined, demolished and nobody is sure where exactly it stood . . . It is believed that the temple was located somewhere on the north-east of the present Kāmākhyā temple. A large number of partly damaged stone statues of beautiful women (Yoginī) has been found in the debris.[45]

In addition to the great *siddha* Matsyendranātha and the Kaula Yoginī tradition, various other *siddhas* are said to have been associated with Assam and even with the early kings of Kāmarūpa.[46] Some of the oldest Tantric songs attributed to the *siddhas* are the *Caryāpadas* (tenth to twelfth centuries), which are composed in a northeastern language that seems to be a mixture of proto-Assamese, proto-Bangla, and proto-Oriya. Two of these highly influential songs are attributed to Luī-pā (a.k.a. Matsyendranātha) who is said to have flourished in Kāmarūpa, and four others are attributed to Saraha, who may have been born in Assam.[47] Many Assamese scholars believe that the Pāla kings, particularly Ratnapāla and Indrapāla, were patrons of the Tantric Buddhist *siddhas* and possibly also practitioners themselves. As S. Sasanananda suggests, "[T]he Pāla line of kings patronized the system of Vajrayāna and some of them became converts and also attained the status of preceptors."[48]

Finally, a number of extremely interesting sculptural figures have been recently discovered in the Ambari region of Guwahati, which date to the twelfth to fourteenth centuries. Among these are a set of male ascetics with long hair piled on top of their heads, pointed beards, long, slit earlobes, and wearing only a small loin cloth (Fig. 4). Based on comparisons with later Tantric figures from other parts of India, art historian Rob Linrothe identifies these as Śaivite *siddhas*.[49] What is perhaps most interesting is that one of these figures is also accompanied by a female, who is either his disciple or consort and therefore indicates the early presence of female *siddhas* in Assam, as well.

The power at the margins: Vedic and indigenous elements in Tantra

One of the most important issues that I think the case of Kāmākhyā and Assam can help illuminate is the question of the non-Hindu or indigenous influence in Tantra. The question of the tribal vs. Vedic origins of Tantra is a long and convoluted debate, which dates almost to the first discovery of Tantric texts by Western scholars. On the one hand, many Western authors like Mircea Eliade assumed that the Tantras must represent some kind of "archaic" or "autochthonous" substratum of religious practice that long predated the arrival of Aryan culture and the Vedas.[50] More recent authors like Vidya Dehejia have suggested that the powerful Tantric current of the Yoginī-Kaula tradition "has roots outside the fold of the orthodox Brahmanical tradition," and indeed, with its "magical rituals and spells, sounds and gestures, is a movement that has deep connections with rural and tribal traditions."[51]

On the other hand, since the time of Sir John Woodroffe and continuing with many contemporary scholars, others have argued that there is little evidence for a tribal basis for Tantra and that this is instead a tradition that grew primarily out of the Vedas and *brāhmaṇic* culture. As Gavin Flood put it, "There is no evidence for a non-Aryan substratum for Tantrism, which must be understood as a predominantly Brahmanical, Sanskritic tradition with its roots in the Veda."[52]

My own opinion is that—at least in the case of northeast India and the worship of Kāmākhyā—the situation is far more complex and most likely involved a more subtle kind of *interaction, negotiation and mutual transformation* between Vedic *brāhmaṇic* and local non-Hindu traditions. As Ronald Davidson aptly observes, Tantric and tribal traditions have long been confused—by *both* Western and Indian observers—because they share a number of basic practices: blood sacrifice, beheading, consumption of meat and wine, etc.

> [T]he entire edifice of "tantrism" has been difficult to separate from tribal religions, for several reasons. First, tribal systems represented the historical "Other" for much of Indian religion, orthodox and heterodox alike. Second, tribal systems engaged in blood sacrifices, including human sacrifice, so those denominations relieving ennui with the beheading of their fellow man (Kāpālikās) were poorly distinguished from tribal systems.[53]

But more important, Davidson suggests, early Tantric leaders like the *siddhas* were actively working among tribal areas, converting indigenous peoples to more orthodox Hindu and Buddhist practice and also accommodating tribal traditions in the newly emerging forms of Tantric practice: "Siddhas became the first line of temporal involvement with tribal and outcaste peoples, appropriated and imitated cult practices objects and sites, and set up preferred siddha religious activities in distant provinces and foreign lands."[54]

Tantra, particularly in heavily tribal areas like the northeast, thus formed a crucial nexus in the larger interaction between Hindu *brāhmaṇs* who were actively Sanskritizing the marginal regions and indigenous traditions that were slowly being absorbed into mainstream Hinduism. As Davidson notes, many of the oldest Tantric *pīṭhas* have some sort of "tribal affiliation" and were originally tribal centers of worship before being assimilated into centers of goddess worship. Thus, one of the four oldest *pīṭhas,* Jālandhara, "where the goddess Mahāmāyā (Vajreśvarī) is worshipped in the modern town of Kangra . . . was probably a Gaddi tribal site before Brahmans and Śaiva sādhus took possession."[55] D.C. Sircar likewise notes examples of indigenous deities being assimilated into the goddesses of the *pīṭhas.* Thus the goddess Rukmiṇī at the *pīṭha* of Ghāṭaśila in Bengal is "apparently the Sanskritized form of the name of the aboriginal deity Raṅkiṇī whose worship is widely prevalent in the Burdwan District of Bengal" and was believed to have been worshipped with human sacrifices up to the nineteenth century.[56]

But nowhere is this indigenous foundation more apparent than in the Kāmākhyā *pīṭha* in Assam. As Debendranāth Bhaṭṭācārya suggests, Assam has long been "the meeting place of various Aryan and non-Aryan peoples," and the worship of Śakti in the region is a complex melding of Hindu and indigenous traditions.[57] Throughout early Sanskrit literature such as the *Mahābhārata,* the realm of Assam or Prāgjyotiṣa is consistently described as a heavily tribal, non-Hindu region, "surrounded by mountain men and Chinese," filled with "barbarians," and ruled by King Bhagadatta, "a strong overlord of the barbarians."[58] Even today, Assam is home to India's richest diversity of indigenous peoples, with 23 recognized tribes coming from a wide array of ethnic and linguistic backgrounds such as Mon-Khmer, Tibeto-Burman, and Shan.

In Assamese texts such as the *Kālikā Purāṇa* and *Yoginī Tantra,* Assam is said to have been originally the land of a group called the *kirātas*—a generic term used to refer to the indigenous, non-Hindu peoples who inhabited the remote mountainous areas and particularly the northeast hills. Many contemporary historians believe that the *kirātas* were probably speakers of a Tibeto-Burman language and ancestors of the Bodo-Kachari peoples of modern Assam.[59] According to the *Kālikā Purāṇa,* the *kirātas* were the first inhabitants of Kāmarūpa and were said to be "shaven-headed and addicted to wine and meat."[60] Likewise, the *Yoginī Tantra* describes the original religion of Assam as *kirāta dharma*, which involved sexual freedom and the consumption of ducks, pigeons, tortoises, boars, and other impure animals:

> In the greatest of all [*pīṭhas*], the *yoginī-pīṭha*, the religion is considered to be that of the *kirātas*. There is no renunciation or long [penance] in Kāmarūpa, O Beloved. Meat is not forsaken there, and there is no celibacy . . . In Kāmarūpa, ducks, pigeons, tortoises, and boars are eaten.[61]

In the mytho-historical account of the *Kālikā Purāṇa*, Kāmarūpa was first conquered by King Naraka—a complex, semi-divine, and tragic figure who was born from the union of the god Viṣṇu and the goddess Earth during the highly inauspicious time of the Earth's menstrual period. At the command of Lord Viṣṇu, King Naraka invaded Kāmarūpa and drove out the indigenous *kirātas*; he then established a number of twice-born families who were masters of the Vedas and the *śāstras*. Thereafter, "[e]veryone became devoted to the study of the Vedas and engaged in offering of gifts and religious duty. In a short time, the land of Kāmarūpa became renowned."[62] Moreover, Viṣṇu also commanded Naraka and his descendents to continue worshipping the great goddess Kāmākhyā, who had already been established in Assam long before the coming of Naraka and his Vedic priests. Indeed, the "mother of the world always dwells there, having assumed the form of Kāmākhyā," and so Naraka was warned never to worship any other deity but this great mother (*ambikā*).[63] As Davidson comments, this narrative seems to frankly admit that the worship of Kāmākhyā was already in practice among pre-Hindu tribal communities in Kāmarūpa before the conquest of King Naraka, who simply continued worship of a goddess who long predated *brāhmaṇic* Hindu traditions: "its prior history as a tribal site of the Kirātas is fully acknowledged . . . [C]aste Hindus simply took the expedient of driving out the tribal occupants and pursued the worship of the goddess along the lines established before the Hindus arrived."[64]

The *Kālikā Purāṇa* also states quite clearly that non-Hindu indigenous rites – especially highly sexual rites – were incorporated directly into mainstream Hindu festivals. Thus, the great festival of Durgā Pūjā is said to be conclude with the wild celebration of the "Śabarotsava," or festival of the Śabara peoples, a mountainous hill tribe often identified with the *kirātas*.[65] The festival culminates in a kind of ceremonial-sexual chaos, as prostitutes, virgins, and dancers join in with music and dance, exchanging rude comments and sexually explicit jokes.[66]

In fact, powerful mother goddesses were worshipped by many of the northeast tribal communities, such as the Bodos, Chutiyas, Jaintias, Khasis, Lalungs, and Rabhas.[67] Thus the Khasis honored Ka blei Synshar, "Goddess of the World," while the Jaintias worshipped a powerful form of Durgā with blood (and at one time human) sacrifice at her temple in Nartiang, Meghalaya. The Chutiya kings, who ruled eastern Assam from the thirteenth to the sixteenth centuries, were known for their worship of the terrible goddess Kecāi Khāti, or "She who eats raw flesh," and her temple near Sadiya was infamous for the regular offering of human sacrifice.[68]

Many historians have suggested that Kāmākhyā herself may have originally been a tribal mother goddess and that Nīlācala hill may have been a sacrificial site for nearby peoples such as the Khasis and Garos.[69] Some trace the name itself to the Khasi goddess *Ka Meikha*, or "old cousin mother."[70] To this day, in fact, many Khasi and Garo folk tales claim that Kāmākhyā was originally a site of their own deities. Thus, one narrative describes Kāmākhyā hill as "the place at which the Khasis halted during their journey from . . . the Himalayas to their present home," and the hill is still referred to as *U Lum Ka Meikha* by many Khasis.[71] The Garos tell a similar tale about Kāmākhyā hill as the place they stopped on their journey through the region and installed the fertility goddess Phojou.[72] To this day, contemporary authorities at the temple, such as the president of the Kāmākhyā Temple Trust Board, assert that "all tribal peoples had been worshippers of Kamakhya,"[73] and that her current worship is simply the continuation of this ancient tradition.

It is worth noting that the Khasis, Garos, Jaintias, and several other tribes of southern Assam and Meghalaya are matrilineal, with descent traced through the mother and property inherited by the youngest daughter. Various authors have speculated that this may have provided a fertile ground for worship of the mother goddess as divine feminine power.[74]

The two faces of the Tantric goddess: loving mother, terrifying destroyer

In sum, the goddess Kāmākhyā is an extremely eclectic figure, who assimilated a variety of older goddesses, both Hindu and indigenous, into her complex form. As we see in popular representations of the goddess today, she is a complex synthesis of a number of mainstream Hindu goddesses, incorporating the iconography of Durgā, Lakṣmī, Kālī, and others into her multi-armed, many-headed form (Fig. 5). Yet she also incorporates more wild and bloody elements drawn from the indigenous traditions of the northeast. As Kakati observes, "All independent deities began to be identified with her as her manifestations. . . . The concept of the Mother Goddess assumed a cosmic perspective and all unconnected local numina were affiliated to her."[75] As we will see in Chapter 3, it seems likely that this assimilation of many local goddesses into one "Great Mother" was also part of the attempt by Assam's kings to assimilate a variety of local communities into a larger political formation under a single ruling power: "The cult of Kāmākhyā belonged to matriarchal tribes like the Khasis and Garos. To win their allegiance . . . royal patronage was extended to the local cult of Kāmākhyā."[76] Conversely, non-Hindu groups like the Ahoms also gradually assimilated their own deities with mainstream Hindu gods and goddesses. Thus the Ahom goddess Lāṅkuri became equated with the supreme Śakti or Durgā; the god Buṛhā Deotā became Śiva; Kṣim Tyāo became Viṣṇu; and so on.[77]

Within the temple itself, Kāmākhyā is represented not by any human image, but by a sheet of stone that slopes downwards from both sides, meeting in a *yoni*-like depression. When she is represented in iconic form, Kāmākhyā appears as an extremely ambivalent goddess, who has two very different sides—a *śānta* or peaceful state and an *ugra* or terrifying state. In the words of Kṛṣṇarāma Nyāyavāgīśa, the well-known Śākta theologian and preceptor of the Ahom king Śiva Siṅgha, the goddess has a twofold nature, at once loving and horrifying, creative and destructive: "She will put on red clothes and red and yellow flower-garlands and bestow sexual pleasure to her devotee. During war and danger, she will throw away her clothes and flowers, will take sword in hand to protect her devotees and take revenge."[78] In her *sānta* state, she is the beautiful Lady of All Desires, Sarva-Kāmeśvarī, "seated on a red lotus in the red-lotus posture, with a fresh and youthful body, her hair untied, wearing a fine necklace, seated on the chest of a corpse, her breasts swelled and high, beautiful, with clothes like the rising sun"[79] (Fig. 6). As the *Kāmākhyā Tantra* describes her, she is the very essence of *kāma* as eros embodied, surrounded by *yoginīs* and Kinnarā women (a hill tribe of the Himalayas) chanting erotic words. Again, we might note here the association of the goddess with tribal groups and the tribal groups in turn associated with eroticism:

> Wearing red garments, offering boons, adorned with a vermillion mark on her forehead, immaculate, the abode of nectar, radiant with a rosy face, adorned with gold, jewels, rubies and other ornaments, supreme, seated on a lion throne made of gold and jewels, etc . . . Beautiful in her entire body, always surrounded by the Vidyā [goddesses], adorned by *ḍākinīs* and *yoginīs*, accompanied by loving women and fragrant with various perfumes . . . Three eyed, infatuating, holding a bow made of flowers, she is praised by the Kinnarā women by the chanting of "*bhaga-liṅga*" [vagina and penis].[80]

In her terrible *ugra* form, however, the goddess appears in her most frightening and destructive aspects. Here she is identified with Kālī, the dark goddess of time and death, "taking up a sword and standing on a naked white corpse, with eyes rolling and hair disheveled,"[81] or the emaciated terrifying Cāmuṇḍā, who smiles ghoulishly as she sits upon a human corpse and drinks blood from a skull-bowl (Fig. 7). As the *Kālikā Purāṇa* describes her,

> When it is the time for love, she abandons her sword and adorns herself with a garland. When she is no longer in a loving mood, she holds a sword. When it is time for love, she is seated on a red lotus placed on the body of Śiva. But when she is no longer in a loving mood, she is seated on a white corpse.[82]

These two sides of Kāmākhyā—as lovingly sensual and violently destructive—recur throughout the mythology and ritual of the goddess, who is worshipped with both sensual rites and sacrifice as the two primary forms through which blood, desire, and power flow to and from the *yoni pīṭha*.

Conclusions: Tantra, power, and the negotiation between indigenous and brāhmaṇic traditions

In sum, the *yoni pīṭha* of Kāmākhyā sheds important and much-needed light on both the origins and the landscape of early Tantra in South Asia. As a whole, the *pīṭhas* comprise a complex matrix of power, a capillary network made up of many sacred nodes in the flow of the goddess' sexo-religio-political energy. But they also comprise a complex social and religious network, where holy men and women from all over South Asia gather in the course of their pilgrimage across the subcontinent. And finally, many of the *pīṭhas* have also served as points of intersection, interaction, and negotiation between the many non-Hindu indigenous populations on the margins of India and the *brāhmaṇic* Hindu traditions coming from central India.

The *yoni-pīṭha* of Kāmākhyā is arguably among the most important nodes in this complex matrix of power. Not only is this perhaps the oldest and most revered Śākta center in the subcontinent, but it also represents a remarkably complex interaction between *brāhmaṇic* and indigenous traditions. This interaction is far more nuanced and interesting than a mere thin veneer of Hinduism pasted clumsily onto a tribal substratum. Rather, it is an extremely complex sort of negotiation between the indigenous cultures of the northeast and the Vedic traditions coming from central India, which evolved over the course of more than a thousand years. At the heart of this negotiation were the *brāhmaṇ* specialists in Vedic ritual and their patrons, the various kings of Assam, almost all of whom came from non-Hindu, indigenous backgrounds.

As we will see throughout the sacrificial rites and the royal patronage of Śākta Tantra in Assam, orthodox *brāhmaṇic* and non-Hindu indigenous influences are intimately linked and help define the unique nature of the goddess in her most powerful forms. The result is hardly a singular, static, or homogenous concept of "Tantra," but rather, a rich, dynamic, and shifting complex of traditions that evolved and changed over hundreds of years, incorporating both traditional Vedic and many indigenous religious practices. This more nuanced and complex view of Tantra as a living, historical phenomenon, I think, helps us understand not just the specific case the *yoni pīṭha* of Kāmākhyā but the broader landscape of Hindu Tantra in South Asia.

In turn, the case of Kāmākhyā can also help us rethink the nature of "power" itself. The concept of *śakti* clearly has much in common with both Deleuze's notion of desire as a productive "flow" and Foucault's notion of power as a decentralized network of fluid "capillary" relations. Indeed, I think the Foucaultian view of power goes a long way to helping us understand *śakti* as a productive, pervasive, and circulating power, a kind of power that is also deeply *corporal* and intimately tied to the body and to sexuality.[83] Yet the concept of *śakti* also points to some key weaknesses of the Foucaultian approach, particularly when applied to non-European cultures. As I noted in the introduction to this book, both the Deleuzian and Foucaultian views suffer from a certain gender-blindness, that is, an inattention to the different constructions of masculinity and femininity and to the differential power relations between the sexes. But at the same time, as critics such as Lois McNay, Jürgen Habermas, and others have argued, Foucault's model of power is in many ways so broad and generalized that it risks losing some of its explanatory value. As McNay notes, "a multiplicity of divergent phenomena are subsumed under a totalizing and undifferentiated notion of power . . . [P]ower is generalized to such an extent that it loses any analytic force."[84] To many critics, Foucault's idea of power seems like an omnipresent, all-encompassing, yet strangely impersonal force, one that acts mysteriously without human agents to exercise it—a kind of "intentionality without a subject" or "action without agency."[85] As such, it risks overlooking the more specific individuals, institutions, state formations, and social relations through which power operates.[86]

In the chapters that follow, I will suggest that we can use the Indian concept of *śakti* in order to critique, refine, and sharpen our understanding of power. Above all, I will argue for a model of power that is at once (a) fundamentally *gendered*, that is, intimately tied to constructions of gender and relations between males and females, and (b) *performative*, that is, continuously reenacted by a wide array of human agents, through the narration of myths, the performance of rituals, and the celebration of festivals.[87] Far from an abstract essence without an agent, power in this case is very clearly embodied in real human agents, ritual acts, and negotiations between a variety of historical actors, from the priests who perform her worship to the kings who sponsor her *pūjās* to the *tāntrikas* who celebrate her secret rites, down to the ordinary male and female devotees who worship the goddess in her popular forms.

The result is a complex capillary network of relations that flows throughout the entire social organism, much as the blood of the goddess flows from the temple during her annual menstruation, through the priests who offer her sacrifices, to the Tantric initiates who perform her secret rites, to the kings who patronize her worship.

Chapter Two

BLOOD FOR THE GODDESS: ANIMAL SACRIFICE AND DIVINE MENSTRUATION

> The gods are pleased by sacrifices; by sacrifice, everything is established. The earth is upheld by sacrifice; sacrifice saves living beings. Creatures live on food, and food grows from rain. Rains come from sacrifice; thus everything is made of sacrifice.
>
> —*Kālikā Purāṇa* (KP 31.7–8)

> The danger which is risked by boundary transgression is power. Those vulnerable margins and those attacking forces which threaten to destroy good order represent the powers inhering the cosmos. Ritual which can harness these . . . is harnessing power indeed.
>
> —Mary Douglas, *Purity and Danger* (1966)[1]

So much of the literature on Tantra has focused so heavily on sex that we have often forgotten what is at least as important an aspect of Tantra as a lived tradition: namely, sacrifice and the ritual offering of blood, which is central to the symbolism and practice of much of South Asian Tantra. As Madeleine Biardeau, Brian K. Smith, J.C. Heesterman, and others have argued, sacrifice (*yajña, bali-dāna*) is a kind of master trope and recurring paradigm throughout the Hindu traditions of South Asia. From the elaborate animal sacrifices of the Vedas and Brāhmaṇas to the internalized sacrifice of yoga and meditation in the Upaniṣads, to the great "sacrifice of battle" in the Epics, to the self-sacrifice of devotional love (*bhakti-yoga*) in the Bhāgavad Gīta, sacrifice is arguably one of the most persistent, unifying themes throughout the many complex traditions that we call Hinduism over the last 3500 years. As Biardeau puts it, "The ritual act, ceaselessly repeated, is the model of all action. The sacrifice, as the mode of communication between the earth and heaven, is the center. Everything could become sacrifice."[2]

Tantra, I would argue, represents one of latest but most interesting variations on this sacrificial theme. Even as animal sacrifice gradually dropped out of mainstream *brāhmaṇic* Hinduism, it survived and resurfaced in the Śākta and Tantric traditions. Thus, the *Kālikā Purāṇa* declares that sacrifice is the origin and foundation of everything; indeed, sacrifice *is* everything. As Ronald Davidson points out, the quintessential Tantric *yoginī* temples, such as the sixty-four *yoginī* temple in Hirapur, contain no depictions of sexual rites and very little erotica, but quite a number of severed heads, suggesting that "sanguinary rites were probably the principal activity practiced"[3] (Fig. 8). However, the kind of sacrifice we see in the Tantric and Śākta traditions also combines elements of Vedic ritual with more explicitly un-Vedic and often highly transgressive elements. Particularly in the case of Kāmākhyā, sacrifice to the goddess includes a number of clearly non-Vedic and impure animals (for example, buffaloes), offered in extremely non-Vedic ways (such as bloody beheading). Many of these sacrificial traditions, we will see, owe far more to the indigenous, pre-Hindu religions of the northeast hills than to any Vedic rite. Again, they reflect the complex negotiation between Vedic and indigenous traditions that epitomizes the hybrid nature of Assamese Tantra, and perhaps South Asian Tantra as a whole.

Overall, the ritual and symbolism at Kāmākhyā center largely on blood as the vehicle—both literal and metaphorical—of the goddess' power. Even today, the dominant motif at Kāmākhyā temple is clearly the color red and its associated symbolism: from the hundreds of red-clad priests and holy men who circulate around the temple grounds, to the generous application of vermilion powder on images of the goddess around the temple (including the prominent menstruating figure on the side of the temple), to the regular offerings of blood sacrifice, to the red cloths handed out at the time of the goddess' annual menstruation, the entire temple complex is a kind of "capillary network" of red- and blood-related symbolism (Figs. 9–10).[4]

In this chapter, I explore two primary aspects of the goddess' symbolism and ritual, both of which center on the circulation of blood: namely, the association of Kāmākhyā with the earth's annual menstruation and the worship of Kāmākhyā with regular offerings of blood sacrifice. Both of these, I suggest, reveal the complex negotiation between Sanskritic Hindu and indigenous traditions that lies at the heart of Assamese Tantra. And both reflect the creative—yet also dangerously impure—power of bodily fluids that are integral to Tantric ritual practice. Both the goddess' annual menstruation and the offering of sacrifice center on the power of the impure, the power inherent in bodily fluids that lie outside the domain of social norms and laws of purity, but that can be unleashed by the logic of ritual inversion. Borrowing some insights from Mary Douglas and Georges Bataille, I will suggest that much of the power of Tantra lies precisely in acts of ritual transgression that deliberately make use of the dangerous yet auspicious fluids that overflow the boundaries of the physical and social body.[5]

As we will see in the following chapters, the paradigm of blood sacrifice and ritual transgression is also a key part of both the royal power of South Asian kingship and the esoteric power of the sexual rites for which Tantra is so infamous in the popular imagination to this day.

Blood of the goddess: Divine menstruation and the capillary flow of power

Since at least the eleventh or the twelfth century, Kāmākhyā has been identified as the supreme locus of the goddess' menstruation, believed to flow from the earth once every year in order to circulate throughout and nourish the world (Fig. 9). To this day, as we will see in more detail in Chapter 7, the most important festival at Kāmākhyā temple is Ambuvācī Melā, which celebrates of the goddess' annual menstruation during the summer month of Āṣāḍha (June–July). Occurring at the beginning of the monsoon season, with the coming of the rains after the heat of summer, Ambuvācī marks the flow of the goddess' life-giving blood to the earth.[6] But it is also a celebration that reflects the profound ambivalence of the goddess' blood and the power that it embodies, a power that is tied to impurity and to the dangerous potency of sexual fluids. Again, as David Shulman suggests, "Power is . . . derived from forces that are contaminating; these forces belong to the violent substratum of chaos out of which the world emerged."[7] And the goddess' menstrual blood is the very essence of this contaminating, chaotic but creative force.

The historical origins of Ambuvācī are by no means clear. Probably the earliest reference comes from the *Devī Bhāgavata Purāṇa* (eleventh to twelfth centuries), where it is described as the aftereffect of the intense love-play between Viṣṇu and the goddess Earth. Assuming his boar (*varāha*) incarnation, Viṣṇu made love to Earth for an entire year of the gods (360 human years). At the end of their dalliance, he worshipped Earth as the supreme goddess and declared that she would be honored on several key occasions: at the beginning of the planting season, at the laying of the foundation of a new home, and at the end of the Ambuvācī ceremony:

> You are the bearer of all things, O Auspicious One, you are worshipped happily by all the sages, Manus, gods, *siddhas* and demons. On the day the Ambuvācī ceremony closes, when laying the entry at the start of building a house, at the start of digging a well and tilling the soil, [everyone] should worship you, with wine, etc. Those fools who do not will go to hell.[8]

The same text also links the Earth's menstrual cycle specifically to the holy *pīṭha* of Kāmākhyā, which is praised as the greatest of all goddess temples and the most powerful place in the world. Thus it is to Kāmākhyā, the seat of the *yoni*, that the goddess comes each month during her period:

> Kāmākhyā, the place of the *yoni-maṇḍala*, the place of the beautiful [goddess] Tripurā Bhairavī, is the best of all places and the original home of [the goddess] Mahāmāyā. There is no better place on earth. The goddess appears there every month during her menstrual period. All the gods dwell there in the form of mountains, and all the great gods dwell in the mountains. There the Earth is known by wise men in the form of the goddess. There is no greater place than Kāmākhyā, the *yoni-maṇḍala*.[9]

It is not entirely clear when Ambuvācī became the primary festival celebrated at Kāmākhyā temple, or whether there was an original festival here during the Purāṇic era that was revived in modern time. However, by the time of later medieval texts, such as the *Kubjikā Tantra*, Kāmākhyā is praised as the greatest of all *pīṭhas*, where the goddess' bloody menstrual cloth will fulfill all one's heart's desires: "The great *pīṭha* of Kāmarūpa fulfills all one's desires. In the *kali* [age], O Goddess, prayer in Kāmarūpa is said to bear quick results. Taking Kāmākhyā's [menstrual] cloth, one should perform prayer and worship. One will attain one's full desires, truly, without doubt."[10]

In order to understand the deeper significance of this festival, however, we need to understand the place of menstruation and menstrual blood in Hindu culture and religious practice. Like all bodily fluids, and particularly sexual fluids, menstrual blood is considered to be an extremely powerful but also deeply ambivalent and impure substance. As Frédérique Apffel Marglin explains, Hindu concepts of purity and impurity are often closely connected to notions of bodily integrity and the boundaries of the physical self; those substances that flow over the boundaries of the body are dangerously polluting: "violations of the boundaries of the body, such as menstruation, elimination, wounds and mutilation, create impurity."[11] Sexual fluids in particular—and most especially menstrual blood—are widely regarded as "polluting, powerful and therefore dangerous substances."[12] Indeed, menstrual blood is at once "sacred and accursed."[13] Just as feces and urine are physical "excesses" that flow over the boundaries of the body, so too menstruation is an excess of blood and is equally polluting. Yet at the same time, it also embodies the raw material and potentiality of new life. As Marglin suggests, menstrual blood may not be pure, but it is highly *auspicious*, that is, revered as powerful and sacred.[14]

Thus, throughout the classical Hindu law books, the *Dharma Sūtras*, menstrual blood and menstruating women are surrounded with all manner of taboos. Touching a menstruating woman is said to be equal to touching an outcaste or a corpse; food touched by a menstruating woman is as impure as food into which hair or an insect has fallen, food touched by someone's foot, or food given by a harlot or a heinous sinner.[15] The menstruating woman is considered impure for three days and is subject to a number of complex prohibitions, such as sleeping on the floor, not eating meat, not bathing in water, not laughing, and so forth.[16] As Madhu Khanna notes, "A woman during menstruation is compared to a fallen woman . . . [The] temporary untouchability attributed to women and the overwhelming number of menstrual taboos imposed on them go to show that the first three days of menstruation were looked upon as dangerous and threatening."[17]

This association of menstruation with both dangerous impurity and auspicious power can still be seen in the modern celebration of Ambuvācī Melā. When Kāmākhyā menstruates for three days each year, she is considered to be in a state like that of any Hindu woman during her menstrual period: she is impure, and the temple must be closed to all visitors for the three days of her menstrual flow. As one contemporary priest, Śrī Gaṅga Sarma, explains, "Mother Goddess

Kamakhya becomes impure due to menses, just like an impurity of woman due to her menstruation . . . During this period . . . the temple doors are closed, and no pilgrim is allowed inside the temple."[18] But this same impure, dangerous, and potentially destructive blood of the goddess is also believed to bring new life to the earth and blessings to her devotees. Thus on the fourth day after her menstruation, the temple doors are reopened, and red pieces of cloth representing the bloody menstrual flow are distributed to the thousands of pilgrims who thereby receive the power and grace of the goddess. As Sarma explains, the red cloth represents the *nirmālī* or *nirmālya* of the goddess' menstrual flow, that is, the sacred "remains" of an offering or sacrifice. It is this bloody remnant of her powerful impurity that brings grace and life to the pilgrims' homes:

> As the sacred remains of this festival, the goddess' red garments (the cloth she was wearing while in her menstrual period) are very fruitful, and the pilgrims wear them as amulets, considering them to be very holy . . . If ordinary people wear this bloody garment on their own bodies with a pure mind, then benefits come from all directions.[19]

Ambuvācī is a particularly clear example of the complex mixture of indigenous pre-Hindu traditions and Tantric influences. As various scholars have observed, the festival is closely connected to the coming of the monsoon rains, to the agricultural cycle, and to larger fertility rites that probably long predate the arrival of Hinduism in Assam.[20] But it also demonstrates the way in which Tantra on the whole seeks to unleash the tremendous power that is associated with impure substances such as menstrual blood, transforming what is normally a source of pollution into a source of divine energy. As Khanna notes, "Whereas the Brahmanical ideology links menstruation to sin, guilt, punishment and fear and . . . regards a woman's body, senses and sexuality as dangerous and threatening, the Śākta Tantras . . . invert the orthodox values to their advantage."[21]

As we will see in the following chapters, this dangerous power associated with menstrual blood is also a central part of Kāmākhyā's worship in both its esoteric and popular forms. On the esoteric level, menstrual blood is one of the key bodily fluids consumed as part of secret Tantric rites (Chapter 4). And on the popular, exoteric level, the blood of the goddess remains to this day the central focus of the summer Ambuvācī celebration, attracting hundreds of thousands of pilgrims who seek the life-giving, creative power of the goddess' menstrual cloth (Chapter 7).

Blood for the goddess: Animal sacrifice and ritual transgression

If the power of the goddess circulates throughout the world in the symbolic form of her annual menstruation, this capillary flow returns to the goddess in the literal form of blood sacrifice. The primary public form of worship at Kāmākhyā is now and has since at least the time of the *Kālikā Purāṇa* been animal sacrifice, which is still today offered numerous times a day throughout the year and hundreds of times on holy days.[22] According to the *Kālikā Purāṇa*, the male gods like Ganeśa, Śiva, and Kṛṣṇa can be worshipped with sweets, chanting, religious vows, etc., but the goddess can only be satisfied with blood.[23]

Animal sacrifice has, of course, been performed throughout the Hindu traditions of India since the time of the early Vedas (1500 BCE), which center in large part around the performance of *yajña* or sacrifice. For the Vedas, the sacrifice is really the principle maintaining the entire universe and, in effect, the "workshop in which all reality is forged."[24] Although animal sacrifice was gradually removed from mainstream Hindu traditions, it has always survived in the marginal areas of India, such as Bangla in the northeast, Kerala and Tamil Nadu in the south, and tribal areas like Assam in the northeast hills. As Biardeau suggests, sacrifice as either a physical ritual or a symbolic trope is a recurring structural theme running throughout Hindu tradition from the Vedas through the Epics, Purāṇas, *bhakti* literature, and the worship of the goddess in the Śākta traditions. Indeed, "Hinduism in its totality is structured around sacrifice."[25]

Above all, animal sacrifice continued and flourished in India's Śakta Tantric traditions, even as it largely declined in the rest of South Asia. As Dehejia points out, the worship of the *yoginīs* in the Kaula tradition has long been associated with the Mahāyāga or "great sacrifice," the ritual offerings of wine, flesh, and blood as the favorite food of these divine female beings. Thus the *Kaulāvalī Nirṇaya* specifies importance of blood and meat (*rudhira* and *māṁsa*) in the worship of the *yoginīs* and Bhairavas.[26] Moreover, as Davidson observes, the great *yoginī* temples such as the Hirapur temple in Orissa prominently feature images of severed heads and other indications of blood rites, suggesting that animal and/or human sacrifice was one of the most important rites performed here. This seems even more likely since these temples also tend to be built in tribal regions were blood sacrifices are also widely performed:

> The primary activity depicted at these sites—beyond the figures of the yoginīs—is the display of severed heads, indicating that sanguinary rites were probably the principal activity practiced. The location of these temples in areas dominated by tribal peoples that were involved in sanguinary rituals suggests that they were constructed with a similar ritual in mind.[27]

As we will see, Tantric forms of sacrifice such as found at Kāmākhyā are really quite different from—and indeed, often deliberate *inversions of*—Vedic sacrificial rites and probably incorporate a large amount of non-Hindu indigenous practices.

Other-worldly salvation and this-worldly power: Origins of Vedic and Tantric sacrifice

One very telling myth from the *Kālikā Purāṇa* explains the origins of both the orthodox Vedic sacrifices and the unorthodox Tantric rites. As we saw in Chapter 1, Lord Viṣṇu is said to have assumed his boar incarnation, Varāha, to couple with the Earth and give birth to king Naraka. That same boar then became Yajña-Varāha, the "boar of sacrifice," and, in turn, Lord Śiva assumed the form of the mythical hundred-legged beast called Śarabha in order to slay Varāha. After a lengthy battle, the boar was killed, and the 1008 kinds of Vedic sacrifice, along with the sacrificial altar and all the implements of sacrifice, were born from the various parts of Yajña-Varāha's dismembered body. Just as the cosmic person, Puruṣa, was sacrificed and dismembered to create the parts of the universe, and just as Satī was sacrificed and dismembered to create the *śākta pīṭhas*, so too, Varāha was dismembered to create all the myriad kinds of sacrifice. From the joint of his eye-brows and nose came the Jyotistoma; from the joint of the jaws and ears came the Vahnistoma; from the joint of his eyes and eye brows came the Vratyastoma, and so forth.[28]

After Śiva discarded his Śarabha form, however, the body of the mythical beast gave birth to another, very different deity and sacrificial rite—namely the terrible form of Śiva as Bhairava, the skull bearer, and the left-hand rites of the Tantric Kāpālikās or "skull-bearers" (Fig. 11). The Kāpālikās, too, have forms of sacrifice, but of a very different, non-Vedic kind. They offer meat smeared with brain and fat, placed in the skull of a *brāhmaṇ;* they worship with wine and human flesh; and their supreme deity is the frightening Bhairava, seated on a human corpse.[29]

In many ways, this myth mirrors the two sacrificial myths we have encountered previously: the Vedic myth of the sacrificial dismemberment of Puruṣa, which creates the universe, and the Purāṇic myth of the dismemberment of Satī, which creates the *śākta pīṭhas*. At the same time, however, this myth also narrates the origins of two very different, even inverse, kinds of sacrifice: on one side, the pure, orthodox Vedic rites are born from Viṣṇu as Yajña-Varāha; and on the other side, the impure, transgressive blood offerings and Tantric rites are born from Śiva as Śarabha. As we saw above, the former are consistently associated with Vedic *brāhmaṇic* culture, while latter are said to be the rites of the indigenous populations (*kirātas*) of the northeast hills.

The Vedic and Tantric forms of sacrifice also bear two very different kinds of fruits. The orthodox Vedic method, which is offered to gods and ancestors, removes the sins arising from debt and karma and quickly leads to liberation.[30] But the left-hand method—which is offered *to the goddess first and foremost, before all the other gods*—only gives liberation "after a long, long time," as one is "reborn on this earth again and again because of the sin arising from debt."[31] As we will below see, however, it *does* bring the worshiper all manner of *this-worldly power and benefits*, including everything from wooing women and subduing lions to conquering kingdoms.[32] In short, the orthodox or Vedic and heterodox or Tantric rites can be summarized in tabular form as follows:

Orthodox/ Vedic ritual	***Heterodox/ Tantric ritual***
Five great sacrifices	Offerings of meat, wine, and sexual union
Based on Vedas and Upaniṣads	Bereft of Vedas
Worship of goddesses Mahāmāyā, Śāradā, etc.	Worship of terrible goddesses Bhairavī, Ugratārā, Caṇḍī, etc.
Worship of Viṣṇu	Worship in Śiva in his terrible form as Bhairava
Use of Vedic *mantras* by Āryan *brāhmaṇs*	Sorcery practiced by *mlecchas*
Achieves freedom from debts to ancestors, sages, gods, etc.	Achieves worldly powers, prosperity, political power, sexual appeal

In sum, as Sanderson notes, "These two poles, of purity and power, were seen as corresponding to the two domains of revealed literature, the Tantric (the domain of power) and the Vedic (the domain of purity)."[33]

Tantric continuations and inversions of the Vedic sacrificial rite

Tantric sacrificial rites of the sort that we find in the *Kālikā Purāṇa* and *Yoginī Tantra* represent both important continuities and profound transformations or even inversions of the Vedic sacrificial rites. With the Vedic tradition, the *Kālikā Purāṇa* agrees that sacrifice is the foundation of the world and essential to the maintenance of the cosmos: "The gods are pleased by sacrifices; everything is founded upon the sacrifice; by sacrifice the earth is upheld."[34] But it also recognizes that act of sacrifice contains an element of dangerous power at its very core.

As J.C. Heesterman has argued, the *brāhmaṇic* ritual itself contained a fundamental ambivalence and inner conflict. The same sacrifice that was said to be the source of all vitality in the universe also centered around the basic reality of death and violence, the impurity and bloodshed that lie at the heart of the ritual: "battle and catastrophe belong to the essence of sacrifice."[35] The later Vedic tradition, Heesterman argues, made a systematic effort to rationalize, marginalize, and ultimately excise the impure aspects of the sacrifice. In place of violent bloodshed, the later *brāhmaṇic* ritual centers on an unbloody, highly sanitized system of ritual rules: "Abstraction enabled the ritualists . . . to do away with the reality of death. Death has been rationalized away."[36] Ultimately, the process of rationalization would culminate in the complete interiorization of the sacrifice that we find in the Upaniṣads: the external rite of animal slaughter was gradually replaced by symbolic sacrifice of yoga, meditation, and offering the breath into the fire of the self.[37]

This profound ambivalence surrounding the violent nature of sacrifice is perhaps most clearly seen in the complex symbolism of the "head of the sacrifice." As Heesterman observes, the head of the sacrifice appears repeatedly in early Indian mythology as a key symbol of the creative, fertile "treasure" of the sacrifice that represents the vital essence of the ritual: "The head is the focus of a rich web of mythological associations. . . . The head . . . contains a treasure or a secret that is the essence of the universe. Everything depends on obtaining the head."[38] Yet ironically, the *brāhmaṇic* ritual contains virtually no reference to the head of the sacrificial victim or how it is to be handled once the victim has been dispatched. Indeed, "the beheading of an animal is expressly said to be a demonic act."[39] In place of the more common act of bloody beheading, the Vedic ritual instead calls for an un-bloody suffocation or "pacification" of the animal outside the ritual enclosure: "What we know as Vedic sacrifice is not sacrifice tout court . . . on a par with its normal practice as we find it to the present day in India . . . Usually the victim is immolated by cutting off the head. . . . but the Vedic texts explicitly reject this procedure. Instead, they prescribe that the victim be killed by suffocation outside the enclosure."[40]

Yet despite this ongoing rationalization of the sacrifice, the problems of violence, bloodshed, and impurity would persist throughout later Indian ritual traditions. As Smith suggests, the central theme of sacrifice "transmigrated throughout the history of post-Vedic discourse" and "plays a crucial role in the self-definition of Hindu religious institutions."[41] And with it, myths of beheading and the underlying fears of sacrificial violence recur throughout the later traditions. They reappear, for example, in the great epic, the *Mahābhārata*—in which the central battle itself becomes a massive sacrifice that grows violently out of control—and they also survive in a range of indigenous tribal traditions on the margins of India, where rituals of animal beheading continue to this day. As Kooij notes, in the non-Aryan folk religion, "bloody rites were quite regular and . . . became more and more important as the Vedic sacrifices fell into decay."[42]

This survival of the themes of sacrifice, impurity, and power is nowhere more apparent than in the case of Tantric ritual, in which the sacrifice reappears both in symbolic and literal forms. Indeed, we might say that even as blood sacrifice began to decline in the mainstream *brāhmaṇic* tradition, in the face of Buddhist and Jain criticisms, and the growing ideal of *ahiṃsa*, it began to reappear (though in a very different form) in the Śākta and Tantric traditions. Sacrifice, in other words, seems to have gone "underground" and then to have resurfaced in the esoteric ritual of the Tantras. Above all, it survived on the margins of India, in the more remote, less accessible, and never entirely "Hinduized" regions like Assam.[43]

The kind of sacrifice we see in the worship of Kāmākhyā, however, is very different from the kind described in the Vedas. The early

Vedic ritual centered on the offering of pure, that is, domestic animals primarily to male deities. According to the *Śatapatha Brāhmaṇa*, pure or domestic animals include humans, cows, horses, goats, and sheep, while impure or wild animals include the *gaura* (a kind of buffalo), the *gavaya* (a species of ox or wild buffalo), the wild camel, and the barbarian of the jungle.[44] Thus we find a series of binary oppositions:

Domestic (pure)	***Wild (impure)***
Man	Barbarian of the jungle
Horse	*Gaura* (kind of buffalo)
Bull Ram	Wild *gavaya* (species of ox or buffalo) Wild camel
He-goat	*Śarabha*[45]

The Brāhmaṇas also warn sternly of the dangers one faces if one is foolish enough to offer any of these impure animals as a sacrifice: "father and son will be set at odds, roads will run apart, beasts and criminals will terrorize the countryside," and so on.[46]

In the Vedic rite, moreover, the animal is not bloodily butchered but instead "pacified," that is, strangled in an *unbloody* manner outside the ritual enclosure before being offered to the (male) deity. Indeed, as Heesterman argues, the Vedic ritual tried to eliminate or "rationalize away" as much of the blood and violence as possible from the sacrifice.[47]

When we turn to Assamese Tantric texts such as the *Kālikā Purāṇa* and *Yoginī Tantra*, however, we find that this Vedic paradigm has been turned completely on its head. Here the most desirable victims are not pure domestic animals but rather wild, dangerous animals, including many of those explicitly listed as impure in orthodox texts. According to the rather motley assortment of victims catalogued in the *Kālikā Purāṇa*:

> Birds, tortoises, alligators, he-goats, and boars, the buffalo, the lizard, the *śoṣa*, as well as the nine kinds of animal, the yak, the spotted antelope, the hare, as well as the lion, fish and the blood of one's own body—these are the eight kinds of sacrifice. And in the absence of these, sometimes even horses and elephants.[48]

Elsewhere, the same text includes tigers, rhinos, and bulls among its list of victims; and equally diverse lists of wild animal sacrifices can be found in many other Tantric texts from the northeast, which also include offerings of mongooses, cows, jackals, and monkeys.[49]

It seems likely that this rather motley list of victims is drawn less from any traditional Vedic rite than from a wide array of local Assamese traditions and the many jungle animals sacrificed by diverse indigenous peoples of the northeast hills.[50] Sacrifices of various wild animals were practiced by most hill tribes prior to the colonial era. The Mechs, for example, worshipped a semi-Hindu form of Śiva with offerings of highly un-Vedic animals like buffaloes and pigeons, while the Kacharis presented him with "offerings of ducks and pigeons, wine and cooked rice and sacrifices of buffaloes and swine."[51] Traces of these indigenous rites can still be seen at Kāmākhyā temple today, where, in addition to the many goats offered each day, there are also sacrifices of fish and pigeons, which are dutifully beheaded by the *bali-katas* along with the usual victims (Fig. 12).

In Assam, Bangla, and parts of South India, the preferred victim is the buffalo—an animal that it is explicitly identified as wild, impure, and unfit by the *brāhmaṇic* texts (Fig. 13).[52] Indeed, the buffalo holds place of special honor at large-scale celebrations like Durgā Pūjā, and it assumes a central importance in the *Kālikā Purāṇa,* which describes its immolation and offering in detail. Here the buffalo is explicitly contrasted with the ultimate sacrificial animal of the Vedas, the horse, and described as the mount of the god of death (Yama), as the best offering to the goddess in her terrible forms, and thus as the destroyer of enemies:

> When a buffalo is offered to the goddess Bhairavī or to Bhairava, he should worship the sacrifice with this *mantra*: "Just as you are hostile to the horse and yet you bear Caṇḍikā, so too you will kill my enemies and bring me prosperity, O buffalo. You are the mount of Yama, you are imperishable with an excellent form. You give life, wealth and fame—hail to you, O buffalo!"[53]

It is significant that the worship of the goddess should center on the sacrifice of the specifically non-Vedic and impure buffalo. In complete contrast to the pure, domestic Vedic victim—who is an embodiment of the original divine sacrifice of the primordial person, Puruṣa—the buffalo is an impure, wild animal that embodies the powers of darkness, evil, and the opposition to the divine order. As Biardeau observes, "The buffalo . . . is a savage beast . . . a stranger to human society and the sacrificial world . . . The Vedic literature . . . does not count it among the permitted animals offered in sacrifice. But it is apt, by this fact, to play the role of the principle that is antithetical to the Goddess, the incarnation of total evil."[54]

Here again we can see the probable influence of indigenous non-Hindu traditions. Among the Nagas and many other hill tribes of the northeast, one of the most important elements of their ritual life is the *mithan* or *gayal* (*bos frontalis*)—the wild buffalo that inhabits the wooded hills of Assam, Bhutan, and northwest Burma.[55] For tribes throughout this range of hills, the *mithan* has long been the most prized sacrificial victim; again, however, the *mithan* is considered an ambivalent and wild sort of creature, betwixt and between the world of men and the world of the jungle, but for that reason also an important liaison between this world and the other-world. As Mark Woodward explains in his study of sacrifice and head-hunting among the Nagas:

> *Mithan* represent a . . . permanently liminal category. They are only semi-domesticated and live in light forests at high elevations. They are located between earth and sky, and between culture and nature . . . They are sacrificed, but never slaughtered simply for food. In feasts of merit they move between earth and sky and . . . are the prime source of wealth and status in both realms.[56]

As such, the sacrifice of the *mithan* is considered an equally ambivalent act: "Killing the animal is both dangerous and taboo, in the same sense that killing or taking the head of a close agnate is."[57] But at the same time, the *mithan* sacrifice is considered integral to the prosperity of the community, and *mithan* skulls are collected and passed on from one generation to the next as a source of magical potency: "Sacrifice generally involves the erection of large wooden posts or stone megaliths through which the animal is sent to the heavens. Rites for captured heads center on a tree that is the center of the village."[58]

This focus on the severed buffalo head is also seen in art from the Pāla era: one tenth- to eleventh-century image from the Kalipahara area of Guwahati, for example, shows the head of the goddess as buffalo slayer seated directly on top of the severed buffalo head, in a style that reflects a strong tribal influence (Fig. 14). However, this focus on the head and skull of the buffalo survives even today in some temples of the goddess in her terrible left-hand Tantric forms. Thus the eighteenth-century Ugratārā temple in Guwahati—one of the most important goddess temples in Assam after Kāmākhyā—is still today adorned with a huge buffalo skull with wide, long horns over its front entry way, directly facing the sacrificial post (Fig. 15). It is difficult not to see direct connections here with the practice of collecting buffalo skulls among the Nagas and other northeast tribes.

Finally, the manner in which the victim is killed in sacrifice to the goddess is also quite different from the Vedic rite. In the traditional Vedic rite, the victim is to be killed with as little bloodshed as possible. As Heesterman argues, the *brāhmaṇic* sacrifice gradually sought to eliminate as much of the impurity from the ritual as possible, replacing a violent beheading with a rationalized, sanitized, "nonviolent" act of suffocating the victim outside the ritual enclosure.[59] In the Śākta sacrifice, conversely, the head of the victim becomes the very center of the entire proceedings. The crucial act is the beheading of the victim with a sword, which is first worshipped as the terrible, thirsty drinker of blood. The sacrificer should sprinkle the animal with water and then honor the sword as the embodiment of lord Śiva in his most frightening and destructive form:

> "You are the tongue of Caṇḍikā, you lead to the abode of the gods. Aiṃ Hriṃ Sriṃ." Meditating with this *mantra*, he should worship the sword [as] black Śiva, whose essence is the black night, terrible, with bloody eyes, adorned with a garland of blood, wearing a garment of blood, with a noose in his hand, drinking blood and eating a lump of raw flesh.[60]

The central act of the ritual, then, is the presentation of the severed head and blood to the goddess (Fig. 16). A burning lamp is placed on its crown, and it offered together with the fresh blood of the victim to the goddess, for whom it is transformed into the sweetest nectar:

> Having worshipped the sword with the *mantra* "Oṃ, Aiṃ, Hrīṃ, Phaṭ," he should grasp the pure sword and behead the excellent victim. Then he should carefully perfume the blood of the victim with water, salt, good fruits, honey, fragrance and flowers and [offer it] with the *mantra* "Oṃ Aiṃ Hrīṃ Śrīṃ. Kauśikī, I am offering the blood to

> you." He should put the blood and the head with a lamp upon it in the proper place.[61]

> Blood that is purified by *mantra* is always praised as nectar. The goddess consumes the head as well as the blood. Therefore, in worship, he should offer the bloody head of the sacrifice.[62]

Ritual beheading and the offering of severed heads, we should note, is also the most common way in which sacrifice is traditionally performed among most of the indigenous religions of Assam and the northeast states. In dramatic contrast to the unbloody pacification of the Vedic sacrifice, Assamese tribes like the Kacharis offer the heads—and "as a rule, only the *heads* of the goats, chickens, etc.,"—together with the blood as gifts to the deity:

> A goat is brought forward and taken up before one of the figures . . . [the priest] with one stroke of the long sacrificial sword . . . severs the victim's head from the body. Most of the blood is held to be offered in sacrifice to the madai [deity], before whose emblem the animal has been slaughtered.[63]

Throughout Indian religions, the head has a central place in a complex web of symbolic meanings and cultural significance. As Brenda Beck observes, the head is often associated with sexual power and the creative but dangerous potency of sexual fluids. In many Indian yogic traditions, the primary aim is to sublimate and redirect the flow of semen to the top of the head; and in many popular traditions, the hair is associated with the ambivalent power of both menstruation and sexual intercourse: "Given this diverse information about the head as the location of sexual force [and] pollution . . . it is not surprising that the beheading of animals is a major sacrificial act at the goddess' festival."[64]

In the South Indian *bhakti* traditions that Beck examines, the sacrificial beheading is a key symbol of the devotee's humility and submission, the sacrifice of one's pride and lower animal nature to the goddess. In the Śākta Tantric traditions, however, the significance of the beheading is quite different. Here the aim is not to eliminate the dangerous forces of sexuality; on the contrary, it is to unleash them as a tremendous source of power. The *tāntrika* does not bow down in selfless humility before the goddess, but rather draws on her awesome strength in the hope that "the entire world will come under his power."[65] Indeed, if one performs the rite, "a king or a prince or women or *yakṣas* or *rākṣasas* or the four classes of demons all will come under his power."[66]

In sum, what we find in the sacrificial ritual described in the *Kālikā Purāṇa* is neither a simple mishmash of Vedic and non-Vedic elements nor a superficial overlay of *brāhmaṇic* Hinduism onto a substratum of tribal ritual. Rather, it is a complex reworking of traditional ritual themes, combined with selected elements of local ritual traditions, centering on the basic dialectic of transgression and taboo. Indeed, we might say that the Tantric sacrificial ritual is based on a series of structural inversions of the Vedic paradigm, which carefully juxtapose categories of purity and impurity in order to shatter the duality between them and unleash the liberating power of the goddess. As we see in the following table, the ritual involves a number of deliberate violations of Vedic practice: a wild, impure animal is substituted for a domestic, pure one; the victim is beheaded in a bloody manner inside the ritual enclosure instead of strangled outside the precincts; the severed head becomes the central focus of the ritual; and the deity to whom it is offered is not the transcendent male god but the goddess in her most violent forms, the goddess who handles impurity and combats the forces of evil:

	Vedic sacrifice	***Śākta Tantric sacrifice***
Status of victim	Domestic (pure) animal	Wild (impure)
means of killing	Unbloody suffocation	Bloody beheading
Role of the head	Ignored	Offered with blood
Deity	Pure male deity	Goddess as handler of impurity

Sacrifice and power: Ritual transgression and the power of the impure

But what is the point of this sort of systematic inversion and transgression of traditional laws of purity and ritual order? Here and throughout the book, I will argue, it centers primarily on the release and channeling of power—the tremendous, creative, and destructive power of the goddess that flows through the cosmos, the body, and the social order alike. As Mary Douglas argued in her classic work, *Purity and Danger*, acts of ritual transgression typically aim to harness the dangerous and yet extremely powerful forces believed to lie on the margins of both the social body and the physical body, the "symbolic filth" or "matter out of place" (what Julia Kristeva calls the "abject"[67]) that lies in the gaps and fissures of the universe:

> The danger which is risked by boundary transgression is power. Those vulnerable margins and those attacking forces which threaten to destroy good order represent the powers inhering the cosmos. Ritual which can harness these . . . is harnessing power indeed.[68]

Blood and other body fluids, Douglas suggests, are often the clearest symbols of the dangerous but powerful forces that transgress and overflow the boundaries of the physical and social body. As such, they can become extremely potent sources of ritual power.[69]

As such, it might be tempting to try to read Tantric ritual as a sort of "carnivalesque" event, in Mikhail Bakhtin's sense of a liberating overturning of conventional social laws, hierarchies, and taboos.[70] But in fact, the sort of ritual that we see at Kāmākhyā is hardly a chaotic, carnivalesque, free-for-all; on the contrary, it is a highly controlled, orchestrated, and carefully performed sort of ritual inversion. For the most powerful form of transgression, as Bataille observes, is seldom a matter of mere hedonism or sexual license; rather, it involves the careful dialectic or play (*le jeu*) between taboo and transgression, sanctity and sacrilege, through which one systematically constructs and then overturns all laws. Indeed, "often the transgression of a taboo is no less subject to rules than the taboo itself."[71] One must first carefully construct and even exaggerate the laws of purity before one can violate them; for it is precisely this dialectic of purity and impurity, law and violation, that unleashes the "explosive surge of transgression" and a sense of supra-human power:

> The regularity of transgressions do not affect the intangible stability of the prohibition since they are its expected complement—just as the diastolic movement completes a systolic one, or just as explosion follows upon compression. The compression is not subservient to the explosion . . . it gives it increased force.[72]

Tantric ritual, we might say, functions like a kind of spiritual slingshot, which is first stretched as tightly as possible and then suddenly released in order to propel the adept into ecstatic liberation. Or to use an even more apt metaphor, it works like a kind of *socio-nuclear fission:* it first exaggerates and then shatters the laws that make up the social organism at the most fundamental atomic level, releasing an explosive burst of energy. As Heinrich Zimmer observes in his classic essay on Tantra, Śākta ritual works precisely by playing upon the complex laws of purity that normally govern the class-based Hindu social order, tapping into the immense reserves of energy that lie bound up in their prohibitions: "How much lies blocked up in every man by the social order! For the vital force (*shakti*) in each of would overflow all measure were it to fulfill its nature, which is totality"; thus Tantric ritual, "by temporarily lifting the rigid rules of morality, by transforming boundaries and fences into roads and gates, by permitting . . . what was ordinarily forbidden" lets loose this vital force.[73] In this sense, the Tantric "path of power" sets itself up in deliberate contrast to the orthodox path of purity. As Sanderson comments, the path of purity seeks to eliminate the dangerous pollution of these marginal forces, but the Tantric path seeks precisely to "unleash all the awesome power of impurity" and so achieve a kind of "unlimited power through a visionary art of impurity." For "the absolute of the impure is absolute Power."[74]

Like many Tantric texts, the *Kālikā Purāṇa* goes into some detail about the various supernatural powers—*siddhis* or yogic attainments—gained through esoteric rites and ritual acts of transgression. Through sacrificial beheading, one unleashes not just the blood of the victim, but also the tremendous, circulating power of the goddess, a power that brings control over all things:

> When offering a sacrifice, one should behead the victim and put a *tilaka* on his forehead with [the victim's] own blood that is on the sword, uttering the *mantra* that controls all things [*sarvavaśyamantra*]. Then the world will be in his power . . . When a man pronounces this *mantra* while secretly putting a *tilaka* [on his forehead], even without worshiping, everything will come under his power for ever. A king or a prince or women or ghosts or demons or the four groups of demons will all come under his power.[75]

Elsewhere, the *Kālikā Purāṇa* promises that the one who performs the heterodox rites will attain all manner of worldly blessings, from a body as beautiful as Madana or Kāma, the god of desire, to the subjugation of rulers, kingdoms, and all living things:

> He is happy and prosperous in this world, everywhere beloved by all; he is radiant with his handsome body like Madana; he subdues kings with their kingdoms and subjects; he attracts all women, who become anxious with lust; he subdues lions, tigers, hyenas, goblins, ghosts and demons; he moves everywhere like the wind.[76]

> He subdues gods, kings, women and others. If the wise man strives, he becomes an eloquent speaker or a king. He lives a long life, becomes prosperous, endowed with wealth and grains; he becomes a poet endowed with wisdom; he is invincible and cannot be defeated by enemies. Thunderbolts do not strike the city where he lives. Poison and weapons thrown by strong hands do not pierce his body and do not harm him. He is victorious everywhere, O Bhairava![77]

Much of the modern scholarship on Tantra has tended to downplay the role of these kinds of worldly powers, typically dismissing them as inferior or even dangerous distractions on the path to spiritual liberation. As Mircea Eliade argued, the true aim of Tantric yoga is liberation from the world of duality and attainment of timeless immortality; thus any practices that seek temporal power or worldly attainments must be "later degenerations" or "symbolic confusions."[78] Even more recent scholars such as Douglas Brooks suggest that these various "accomplishments (*siddhi*), including the power to acquire any worldly desire, are usually considered . . . secondary accretions on the path to liberation."[79]

I would argue, however, that these sorts of occult powers cannot be dismissed so easily. Rather than mere accretions, they are an integral part of Śākta Tantra and a critical element in Tantra's very this-worldly notion of power. Tantric practice does not simply liberate the *sādhaka* into an other-worldly state of bliss; rather it infuses him with a mastery over the temporal world and the social order. As Flood suggests, "[P]ower suffuses the concerns of the tantric traditions. The Tantras offer their followers power to achieve world transcendence or magical power over supernatural entities in order to achieve worldly success."[80] Beyond the *Kālikā Purāṇa,* most of the other major texts from Assam such as the *Kaulajñāna Nirṇaya* go to great lengths to describe the various supernatural powers the adept will acquire: these range from the power to see from a long distance, the power to enter into another's body, the attainment of great speed, control over decay and death, control over creation and destruction, and the power to become like Śiva himself[81]; the power to bring others under control, the power to make others unconscious[82]; the attainment of popularity, mastery in poetry, and so on.[83] The *Kāmākhyā Tantra* likewise promises the power to enchant and control everything from sovereigns, kings and ministers to the city and the entire kingdom, along with all the king's courtesans and wives.[84] In sum, far from marginal or secondary to the goal of other-worldly transcendence, these kinds of this-worldly powers are central to the unique power of Tantra and its attempt to unleash the tremendous energy of the goddess that lies bound up in cosmos, the social order, and physical body alike. For, as Shulman aptly observes, "in a religion that ultimately asserts the divine nature of terrestrial existence, power—however dark its workings, however terrible its effects, never loses its sacred character."[85]

Conclusions: Vedic, indigenous, and Tantric elements in the Śākta tradition

In sum, both the annual celebration of Kāmākhyā's menstruation and the offering of animal sacrifice center on the tremendous, creative, but also profoundly ambivalent power of the goddess. Embodied in the literal and symbolic form of blood, power flows through a circulating, capillary network of relations that extends from the goddess, through her priests, to the devotees and *tāntrikas* who worship her. And in both the annual celebration of Ambuvācī and the offering of sacrifice, this power is inherently tied to impurity. Indeed, it is precisely through the systematic manipulation of impurity—in the form of menstruation and the offering of impure animals by acts of bloody beheading—that one can tap into and unleash the tremendous energy of the goddess that lies within the cosmos, the social structure and the physical body.

In both these cases, however, we also see a complex interplay between Vedic, Tantric, and indigenous practices, which together make up the rich tradition of goddess worship in Assam. Ambuvācī itself is the fusion of indigenous agricultural rites with Tantric ideas surrounding the power of menstrual blood, along with a variety of *brāhmaṇic* elements from mainstream Hinduism. Likewise, the practice of animal sacrifice is a clear example of the complex melding of indigenous, Vedic, and Tantric ritual. From the offering of wild and impure animals, to the act of bloody beheading and the focus on the severed head, the Assamese tradition reflects a negotiation between non-Hindu traditions and Vedic *brāhmaṇic* elements that evolved over hundreds of years. As such, it reveals the complex dynamics of the heterogeneous body of traditions we call "Tantra"—and of "Hinduism" as a whole—as it exists in its lived compromises and contradictions.

As we will see in the following chapter, this association between impurity and power and this complex negotiation between Vedic and tribal traditions also lies at the heart of kingship and political power in Assam. Indeed, the king is in many ways both the embodiment of the impurity of power/power of the impure and the key figure in this ongoing negotiation between Vedic and non-Hindu traditions in the northeast.

Chapter Three

GODDESS OF POWER: TANTRA, KINGSHIP, AND SACRIFICE IN SOUTH ASIAN HISTORY

> Power, in the form of wealth, is the most important goal for a king—because it is the basis of social life.
>
> —*The Kāma Sūtra*[1]

> By performing sacrifices and offering gifts, one becomes a king in this world . . . By means of these rites and by performing sacrifices, O ruler, your enemies are destroyed and you will achieve kingship, without doubt.
>
> —*Kālikā Purāṇa* (KP 85.79-80)

As a path of power, centered on the goddess as the embodiment of *śakti* in both its spiritual and material forms, Hindu Śākta Tantra has often been closely related to kingship and political rule in various periods of South Asian history. For *śakti* is not simply a spiritual or transcendent sort of metaphysical energy; it is also the material power that flows through the social body and the state as well as the physical body and the cosmos. As we saw in the previous chapter, Tantric texts promise the adept not just other-worldly benefits but also very this-worldly kinds of attainments, including the power to assume the throne and defeat enemy kings. Conversely, as Charles Orzech notes in his study of Chinese esoteric Buddhism, the *tantras* "were among the most important vehicles for the spread of Indian political and religious ideas throughout East, Central, and Southeast Asia."[2] Indeed, the king is, in many ways, the "Tantric actor par excellence,"[3] the ideal embodiment of the *śākta* as seeker of power and the male consort of the land represented by the goddess. As Flood observes, "The transgressive violence and eroticism of Tantric deities became tapped and controlled by the institution of kingship."[4]

Perhaps nowhere is this connection between Tantra and kingship more apparent than in the case of Assam, where the worship of the goddess Kāmākhyā was closely tied to political power, from the mythical demon-king Naraka down to the last of the Ahom kings before British colonial rule. As the embodiment of divine desire and power, Kāmākhyā formed a key religio-political center during several of Assam's ancient and medieval dynasties, such as the Pālas, Kochs, and Ahoms. Yet at the same time, Kāmākhyā was also a central point of interaction between the various indigenous communities of the northeast and the *brāhmanic* forms of Hinduism coming from Bengal and central India. This complex interaction between Tantra and kingship is apparent as early as the *Kālikā Purāṇa*, which not only narrates the conquest of Assam by king Naraka but also devotes its last several chapters to the seemingly secular matters of statecraft, politics, and military strategy.[5] Clearly written for a king, the *Kālikā Purāṇa* combines elements of Vedic ritual, non-Hindu tribal practices, left-hand Tantra, and the rules of statecraft.

Similarly, the second most important Tantric text composed in Assam—the *Yoginī Tantra*, from the sixteenth or the seventeenth century—also provides a mytho-historical narrative of medieval Assam, recounting the divine origins of the Koch king Viśva Siṅgha and the violent struggles for power between the Kochs, Ahoms, and Mughals that took place in the sixteenth century.[6] The inner wall of the present temple still bears an inscription dedicated to Viśva's sons, Naranārāyaṇa and Chilarai, who rebuilt the complex in the sixteenth century and were praised as generous patrons of the goddess.

However, one of the most important and recurring themes throughout the Assamese literature is the profound *ambivalence of kingship*. For while he is the embodiment of worldly power and strength, the king is also—like the goddess Śakti herself—tied to the inevitable realities of violence, bloodshed, and impurity. In the particular case of Assam, moreover, the king is consistently linked to powerful but also impure traditions such as indigenous religions, non-Vedic rituals, and the deeply ambivalent power of sacrifice. From the time of the *Kālikā Purāṇa* down to the nineteenth century, in fact, the institution of kingship was closely linked to the offering of human sacrifice, a practice that probably shows the influence of several indigenous tribes of the northeast.[7] Again, this reflects the unique *power of Tantra,* as a tradition that appropriates, harnesses, and transforms the dangerous but life-giving forces at the margins of the social body.

Goddesses, kings, and political power

Kingship in Assam is at once a reflection of wider South Asian ideals of kingship and a unique instantiation of those ideals in the specific case of northeast India, with its complex history of negotiations between Hindu and non-Hindu indigenous traditions. On the one hand, since the time of the Varman dynasty (fourth to seventh centuries), the kings of Kāmarūpa have largely fit the model of the ideal king described in the Epics and Purāṇas. Throughout the Purāṇas, the king is praised as at once powerful, divine, and yet potentially dangerous, a being "endowed with divine luster . . . As he controls the people, he is Vaivasvata (the son of Vivasvān, the sun). As he burns evil, he is Agni, the fire-god; and as he gives gifts to *brāhmaṇs,* he is Kubera, the god of wealth"; and yet, "if he is sinful . . . rains stop in his kingdom."[8]

Particularly in the Śākta or goddess-centered traditions, the king is also imagined as the male counterpart to the goddess as nature, earth or the land. As Thomas Coburn notes, the interplay between the goddess and the king may well be "one of the important continuities in Indian religion" and a key to the "growth of the cult of a buffalo-killing Goddess from local to pan-Indian scope between the ninth and sixteenth centuries."[9] As the embodiment of the earth, land, and nature, the goddess is the ultimate symbol of the kingdom that is wedded to and gives power to her human consort, the king: "The goddess, she who slays the buffalo demon and who gives victory to the king, is therefore that very Nature in which men have their place and from which they await the satisfaction of their needs."[10] Thus the Śākta and Tantric traditions continue many themes from earlier Vedic and Purāṇic models of kingship, such as the ideal of the king as supreme sacrificer; but they also add the ideal of the king as Tantric hero who can harness the tremendous energy of the goddess as the embodiment of divine power. As Flood suggests, the medieval period in India saw the rise of a more "aggressive, power-hungry" concept of lordship, which sought to appropriate the erotic violence of the goddess in the person of the king: "The king is also the patron of ritual, who assumes the classical Vedic role of the patron of the sacrifice . . . But the new Tantric conception of kingship saw the king as a deity warrior whose power is derived from the violent erotic warrior goddesses . . . The power of the king was linked to the power of the Goddess."[11]

Not surprisingly, Tantric worship became increasingly popular in royal and aristocratic circles throughout India during the early medieval period, from the Chandella kings of Khajuraho, to the Kalacuris of Tripurī, and the Somavaṃśis of Orissa.[12] The worship of the quintessentially Tantric goddesses, the *yoginīs*, also owed much to royal patronage in these same regions. Various *tantras* promise that a king who worships the *yoginīs* will see his "fame reach to the four oceans," making him "king of all kings" (*rājendraḥ sarvarājānām*): "such worship will enable the king to achieve success in his military campaigns and to ward off invasion from neighboring kingdoms."[13]

Tribals, kings, and goddesses in Assam

Something we see in several Tantric regions is the complex tension and negotiation between non-Hindu tribal kingship and mainstream *brāhmaṇic* traditions. The worship of powerful Tantric goddesses is often a complex point of intersection between indigenous kings and the priests who would convert them and win their patronage. A classic example is the case of the Chandellas. An originally non-Hindu tribe of the Gond ethnicity, the Chandellas carved out a kingdom in central India in the ninth century and gradually adopted *brāhmaṇic* traditions. Today they are perhaps most famous for building the spectacular erotic temples at Khajuraho and for establishing one of the most important early Tantric temples of the 64 *yoginīs*.[14]

This dynamic between tribal kings and the patronage of Tantric deities is perhaps nowhere more apparent than in Assam. Throughout the northeast region, non-Aryan ruling families were progressively brought within the *brāhmaṇic* fold and given a divine ancestry going back to Hindu deities. This began with oldest known historical dynasty of Kāmarūpa, the Varmans (fourth to seventh centuries), who are believed to have been non-Hindu people but traced their origins to the mythical king Naraka, the ambivalent divine-demonic son of Viṣṇu. Likewise, the second major dynasty, the Śālastambha (seventh to ninth centuries) is explicitly referred to as a *mleccha* or non-Hindu, tribal, barbarian dynasty; yet it too would claim to be descended from the dynasty of Naraka.[15] Virtually all later indigenous kings of the northeast claimed some similar divine descent once they began to patronize *brāhmaṇic* traditions. Thus the Manipuris linked their kings to Arjuna, the Koch kings traced their origin to Śiva; the Chutiyas began worshipping Hindu deities and traced their origin to Indra; and the Ahoms not only traced their lineage to Indra but also identified their own deities with Hindu gods and goddesses, such as Chao-pha for Indra, Khan-Khampha-pha for Devī or Śakti, etc.[16]

However, Śākta Tantra appears to have reached its peak under the kings of Assam's Pāla dynasty (tenth to twelfth centuries). As we saw in Chapter 1, it was under the Pālas that the *Kālikā Purāṇa* was composed and Assam's sculpture and architecture reached their pinnacle. The great Pāla kings, Ratnapāla, Indrapāla, and Dharmapāla, clearly fit the model of the divine ruler who is at once the patron of sacrifices and also the Śiva-like consort of the goddess/kingdom. Indeed, many Assamese scholars believe that Indrapāla and others in his line were public patrons of orthodox rites and private patrons of the *tantras:* "what appears to be most likely is that the Kāmarūpa kings received Tantric *dīkṣa* [initiation] only in their private life while in public they remained followers of Brahmanical faiths."[17] Throughout the copper plate grants that survive from ancient Assam, the Pāla kings are identified as Parameśvara, the Supreme Lord, meaning both Śiva and the king; they are equal to Kāma in sexual prowess; they are supreme patrons of sacrifices; and, above all, they are indomitable in battle. For "war was the sport of kings, and success in war and valour in battle was the rulers' highest ambition."[18] Thus King Ratnapāla (ca. 920–60) is described as a descendent of the demon-king Naraka, but he is also a destroyer of demons and so wears a garland made of the heads of "kings defeated in battle"[19]:

> Even being the Parameśvara, he is the promoter of joy in Kāmarūpa. Even belonging to the family of Naraka he causes the pleasure of the enemy of Naraka [Viṣṇu] ... Even being a *vīra* [warrior] he moves like an intoxicated elephant. His beauty surpasses even that of Cupid ... His valor is productive of the conquest of the whole world. ... He is an Arjuna in fame, a Bhīmasena in the battlefield, the god Yama in anger, a forest fire in respect of the grasses in the form of enemies.[20]

Ratnapāla's son Indrapāla (ca. 960–90) is widely believed to have been a patron of Śākta Tantra, and it seems that the worship of the goddess (Mahāgaurī or Kāmākhyā) and her consort (Śiva or Kāmeśvara) was popular in kingdom during his reign. The king himself is said to have been "learned in *pada* (grammar), *vākya* (rherotic), *tarka* (logic) and *tantra*."[21] And Indrapāla is praised in no less spectacular terms as both a supreme lover, "to the damsels like Kāmadeva,"and a supreme warrior, omnipotent in battle: "He vanquished the enemy by dint of his might, which was increased with the three *śaktis*," namely, the three royal powers of *prabhuśakti* or power of the king, *mantraśakti* or power of good counsel, and *utsāhaśakti* or power of energy.[22]

The greatest of the Pāla kings was Dharmapāla (ca. 1035–60), during whose reign the *Kālikā Purāṇa* was likely composed. Like his predecessors, Dharmapāla is celebrated as a "vanquisher of enemies" and a consort of the goddess in war: "On the battlefield beautiful with flower-like pearls struck off from the heads of elephants killed by the blows of his sword, king Dharmapāla alone remained victorious to sport with the goddess of wealth born of battle."[23]

Even after the collapse of the Pāla dynasty and the fragmentation of the early Kāmarūpa kingdom, this association of kingship with the goddess, with bloodshed, and with terrible power would continue in the medieval dynasties of Assam. As we will see below, the Koch kings Viśva Siṅgha and Naranārāyaṇa Siṅgha resurrected the worship of the goddess in the sixteenth century, as did the Ahom kings Rudra Siṅgha and Śiva Siṅgha in the eighteenth century. Both the Kochs and Ahoms were, again, non-Hindu tribal kings who adopted *brāhmaṇic* traditions and patronized a kind of hybrid goddess worship woven of both indigenous and mainstream Hindu traditions.

The impurity of power: Kingship and the necessity of violence

Both Hindu mythology and the historical narratives of Assam closely link kingship with the goddess—though in complex and ambivalent ways, for the king is consistently portrayed as both a devotee of the goddess and a man flawed by sin and weakness. Like the goddess herself, the king is inevitably tied to the realm of bloodshed and the impurity that comes with it. As early as the *Laws of Manu* and the *Mahābhārata*, the king was conceived as a deeply ambivalent character who wields a dangerous and frightening power. This is what Heesterman calls the "conundrum of the king's authority," or the "ambivalent numinosity" of the king, who is seen as terribly powerful in both a positive and a negative sense. On the one hand, the king protects the people, maintaining the order of the universe; indeed, he is *dharma* incarnate. But on the other hand, the king is "roundly abominated. That he is simply the 'eater of the people' who devours everything he can lay hands on is already a cliché in the Vedic prose texts . . . [T]he king is put on a par with a butcher who keeps a hundred thousand slaughterhouses."[24]

Likewise, the *Kālikā Purāṇa* consistently portrays the king as a being of dangerous power whose strength and self-will always threaten to bring his own downfall: "The power of kings is like the heat of the sun. If there is pride in it, he should abandon it like a diseased body"; indeed, "the self-will of kings will always destroy them. The self-willed prince surely goes astray."[25] Above all, the king is inevitably tied to impurity because of his involvement in punishing criminals, offering blood sacrifice, and waging war: "Kings immediately become impure when passing judgment, when consecrating an image, when performing sacrifice, or when invading an enemy kingdom."[26] That is why the king needs to support his *brāhmaṇs,* who alone can purify him of the evil deeds that he must inevitably perform. As Heesterman notes, "The king . . . desperately needs the Brahmin to sanction his power by linking it to the Brahmin's authority. The greater the king's power, the more he needs the Brahmin."[27]

In part, this complex relationship between kings and *brāhmaṇs* in Assam reflects a larger tension between power and purity in South Asian Hindu traditions as a whole. Since the earliest Vedas, the *brāhmaṇ* was associated with purity and goodness (*sattva*) and the king with power and strength (*rajas, vīrya, ojas*); and the sacrificial ritual, as Romila Thapar suggests, served as a key exchange of material and symbolic capital between the pure priest and the powerful king: "The *brāhmaṇa* had a relationship with the *kṣatriya* embodying political power. The sacrificial ritual was an exchange in which . . . the priests were the recipients of gifts and fees and the *kṣatriya* was the recipient of . . . status and legitimacy."[28] But at the same time, in the Assamese tradition, we also see a deep tension between *brāhmaṇic* Hinduism and the local indigenous traditions of the northeast that were slowly being brought into the Hindu fold. Again, this clearly reflects the real political history of the region, since most of Assam's kings came from tribal backgrounds and brought with them a variety of indigenous rituals and deities that were never fully "Hinduized." And it is reflected throughout the narratives of Assam's great mythic and historical kings.

Naraka, the demon king

As we saw in Chapter 1, the first devotee of the goddess was king Naraka, who is said to have founded the first kingdom in Assam, then known as Prāgjyotiṣapura. An ambivalent character from the very beginning, Naraka was born the son of Lord Viṣṇu in his boar incarnation, who united with the goddess Earth during the highly inauspicious time of her menstrual period. Indeed, it was precisely because he was conceived during Earth's menstruation that this son of a god was doomed to become demonic: "Because [he was born] in the womb of a menstruating woman by the seed of the boar, although the son of a god, he became a demon."[29] From his origins, however, Naraka was also associated with the sacrificial ritual and was in fact born upon the sacrificial ground of King Janaka.[30] Thus he was from his birth an impure but dangerously powerful being.

According to the *Kālikā Purāṇa*, Naraka conquered the indigenous peoples of the region, slew Ghaṭaka, the king of the *kirātas*, and established *brāhmaṇic* traditions in the realm. His father Viṣṇu gave him a special weapon called none other than *śakti*, made him ruler of Kāmarūpa, and instructed him to worship Kāmākhyā on the great mountain Nīlakūṭa.[31] The kingdom flourished until the arrogant Naraka forged an alliance with Bāṇa, a demon king in the non-Hindu tribal region of Sonitpura in eastern Assam. Thereafter, he became "inimical to gods and Brahmans . . . He destroyed heaven and earth, carrying his torture and destruction everywhere."[32] Thus he was cursed by the sage Vasiṣṭha that so long as he lived, the goddess would remain hidden. In fact, the goddess does seem to have gone into hiding for some time, as there is no clear mention of Kāmākhyā or her temple between the time of the *Kālikā Purāṇa* (tenth to eleventh centuries) and the rebuilding of the present temple (sixteenth century).[33]

Another popular story about a demon king and the goddess is told about both Naraka and the tribal ruler of Sonitpur, Bāṇa. In the latter version of the legend, the arrogant king Bāṇa wished to see the goddess. She told him she would reveal herself to him only on the condition that he could build a stairway up the hill to the temple in one single night before the first cock's crow in the morning. The king worked all night with his men, building the staircase almost to the top, and then, just before he laid the last stone, the goddess miraculously caused the cock to crow. Thus "the Goddess got a stairway to her temple without having to show herself to the *ashura* king."[34] Much the same story is also told of Naraka, except in this case the demon-king wants not just a vision of the goddess, but the goddess herself as his bride. Again, the goddess in this narrative magically causes the cock to crow just before the king can finish his task, rebuking him for his demonic arrogance: "Hey proud demon, your request has been denied."[35]

In sum, each of these narratives links the pride of the king—and specifically the pride of a king who either is himself non-Hindu or else who makes deals with a tribal king. And in each case, the king is punished by being denied access to the goddess. Ironically, however, the demon king was to have a long legacy in Assam, as virtually all the later kings of ancient Kāmarūpa, from the Varman dynasty (fourth to seventh centuries) to the Pāla dynasty (tenth to twelfth centuries) traced their lineage to Naraka. Perhaps the most mysterious and little-understood of the early Kāmarūpa dynasties was the Śālastambha kingdom, which flourished from the seventh to ninth centuries. According to two copper plate inscriptions from the ninth and eleventh centuries, the Śālastambhas claimed to be descended from the demon king Naraka. But, like Naraka, they too suffered some unknown curse (the portion of the plate that presumably explains why the dynasty became *mleccha* is damaged and unreadable) and were doomed to be called *mlecchas*, that is, non-Hindu barbarians. King Śālastambha himself became "lord of the *mlecchas*."[36]

Viśva Siṅgha, the son of the cursed yoginī

According to a widespread series of legends and semi-historical narratives, the temple of Kāmākhyā was rediscovered and her worship reinstituted in the sixteenth century by Viśva Siṅgha (1515–40) of the Koch kingdom immediately adjacent to Kāmarūpa (modern Cooch Behar). Apparently, the original temple had been destroyed by some natural disaster or invasion and was not rebuilt until Viśva and his sons conquered the region.[37] Again, Viśva Siṅgha embodies the tensions between Hindu and tribal traditions and the dangerous power of kingship. As Subhajyoti Ray suggests in his study of northern Bangla and Assam, the Koch kingdom is yet another example of the "gradual process of 'Hinduisation'" of a tribal group that progressively replaces indigenous practices with mainstream Hindu traditions. Like many other northeast tribes, the Kochs did so by claiming a divine lineage descending from the gods.[38] But it is a complex and ambivalent lineage, also linked to sin, curses, and their non-Hindu tribal past.

The *Yoginī Tantra*, for example, provides a mytho-historical narrative for the birth of king Viśva, which, again, involves the themes of Hindu–tribal tensions and the legacy of a curse. Here we learn that Viśva was the son of a beautiful, powerful, and wise *yoginī* name Revatī, who lived "in the land of Koch, adjacent to the *yoni* cave. She was honored as a beautiful *yoginī*, but she assumed the body of a *mleccha*."[39] Both charming and wise, versed in both the Vedas and Āgamas, the *yoginī* engaged in joyful love-play with Lord Śiva himself. But when a powerful sage came to her seeking alms, she ignored him, and the sage therefore cursed her to become a *mleccha*, that is, a non-Aryan, outcaste, or barbarian. The child born of her love-play with Śiva was Vinu Siṅgha (a.k.a. Viśva Siṅgha), who conquered the Saumaras (Ahoms) and the other tribes of the region and established a mighty lineage of Kuvācā (Koch) kings. As Lord Śiva praised the king and his descendents,

> His many sons were great kings of the earth. The Kuvācās were all righteous kings and fierce in battle . . . Just like my son, Bhṛṅgarīṭa, Vinu is my offspring. So too, at the end of the age, Vinu will achieve supreme perfection. The descendents of that family are all kings and dwell on Mount Kailāsa.[40]

Indeed, because Viśva took birth in Kāmākhyā out of his own desire (*svasya kāmasya*), so too, all his descendents were destined to be *kāmapālakās*, meaning both "kings of Kāmarūpa" and "kings of desire."[41]

Viśva's rediscovery of Kāmākhyā temple is a popular and often repeated narrative (even making its way into modern popular film[42]). According to one widespread narrative, the king was leading his armies into Assam to wage war against the tribal kingdoms of the region, when he lost his way in the forest. There he came upon an old woman who gave him water from a sacred spring. The spring, she said, flowed from the goddess' own *yoni* and marked the spot at which the original Kāmākhyā temple stood. The king prayed to the goddess, offered the sacrifice of a pig and a cock, and vowed that, if she would aid him in battle, he would build her a new temple made of gold. The king was indeed victorious and established a new kingdom in Assam with Kāmākhyā at its religio-political center.[43] However, like Naraka before him, Viśva represents a complex negotiation between non-Hindu indigenous cultures and Hindu traditions imported from central India. Indeed, the new Kāmākhyā temple was established directly amidst and on top of existing tribal ritual practices. According to historical accounts from Cooch Behar, Viśva "built this temple over a mound where the inhabitants of the nearby Nilachal hill used to sacrifice pigs, fowls and other animals and . . . imported numerous brahmans from Kanauj and Benaras and other centres of learning to run it."[44] Here we see a classic example of the complex negotiation between indigenous and *brāhmaṇic* traditions in Assam: the tribal king claims a mythical descent from Śiva and then transforms the goddess' temple from a site of tribal sacrifice into a center of *brāhmaṇic* rites.

Naranārāyaṇa, the cursed king

A similar set of narratives, with a similar tension between *brāhmaṇic* and tribal traditions, surrounds Viśva's son, Naranārāyaṇa Siṅgha (1540–86). It was Naranārāyaṇa and his brother Chilarai who brought most of the region under a single rule, subduing the Ahoms, Manipuris, Kacharis, Jaintias, and Tripuris.[45] In 1565, they rebuilt Kāmākhyā temple, whose inner wall still contains an inscription celebrating their glory as supreme heroes and devotees of the goddess:

> Glory to the king Malladeva [Naranārāyaṇa] who, by virtue of his mercy, is kind to the people, who in archery is like Arjuna, and in charity like Dadhichi and Karṇa; he is like an ocean of all goodness, and he is versed in many *śāstras;* his character is excellent; in beauty he is as bright as Kandarpa, he is a worshipper of Kāmākhyā. His younger brother Śukladeva [Chilarai] built this temple of bright stones on the Nīla hill, for the worship of the goddess Durgā in 1487 Śaka [1565 CE]. His beloved brother Śukladhvaja again, with universal fame, the crown of the greatest heroes, who, like the fabulous Kalpataru, gave all that was devoutly asked of him, the chief of all devotees of the goddess, constructed this beautiful temple with heaps of stones on the Nīla hill in 1487 Śaka.[46]

Like Naraka, Naranārāyaṇa also had a complex relationship with the indigenous peoples of Assam. Although he was famed for his conquest of many indigenous kings, Naranārāyaṇa was also known for his tolerance of indigenous traditions. According to one well-known story, on the eve of battle with the Ahoms, Naranārāyaṇa allowed his Kachari soldiers to worship Śiva in their own indigenous mode, alongside his *brāhmaṇic* method of *pūjā:*

> Besides the Vedic rites there were and even now are various tribal modes of worship of Shiva. On the eve of his expedition against the Ahoms, as recorded in the *Darang Rajvasmsavali*, King Naranarayana of Koch-Bihar worshipped Shiva according to accepted *sastric* rites. But at the insistence of his Kachari soldiers, the sacrifice of swine, buffalo, he-goats, pigeons, ducks and cocks and offering of rice and liquor and also dancing of women (*deodhai*) were allowed. By edict he allowed this form of Siva worship in the north bank of the Brahmaputra river.[47]

Like Naraka, however, Naranārāyaṇa was also a flawed king, whose pride eventually led to a terrible curse. According to one widespread story, a pious *brāhmaṇ* named Kendukalai received a vision of the goddess. Upon hearing of this vision, Naranārāyaṇa also wished to see Kāmākhyā and demanded that the priest help him pray until the goddess revealed herself. The goddess, however, became so furious at his audacity that she beheaded the priest and cursed the king: thenceforth, if he or any of his descendents ever visited the temple they would be doomed.[48]

Rudra and Śiva Siṅgha: The Ahom kings and the "cult of strength"

This intimate connection between kingship and the goddess continued even after the defeat of the Koch Behar kings by the Ahoms in the seventeenth century. Although originally a non-Hindu people derived from the Tai or Shan race, who first entered Assam in the thirteenth century, the Ahoms adopted many *brāhmaṇic* traditions and worship of Kāmākhyā after they conquered the region.[49] The Ahoms brought in new priests from Bengal and other parts of India and constructed hundreds of temples throughout the region. As part of their complex blending of Hindu and indigenous traditions, they not only identified Ahom gods with Hindu deities, as we saw above, but also gave both a traditional Ahom and a Sanskritic Hindu title to each of their kings, who thus embodied fusion of Ahom and *brāhmaṇic* traditions.[50]

The greatest of the Ahom kings was Rudra Siṅgha (Siu-Khrung-Pha, 1696–1714), who ruled during the zenith of Ahom power, subjugated the neighboring Jaintia and Dimasa kingdoms, and raised a vast army against the Mughal empire. According to one widespread narrative, Rudra decided that he should adopt *brāhmaṇic* rites and worship of the goddess, thus being initiated into the "cult of strength or Śakti."[51] Too proud to receive initiation from any of his subjects, however, he invited a famous Śākta priest named Kṛṣṇarāma Bhaṭṭācārya to come to Assam from Bengal, promising him the care of Kāmākhyā temple itself. Even then, the king had second thoughts and changed his mind, sending the priest away. But then the king received a cataclysmic warning that he took to be a sign from the gods that he had offended them:

> After the priest departed there was a severe earthquake that shattered several temples. Rudra Singh thought he had attracted divine displeasure by hurting a favorite of God and recalled the Mahant and satisfied him by ordering his sons . . . to accept him as their Guru.[52]

Kṛṣṇarāma was subsequently given management of Kāmākhyā temple by Rudra's son, Śiva Siṅgha (1714–44), perhaps the greatest patron of Śāktism among the Ahoms. Kṛṣṇarāma's descendents, in turn, became known as the Parvatīya Gosāiṅs, whose method of worshipping Kāmākhyā is said to have continued down to the present era.[53] Ironically, however, many contemporary Assamese historians also blame Śiva Siṅgha for the eventual decay and "final crash" of Ahom rule, largely because of his over-indulgence in Tantra and "absorption in the Śākta cult":

> Shiva Singha used to spend most of his time in Shakta worship . . . The Ahoms in their fanatic zeal for their new religion had turned indifferent to the political consequences of their actions. The Ahoms now became unmindful of the effects of their religious conduct on the stability of the government . . . Such patronage now became the criterion of excellence of kings and individuals rather than . . . state service.[54]

Thus, in each of these narratives, we can see a consistent structural theme that centers around kingship, the goddess, and a basic tension between Hindu and tribal religious practice. In each case—Naraka, Bāṇa, Viśva Siṅgha, Naranārāyaṇa Siṅgha, and Rudra Siṅgha—the king worships the goddess and conquers his enemies; but in each case, the king also has some flaw that prevents him from seeing the goddess or worshipping her properly; and in each case, this flaw centers on the king's relation to indigenous traditions, whether by making alliances with tribal kings, allowing tribal practices to continue, or by his own non-Hindu origins.

King	Great deed	Sin or fault	Punishment	Brāhmaṇic vs. tribal tension
Naraka	Founds kingdom of Kāmarūpa, worships Kāmākhyā	Makes pact with tribal king	Goddess hidden from him	Pact with tribal king
Bāṇa (or Naraka)	Builds stairway to Kāmākhyā temple	Demands vision of the goddess	Goddess hidden from him	Demonic tribal king
Śālastambha	Conquest of Kāmarūpa	Unknown	Cursed to be *mleccha*, non-Hindu barbarian	Founds *mleccha* dynasty
Viśva Siṅgha	Rediscovers Kāmākhyā temple	Mother offends holy man	Mother is a *mleccha*	Wars against tribal kings; child of a god and a *mleccha*
Naranārāyaṇa Siṅgha	Rebuilds the temple	Demands a vision of the goddess	Descendents cannot visit the temple	Defeats tribal kings, but allows soldiers to worship in tribal mode
Rudra Siṅgha	Patronizes *brāhmaṇs*, builds temples	Tribal origin; offends priest	Dies without receiving initiation	Non-Hindu tribal origin

In sum, the king in these narratives is always an ambivalent character, a devotee of the goddess, but also a flawed being tied to impurity, sin, and non-Hindu indigenous traditions.

There are good reasons for this connection between the political power of the king and the spiritual power of the goddess—and also for the ambivalent status of the king. As Coburn notes, the goddess and the king mirror one another in many ways, sharing a "common character as both valorous and irascible."[55] The goddess is, after all, the embodiment of the earth and the land, of which the king is the ruler and protector. The goddess, moreover, embodies a fierce and awesome source of power, the power to destroy demons, to cleanse the world of evil, and, by extension, to defeat one's enemies and rival kings. As Biardeau notes, "she is closer to earthly values . . . but she is more apt to make use of the violence without which the earth could not live."[56] But more important, the king also embodies many of the same tensions as the goddess. Above all, he reflects the tension between dangerous impurity and terrible power, between the polluting flow of blood and the strength to destroy enemies. Like the goddess, the king is bound to the world of warfare, battle, violence, and inevitable impurity that is necessary to the functioning of the state.

Kingship and sacrifice: Impurity, violence, and power

These three related themes of kingship, impurity, and the *brāhmaṇic*–tribal tension all come together in the ritual of sacrifice, of which the king is the supreme patron. Virtually all of the inscriptions and textual evidence from Assam, from ancient Kāmarūpa down to the Ahom era, consistently link the king with the bloodshed of sacrifice and war. Thus the earliest copper plate inscriptions from the Varman dynasty portray the Varman kings as patrons of the great royal rite, the horse sacrifice, which was performed as a prelude to the conquest of new regions. Indeed, Mahendravarman was praised as the "repository of all sacrifices" (*yajñavidhīnāmāspadam*)[57] and his mother as "the goddess of sacrifice"[58] (*yajñadevī*), because of their generous patronage, as were their descendents: "Mahendravaman is said to have performed two horse sacrifices, Bhūtivarman one and Sthilavarman two sacrifices. This sacrifice was always preceded by some conquests."[59]

This link between kingship and sacrifice is also seen throughout the copper plate grants of Assam's Pāla kings (tenth to twelfth centuries), who are endlessly praised as patrons of sacrifice. Thus Ratnapāla (920–60) "caused the whole world to be crowded with white-washed temples of Śiva, the dwellings of *brāhmaṇs* to be stuffed with various types of wealth, the places of sacrifice to be littered with sacrificial posts, the sky to be filled with sacrificial smoke."[60] Likewise, Harṣa Pāla (1015–35) is praised as making offerings of enemy blood, spilled on all sides in the great sacrifice of battle: "In the battlefields he, by breaking with weapons the foreheads of the enemy elephants, repeatedly made offerings of drinks to the demons on all sides, who being thirsty drank up hurriedly the lukewarm blood mixed up with a profuse quantity of froth."[61]

Kingship and sacrifice in the Kālikā Purāṇa

Probably composed during the reign of the Pāla kings of the tenth and eleventh centuries, the *Kālikā Purāṇa* makes the most explicit link between kingship, sacrifice, and dangerous power. Throughout the text, blood sacrifice is identified with both the attainment of political power and the conquest of enemies in battle: "By sacrifices one attains liberation. By sacrifices one attains heaven. By offering sacrifice a king always conquers enemy kings."[62] Indeed, a large portion of the *Kālikā* is devoted to the complex details of kingship, statecraft, politics, and military strategy. Like the classic Hindu political text, the *Arthaśāstra*, the *Kālikā Purāṇa* provides detailed directions on economic affairs, agriculture, forts, farms, taxes, and especially warfare. For "kings should always be engaged in war. If one concludes he can obtain land, wealth, or allies, there should be wars."[63] At the same time, the text emphasizes that the king must also be a good patron of *brāhmaṇs*, carefully listening to their teachings and funding their ritual performances.[64] Here we see, again, that the Śākta traditions of Assam are the result of a complex negotiation between the Sanskrit-trained priests who composed these texts and the local kings whose patronage they sought.

Following the ancient Indian social model, which dates back to the early Vedas, the *Kālikā Purāṇa* imagines the kingdom as an alloform of the human body. In the well-known myth of the *Ṛg Veda* mentioned above, the entire universe is born from the sacrifice and dismemberment of the primordial person, Puruṣa, who is ritually divided up into the various forms of both cosmic and social hierarchies. Puruṣa's body forms of the paradigm for the cosmic hierarchy of heaven, atmosphere, and earth as well as for the hierarchy of the social classes: *brāhmaṇs* become the head, the *kṣatriyas* become the torso, the *vaiśyas* become the legs, and the *śūdras* become the feet of the body politic. Similarly, the ideal kingdom is conceived on the analogy of a human corpus with its even limbs: "The king, the ministers, the kingdom, friends, the treasury, the army, and the citadel—these seven are known as the limbs of the kingdom [*rājyāṅgam*]."[65] As B.K. Sarkar comments, "This conception is not merely structural or anatomical but also physiological . . . It embodies an attempt to classify political phenomena in their logical entirety."[66]

Just as the proper maintenance of the Vedic universe was said to depend on the regular performance of rituals, so too the proper order of the sociopolitical universe relies on the king's generous patronage of sacrifice. And just as the Vedic sacrifice was believed to regenerate and reunify the cosmic body of the first sacrificial victim, Puruṣa, so too, the sacrifice performed by the king is necessary of the ongoing unity and vitality of the body politic. Indeed, he would risk disaster and ruin if the sacrifice were not performed:

> Having performed these [rites], his army, kingdom and treasury increase, but if these sacrifices are not performed, famine, death, etc will occur . . .[67]

> By performing sacrifices and offering gifts, one becomes a king in this world. Therefore to have a kingdom one should follow *dharma*. By means of these rites and by performing sacrifices, O ruler, your enemies are destroyed and you will achieve kingship, without doubt. The [enemy] king does not follow the *dharma* of a king or perform *aśvamedha* sacrifices, etc, therefore you should perform all these, O best one![68]

Many of the rites described in the *Kālikā Purāṇa* are specifically designed to ensure the prosperity of the kingdom and the conquest of enemies. During the autumnal worship of Durgā, for example, the king should prepare a horse sacrifice that will "increase his strength" and determine his success in war.[69] In other rites, the king should fashion an earthen image of his enemy and magically infuse it with the enemy's spirit. Finally, he should "pierce its heart with a trident and sever its head with a sword," before marching against his enemies on horseback.[70]

Above all, the power of blood sacrifice can be harnessed by the king and turned directly against his enemies in battle. Whereas the Vedic sacrifice had, on the offering of a pure victim, identified with the divine offering of Puruṣa, the Śākta sacrifice centers on an impure, demonic victim—ideally, a buffalo—identified with the evil and danger of a hostile king. And the deity worshipped here is not a pure male god, but rather the goddess in her most terrible, blood-thirsty, left-hand forms as the destroyer of evil:

> A king may offer sacrifice for his enemies. He should first consecrate the sword with the mantra, and then consecrate the buffalo or goat with the name of the enemy. He should bind the animal with a cord around his mouth, reciting the *mantra* three times. He should sever the head and offer it with great effort to the goddess. Whenever enemies become strong, more sacrifices should be offered. At such times, he should sever the head and offer it for the destruction of his enemies. He should infuse the soul of the enemy into the animal. With the slaughter of this [animal], the lives of his unfortunate enemies are also slain. "O Caṇḍikā, of terrible form, devour my enemy, so and so"—this *mantra* should be repeated. . . . . "This hateful enemy of mine is himself in the form of the animal. Destroy him, Mahāmārī, devour him, devour him, *spheṇg spheṇg*!" With this *mantra*, a flower should be placed on his head. He should then offer the blood, with the two-syllable [*mantra*].[71]

Here we see that the ritual explicitly manipulates the transgressive forces of impurity, bloodshed, and the severed head in order to unleash the violent power of the goddess in her most terrible Tantric form, now turned against an enemy in battle.

This link between kingship, power, and sacrifice (especially buffalo sacrifice) persisted long after the time of the *Kālikā Purāṇa* and the end of the Pāla dynasty. Even as late as 1781 when the Ahom king Gaurīnatha Siṅgha (Chāophā Shuhitpungngam Mung) assumed the throne, the coronation culminated with the royal sacrifice of a buffalo: "For seven days and nights, drums were beaten, gongs were struck, and flutes were blown . . . At the time of ascending the throne, the king pierced to the death a buffalo. All the great men of he country were entertained with feasts for seven days."[72] Up to the end of Ahom rule, sacrifice remained closely tied to royal power, believed to be "conducive to the welfare of the kings and their people," and "performed for bringing victory to Ahom arms or in celebration of victories in war."[73]

In fact, the link between Kāmākhyā, kingship, and sacrifice has even survived into the twenty-first century. During the Ambuvācī celebration in 2002, King Gyanendra and Queen Komal of Nepal visited the temple with the intention of offering animal sacrifice. However, the plan drew such protest from animal rights groups that the king himself offered the substitute of vegetarian offerings and left the site before a buffalo, a sheep, a duck, and a goat were sacrificed on his behalf.[74]

Human sacrifice and kingship in Assamese history

According to Assamese texts like the *Kālikā Purāṇa* and *Yoginī Tantra*, the supreme sacrifice that can be offered by a king is that of a human being. Indeed, human sacrifice receives a great deal of attention in the *Kālikā Purāṇa*, where it is said to be the most perfect offering and greatest source of power: "With a human sacrifice, performed according to ritual precepts, the goddess is pleased for a full one thousand years, and with three humans, for 100,000 years. With human flesh, Kāmākhyā and Bhairavī, who assumes my form, are pleased for three thousand years."[75] The *Yoginī Tantra* likewise declares that the sacrifice of a human boy (*narasya kumāra*) is the highest of all sacrifices, worth more than the offering of any number of yaks, tortoises, rabbits, boars, buffaloes, rhinos, or lizards.[76] As Wendell Beane points out, human sacrifice had deep roots in the political history of Assam, closely tied to power, warfare, and royalty: "The sacrificial cults had royal patronage, and sacrifices were demanded of the most loyal officials . . . [T]he occasion tended to coincide with calamities such as war or for obtaining wealth."[77]

But did human sacrifice ever really take place? It is tempting, of course, to dismiss accounts of human sacrifice as mere mythological fantasy or British colonial paranoia (which in some cases they were, as we will see in Chapter 6). However, there seems to be sufficient evidence from textual and ethnographic that suggests that human sacrifice did indeed occur among several indigenous communities of the northeast and was carried over into Śākta Tantra.

Vedic and indigenous roots of human sacrifice

The practice of human sacrifice, I would argue, is another example of the rich intermingling of traditional Vedic rites with indigenous practices of the northeast hills. Human sacrifice is clearly mentioned in the Vedas and Brāhmaṇas, and the human being is even listed as the first among animals fit for sacrifice. Yet paradoxically, consumption of human flesh is explicitly considered taboo throughout the same literature.[78] As Heesterman suggests, the sacrifice of a human being is part of the same basic conflict at the heart of the sacrifice—the problem of violence and impurity at the center of a ritual that is supposed to be life-giving and pure. As we saw in Chapter 2, human sacrifice, like animal sacrifice in general, was gradually eliminated in mainstream Hindu traditions, as the sacrifice was increasingly domesticated and the violent elements were gradually replaced by a logical system of ritual procedures.[79]

Yet human sacrifices continued throughout many non-Vedic indigenous traditions, particularly in remote, mountainous regions like Assam. Several of the northeast tribes, such as the Nagas and Garos, were head-hunters with a long tradition of collecting human heads. And human sacrifice was widely practiced by many other northeast tribes such as the Jaintias, Khasis, and Chutiyas.[80] As Briggs points out, the rite of human sacrifice described in the *Kālikā Purāṇa* has little in common with any Vedic ritual, but quite a lot in common with non-Hindu indigenous practices: "though they may be performed by non-Aryans under Brahmanic auspices, they form no part of the Aryan religion. But they are recommended to princes and ministers . . . The ritual bears little resemblance to Vedic sacrifices, and the essence of the ceremony is the presentation to the goddess of the victim's severed head."[81] Again, the rite of human sacrifice described in texts like the *Kālikā Purāṇa* and *Yoginī Tantra* is likely the result of a complex interaction between Vedic and indigenous traditions, through which Vedic paradigms that were later rejected by the mainstream tradition were reworked within a more accommodating religious framework.

The *Kālikā Purāṇa* makes it clear that human sacrifice is at once an extremely powerful and yet also dangerous and potentially polluting act. In fact, a *brāhmaṇ* cannot offer a human victim without losing his priestly status.[82] Members of the *kṣatriya* class may offer human sacrifice, but only with the permission of the king, who alone can sanction such a rite. Above all, in times of political turmoil such as anarchy or war, it is the king alone who may perform the *puruṣamedha:*

> The prince, the minister, the counselor, and the *sauptika*, etc., may offer human sacrifice [in order to attain] kingship, prosperity and wealth. If one offers a human being without the permission of the

> king, he will find great misfortune. During an invasion or war, one may offer a human being at will, but only a royal person [may do so], and no one else.[83]

The preferred human victims, moreover, are said to be neither a priest nor an untouchable, but ideally "the mercenaries of enemy lands, who are captured in battle."[84]

Overall, this ritual is surrounded with an aura of fear and danger. It must be performed in the cremation ground.[85] As the locus of human remnants and the ashen leftovers of bodies, the cremation ground is a place of utmost impurity in the Hindu religious imagination and is the dwelling place of Śiva in his terrible form as Bhairava.

The human victim, however, is described in terms that draw explicitly on the classical ritual of the Vedas. Indeed, the victim is a representation of the primordial sacrificial victim, Puruṣa, who was slain and dismembered to create the various parts of the cosmos at the beginning of time. In the consecration of the victim, all the gods and aspects of the cosmos are ritually identified with various parts of the body, infusing the sacrifice with the powers of the universe and, in a sense, reconstructing the original cosmic victim. Thus, one should worship Brahmā in the cavity of the skull, the earth in the nostrils, the sky in the ears, water on the tongue, Viṣṇu in the mouth, the moon on the forehead, and Indra on the check, declaring, "O, most auspicious one, you are the supreme embodiment of all the gods!"[86] Still more important, the king also identifies himself with victim, who is offered in his place in order to insure the protection of his kingdom and wealth:

> Save me, taking refuge in you, together with my sons, livestock and kinsmen. Save me, together with my kingdom, ministers and fourfold army, giving up your own life, for death is inevitable . . . Do not let the demons, ghosts, goblins, serpents, kings, and other enemies attack me, because of you. Dying, with blood flowing from the arteries of your neck and smearing your limbs, cherish yourself, for death is inevitable . . .
>
> The one worshipped in this way has my own form and is the seat of the guardians of the four quarters. He is possessed by Brahmā and all the other gods. Even though he was a sinner, the man worshipped in this way becomes free of sin. The blood of this pure being quickly becomes

> nectar. And the great goddess, who is the mother of the universe and also herself the universe, is pleased.[87]

What we have here, then, is a complex series of homologies that symbolically link the body of the victim, first, with the body of the cosmic or the cosmic man, Puruṣa; second, with the body politic of the kingdom; and finally, with the body of the king himself. And just as in the Vedic sacrifice, the universe is reintegrated through the performance of the ritual and the reconstruction of the cosmic man, so too, in this sacrifice, the kingdom and the body politic are rejuvenated and preserved through the offering of this now-divinized victim. As in the case of other Tantric sacrifices, the focal point of the human sacrifice is the ambivalent but powerful offering of the severed head. Indeed, the sacrificer must carefully observe exactly how and where the severed head falls, for the *Kālikā Purāṇa* provides a long list of various good and bad omens associated with its direction, the sound that it emits, and how the blood flows out, along with their portents for the future of the kingdom.[88] Ultimately, by standing in all-night vigil holding the severed head as the supreme gift to the goddess, the king achieves the highest fruit of the sacrifice:

> If the adept stays awake all night holding the head of a human being in his right hand and the vessel of blood in his left, he becomes a king in this life, and after death, he reaches my [Śiva's] realm and becomes lord of hosts.[89]

Here again we see the circulation of divine power between the goddess and her devotee, flowing through the physical medium of blood.

Kingship, human sacrifice, and the power of the impure

Much of the efficacy of rituals like human sacrifice, I would argue, lies precisely in the use of impurity and the dangerous power that such transgressive acts unleash. As we have seen above, the king himself is a complex figure, often associated with impurity, bloodshed, and death. Forced by his *dharma* to deal with the impurity of war, conquest, and punishment, the king is likened to an "eater" of the people and a "butcher."[90]

For the early *brāhmaṇic* tradition, priestly ritual serves as the expiation for the inevitable impurity that comes with the office of the king:

"The guilt of the warrior or the evil of the sacrificer was easily removed by the priest in Vedic times."[91] As Heesterman argues, however, the *brāhmaṇic* tradition would gradually seek to eliminate as much impurity and violence from the ritual as possible—ultimately even excluding the impure king from the sacrificial arena: "The elimination of conflict. . . resulted in the internal contradiction of Vedic ritualism. This has already come out in the fact that the *kṣatriya*—the king who. . . is the ideal sacrificer—is. . . excluded from the *agnihotra* . . . The *kṣatriya* perpetrates many impure acts, he kills and plunders."[92]

For the later Śākta Tantric, however, the sacrifice seems to function quite differently. Indeed, the Tantric sacrifice actually seizes on and exploits the transgressive nature of ritual violence, precisely in order to unleash its dangerous power. Tantric ritual turns to the dark and furious energy of the goddess in her most terrifying forms—as Kālī, Cāmuṇḍā, and Caṇḍikā—to let loose their violent power. As Biardeau suggests, the goddess in her aggressive, militant forms is the supreme symbol of a kind of necessary violence: she is the one who deals in bloodshed, battle, and impurity in order to preserve the cosmic order:

> When we pass from bhakti to Śāktism . . . she becomes the preeminent divinity, the Śakti who is superior to Śiva, and this reversal of the hierarchy is accompanied . . . by a reversal of dharma: what was prohibited becomes permitted, the impure becomes pure. She is closer to earthly values . . . but she is also more apt to make use of the violence without which the earth could not live.[93]

We might also say that the goddess represents the violence without which the kingdom and the political order could not be maintained.

The Tantric traditions, however, make no attempt to rationalize this violent impurity, but instead seek to transform it into a tremendous source of power. The one who knows how to harness this violent power can become a master of this world, a hero in statecraft and war. The *Kālikā Purāṇa* makes this abundantly clear, often making an explicit appeal to the desires of the royal classes: "He who performs this [sacrifice] enjoys all the pleasures of this world and after death remains in the abode of the goddess for the three ages and then becomes a sovereign king on earth."[94] Ultimately, the king who performs these rites will achieve success in everything—not only "all the objects of his wishes and Śiva's form in the afterlife" but also supreme success in battle and virtual invincibility against any foe: "he has the power to subdue gods, kings, women and others . . . He lives a long life, becomes prosperous, endowed with wealth and grain; he becomes . . . invincible to enemies."[95] Ultimately, "that hero, like me [Śiva] enters into battles. The weapons of the enemies become like grass upon a fire . . . The Tiger among men becomes strong and virile."[96]

Human sacrifice in medieval Assam

Human sacrifice appears to have continued throughout the northeast region long after the period of the *Kālikā Purāṇa* and the Pāla kings, persisting up to the arrival of the British empire. As late as the nineteenth century, the Jaintia kings offered human victims to the goddess Durgā at her mountain temple near Nartiang, Meghalaya. Still today, one can see the ritual mask allegedly worn by human victims and the sacrificial hole into which the heads were offered, sending them down to the river far below the temple (Fig. 17).[97] As we will see in Chapter 6, the practice apparently continued up until the 1830s when the British authorities put a stop to it after four British subjects were kidnapped and taken to be offered to the goddess.[98]

The Ahoms, too, are said to have performed several human sacrifices, particularly during their war with the invading Muslims in the early seventeenth century. On the eve of the great Saraighat battle, the Ahom commanders and soldiers were said to have knelt at Kāmākhyā temple, praying to the goddess: " 'O mother Kāmākhyā, eat up the Moghuls and give us victory.' This no doubt put courage and confidence in the hearts of the Assamese army."[99] According to the Ahom *burañjīs*, the defeated Muslim commanders were subsequently sacrificed, beheaded, in some cases flayed, and offered to Kāmākhyā by the Ahom kings:

> Near the principal shrine of Kamakhya is the smaller temple of Bhairavi . . . here human sacrifices were once held. In 1615 Karmachand, son of Satrijita, a commander of an invading Musalman army, was sacrificed to the goddess Kamakhya.[100]

In 1616 King Pratap Siṅgha (Chāopā Shushengphā) is even said to have made a garland of severed heads from the Muslims slain in the sacrifice of battle—an act that is clearly a tribute to the goddess in her terrible forms as Kālī and Cāmuṇḍā, with her own dripping garland of severed heads:

> The king came back to the capital and offered oblations to the dead and sacrifices to the gods. In the month of Dinshi (Phalgun) the heavenly king made a "Mundamala" (garland of heads) with the heads of the deceased Musalmans.[101]

However, the most infamous example of human sacrifice in medieval Assam is the worship of the terrible goddess Kecāi Khātī, "the eater of raw human flesh," by the Chutiya kings of eastern Assam.[102] Annual sacrifices of human victims—usually criminals sentenced to capital punishment—were apparently offered at the Tāmreśvārī temple near the town of Sadiya. Details of the offerings are found both in various British colonial accounts and in manuscripts such as the *Tikha Kalpa*, which was found in the Manipur State Library. According to this text, "Human sacrifices are made, after the royal consent has been obtained, on the occasion of public calamities such as war or for the purpose of obtaining great wealth."[103] As the sacrificer offered the victim, he was to pray as follows: "O Goddess, living on the golden mountain, I offer this sacrifice to thee! He is good and stout and without blemish, I bind him to a post. I offer this sacrifice to remove my misfortune."[104] Again, the central act was the beheading of the victim, whose severed head was then added to a heap of skulls that were "piled in view of the shrine."[105]

With the coming of British colonial rule and the end of royal power in the northeast, the practice of human sacrifice largely died out by the early nineteenth century. However, there are in fact still periodic rumors of the rite being practiced secretly around Kāmākhyā, and the region retains its aura of blood rites and dangerous but tremendous supernatural power to this day. As recently as 2003, in fact, a man was arrested for attempting to sacrifice his daughter during the Ambuvācī celebrations in the hopes that the goddess "would bestow him with tremendous powers."[106]

Conclusions: The ambivalence of kingship and the impurity of power

In sum, the Śākta traditions of Assam represent a striking example of the complex relations between kingship, sacrifice, impurity, and power that characterize the Tantric traditions of South Asia as a whole. They reveal the intimate associations between the king as the embodiment of the male deity (Śiva, Kāma, Kāmeśvara) and the goddess as the land and divine power (Śakti, Kāmākhyā, Kāmeśvarī). The two are joined symbolically and ritually through the circulation of *śakti*, which is embodied above all in the circulation of blood—namely, the blood that flows from animal (and human) victims, and the blood that flows from enemies slain in the sacrifice of battle.

However, the Assamese traditions also highlight another key aspect of this circulation of power and blood: namely, the impurity of power, the association of the king with the dangerous pollution that comes with sacrifice and war. Throughout the narratives of kingship from Assam, from the *Kālikā Purāṇa* to the *Yoginī Tantra*, from mythic king Naraka down to Rudra Siṅgha, the king is repeatedly associated with impurity and bloodshed. Finally, the Assamese traditions also highlight the complex tension between indigenous, non-Hindu traditions and the *brāhmaṇic* Sanskritic traditions that lies at the heart of Śakta Tantra in this region. Indeed, the long history of Tantra in the northeast could be described, in part, as a complex negotiation between the Assam's many non-Hindu kings and the *brāhmaṇs* they patronized. Again, this is also a complex tension between purity and power.

As we will see in the following chapter, much the same logic of sacrifice, the circulation of blood, and the inherent impurity of power also lies at the heart of the esoteric sexual rites that constitute the most poorly understood aspect of Tantric practice.

Chapter Four

THE SACRIFICE OF DESIRE: SEXUAL RITES AND THE SECRET SACRIFICE

> Merely by worshiping the *yoni*, the worship of Śakti is surely performed. The adept should worship with the blood flowing from the sacrifices of birds, etc, and with the words "*yoni, yoni*," while muttering his prayers.
>
> —*Yoni Tantra* (YT 3.16–17)

> The totality . . . is reached only at the price of a sacrifice: eroticism reaches it precisely inasmuch as love is a kind of immolation.
>
> —Georges Bataille, *The Accursed Share*[1]

Surely the most complex and controversial aspect of Tantra—and also the primary reason for its frequent misunderstanding among both Western and Indian audiences—is the role of sexual rites in Tantric practice. From the first Christian missionaries and Orientalist scholars writing about Indian religions to the most recent New Age appropriations, from the worst to even some of the best of contemporary scholarship, Tantra has consistently been defined primarily by its sexual component. The same tradition that was once decried by Orientalist scholars and missionaries as a perverse indulgence in "orgies with wine and women"[2] has been more recently celebrated by contemporary American readers as "the art of sexual ecstasy" that now helps us explore "the path of sacred sexuality for western lovers."[3]

And yet, anyone who actually sits down to read the many Sanskrit *tantras* quickly discovers that most of them have relatively little to say about physical sexual intercourse. For example, two of the largest and most comprehensive Tantric compendia from northeast

India are the sixteenth-century *Bṛhat Tantrasāra* and the nineteenth-century *Prāṇatoṣiṇī Tantra*: the former is a 752-page text, of which roughly 10 pages concern sexual rites; the latter is a 565-page text, of which roughly 5 pages concern sexual rites.[4] The rest of these texts deal with the far less "sexy"—and often rather boring—details of *mantras, yantras,* meditations, and worship of various deities, the six acts of magic, and so on. And when they *do* talk about sexual rites, they typically do not do so in a way that we today would consider particularly "sexy." As Agehananda Bharati commented to an audience of American spiritual seekers in 1975, "Most of you . . . believe that the sexual element in Tantra is somewhat *nice* and *romantic* and lovely and full of nice warm love-making. Nonsense."[5] Many of the oldest accounts of Tantric sexual rituals, as David Gordon White has shown, are not really concerned with sexual pleasure or eroticism, but rather with the generation of the male and female sexual fluids, which are orally consumed as part of a sacramental rite.[6]

In this chapter, I argue that Tantric sexual rites are really not primarily about "sex" at all—at least not in the contemporary understanding of genital orgasm and sexual pleasure; rather, they are *the esoteric counterpart to the public offering of blood sacrifice.* Again, as we saw in the previous chapter, the theme of sacrifice runs throughout the long history of Hindu traditions, from the Vedic offering of animals to the offering of devotion in later *bhakti* traditions, from the sacrifice of one's actions in *karma yoga* to the "sacrifice of battle" in the *Mahābhārata.* And it resurfaces in a new guise in the Tantric offering of sexual fluids in secret ritual, the *kulayāga* or esoteric sacrifice.[7] As Bharati put it in his classic work on Tantra, "For the Hindu . . . the notion of ritualistic sacrifice is all-important. In fact, the idea of sacrifice (*yajña)* being at the base of every religious act has remained focal in Hinduism, even though the interpretations have changed."[8]

Kāmarūpa, as the land of desire, has long been identified as both the original heartland and the ultimate symbol of Tantric sexual rites. And Kāmākhyā herself is the very embodiment of desire in its most sensual and creative form.[9] But what we see in the Assamese tradition, I think, is an important *historical shift* in the understanding and uses of this power of desire. Specifically, there is a shift from a central focus on animal sacrifice of the sort we saw in the tenth- to eleventh-century *Kālikā Purāṇa* to a focus on the internalized sexual sacrifice or "sacrifice of desire" that we see in sixteenth-century texts like the *Yoni Tantra* and

Kāmākhyā Tantra.[10] The *Kālikā Purāṇa* acknowledges but only briefly mentions sexual rites[11]; even the key early Tantric text, the *Kaulajñāna Nirṇaya*, never enters into the details of sexual intercourse, even when it mentions consumption of sexual fluids.[12] Yet, in later texts such as the *Yoni Tantra* and *Kāmākhyā Tantra*, sexual union becomes central. Here the sexual rite itself is described as a sacrificial offering, both *accompanied* by animal offerings and *symbolically analogous* to blood sacrifice.

What accounts for this shift toward an increasingly internalized interpretation of the sacrifice and a more explicit focus on sexual rites? Part of the shift is likely due to influences from the Kashmir Śaivite tradition, which, as White has argued, reflects a progressive "aestheticization" and "sublimation" of Tantric sexual rituals after the eleventh century.[13] But in the particular case of Assam, I would suggest, it also reflects the changing political dynamics of the northeast region. Under the powerful Pāla dynasty, Śāktism received strong political support, and the primary focus of the goddess' worship was the public performance of animal sacrifice as described in the *Kālikā Purāṇa*. With the collapse of the Pālas and the end of the early Kāmarūpa dynasties, Assam's political history became far more fragmented, and Kāmākhyā temple itself was destroyed sometime between the twelfth and the sixteenth centuries. The more "sexo-centric" texts like the *Yoni Tantra* and *Kāmākhyā Tantra* were composed during the sixteenth and seventeenth centuries, a period when the northeast was divided into several competing and warring kingdoms such as the Koches, Ahoms, and Chutiyas, with occasional Mughal invasions. It seems likely that the primary focus of worship shifted from large-scale public sacrifices at the physical *pīṭha* to the more individualized, interior sacrifice of sexual rites at the secret *pīṭha* of the female body.

But despite its internalization, the secret sexual rite centers once again on the *flow and circulation of blood*. In this case, it is the blood flowing from the female partner as the human embodiment of the goddess, which is collected and orally consumed in esoteric ritual. Again, following Deleuze, we could say that *kāma* in Tantric ritual is a kind of "desire" that includes but also far transcends the level of mere sexual desire; instead, it is a *vast, circulating flow of productive energy* that can be released and channeled in various ways. In Deleuze's terms, "desire is less a struggle to monopolize power than an exchange that intensifies and proliferates energy and power into a state of excess."[14]

Like the offering of highly un-Vedic victims such as buffaloes in blood sacrifice, however, this esoteric ritual also centers on the systematic use of impurity (such as consumption of menstrual blood and sexual fluids) and deliberate acts of transgression (such as violation of class laws). And like the offering of blood sacrifice to the goddess, the aim of these acts of transgression is the unleashing of power—the power at the margins, the power of fluids, substances, and beings that *overflow* the boundaries of the individual social body. But its ultimate goal, I will suggest, is not simply the acquisition of this-worldly power. Rather, it is a kind of "*unlimited transgression*" that oversteps the very boundaries of the finite self in the realization of one's own godhood.

The origins of sexual rites: The right and left-hand paths

Sexual rites, according to the *Kālikā Purāṇa*, belong to a form of worship broadly known as "left-hand" (*vāma*) practice and contrasted with the "right-hand" (*dakṣiṇa*) form of worship. In most Tantric traditions, the "right" and "left-hand" methods usually refer to two different interpretations of Tantric practice. The left-hand is typically said to involve a literal use of substances that are normally prohibited by mainstream social and religious standards. The most infamous of these are the five Ms (*pañcamakāra*) or five things that begin with *ma-* in Sanskrit, namely, *māṃsa* (meat), *matysa* (fish), *madya* (wine), *mudrā* (usually said to be parched grain, but exact meaning much debated[15]), and *maithuna* (sexual intercourse). The right-hand path, conversely, typically interprets these forbidden substances symbolically or metaphorically, using them to refer to internal spiritual states rather than literal transgressive acts.[16]

However, in Assamese texts like the *Kālikā Purāṇa*, *vāma* and *dakṣiṇa* are used in a slightly different way. Here, the "right-hand" form of worship refers specifically to orthodox ritual practice, that is, the observance of the Vedic sacrifices and traditional social norms. The *vāmācāra*, conversely, refers here to "heterodox" worship and the performance of socially transgressive rites such as the consumption of meat, wine, and engagement in sexual rituals. Indeed, the *Kālikā Purāṇa* appears to reflect a need on the part of Assamese Hindus to negotiate between the older *brāhmaṇic* traditions and the newer, more radical, and explicitly transgressive practices of left-hand Tantra. As Kooij notes, the *Kālikā Purāṇa* wants to "accept that heterodox cults are really worth while, although it remains true to the general tendency found in the Purāṇas to stimulate the performance of the old brahmanical sacrifices and the attendance to the established forms of social behavior."[17] Thus, the text insists that one should still perform the five great sacrifices to sages, gods, ancestors, men, and demons that comprise right-hand practice. But it also notes that some fierce deities, such as the terrible goddesses Ugratārā, Caṇḍī, Ucchiṣṭa Bhairavī, and Śiva in his wrathful Bhairava form, can only be worshipped in the left-hand method. Kāmākhyā herself, interestingly enough, should be worshipped with both the left and right-hand methods.[18] In these transgressive left-hand rites, the practitioner first invokes and then identifies himself with Bhairava in order to engage in the use of wine, meat, and sexual union:

> For the sake of eating meat, drinking wine and enjoying sexual union with women at pleasure, I assume the form of great Bhairava. One should always worship [Bhairava] in the left hand form using meat, wine, and so forth.[19]

Finally, while right-hand performance of *brāhmaṇic* rites will remove ones debts and bring rewards in the afterlife, the more transgressive left-hand rites promise much more immediate, this-worldly sorts of rewards; indeed, like the transgressive offering of blood sacrifice, the left-hand rites offer tremendous material power: "He gains a body radiant like Kāma's. He subdues kings together with kingdoms. He enchants women, who are filled with desire. He can control lions, tigers, hyenas, ghosts, spirits and ghouls and travel with the speed of the wind."[20]

Interestingly enough, the *Kālikā Purāṇa* also explicitly links the origins of left-hand Tantra to non-Hindu, outcaste, tribal, or barbarian peoples, namely, the *mlecchas*. In this account, the people of Kāmarūpa had become so holy because of the greatness of Kāmākhyā that Yama, the god of death, was losing all his power there and had no souls to drag down to his realm. Therefore, he implored Brahmā and Viṣṇu to help him, and they in turn assigned Śiva the task of driving all the people from Kāmarūpa. Śiva thus sent his army of hosts along with the terrible, frightening goddess Ugratārā, to drive out the inhabitants of the realm. Unfortunately, they also caught hold of the great sage

Vasiṣṭha, who became so furious that he cursed Ugratārā, Śiva's hosts, and Śiva himself: henceforth, they would all become *mlecchas* and Śiva himself would be worshipped by *mlecchas* in the left-hand method:

> O Vāma [follower of the left-hand path], because you have seized me, a sage, in order to drive me away, you will henceforth be worshipped in the left-hand method. Because these wretched hosts have been wandering around like *mlecchas*, let them be *mlecchas* in Kāmarūpa. Because Mahādeva, like a *mleccha,* tried to expel me, a sage, rich in austerity, self-restrained and versed in the Vedas, let Śaṅkara be the favorite of the *mlecchas*, wearing ashes and bones. And may this place renowned as Kāmarūpa remain hidden by the *mlecchas* until Viṣṇu returns here.[21]

As we saw above, there has been much debate about the possible non-Hindu or indigenous roots of the more transgressive aspects of Tantra.[22] The *Kālikā Purāṇa*, at least, makes this link quite directly. As we saw in Chapter 1, the text tells us that the wine-drinking, meat-eating, sexually promiscuous *kirātas* or tribal hill peoples were the original worshipers of Kāmākhyā; and now it suggests that it was originally the *mlecchas* who worshipped Bhairava in the left-hand method. This connection of left-hand rites with indigenous religions may or may not be historically accurate; but it does reinforce the idea that such rites center on the "power at the margins," that is, the power inherent in those forces that lie outside of mainstream society and laws of purity.

Varieties of sexual experience: Initiation, yoni pūjā, and cakra pūjā

While early Assamese texts like the *Kālikā Purāṇa* mention the origins of left-hand rites, they have relatively little to say about the specific details of sexual union. Yet in later texts from the sixteenth-century northeast, such as the *Yoni Tantra* and *Kāmākhyā Tantra,* sexual rites become central as the primary embodiment of the goddess' *śakti,* and the supreme "sacrifice of desire" is described in more graphic detail. Thus, we see a progressive shift from literal sacrifices performed at the great *pīṭha* of the goddess' *yoni* to sexual sacrifices offered to the individual *pīṭha* of the female partner. However, sexual rites are by no means singular or homogenous in form, but really quite varied even within a single tradition such as Assamese Śākta Tantra. The

Yoni Tantra and *Kāmākhyā Tantra* describe at least three different contexts in which sexual rites might occur: the *abhiṣeka* or initiation of a new member into the Tantric lineage *(kula)*; the ritual of *yoni pūjā* or worship of the female sexual organ; and the *cakra pūjā* or "circle worship," involving multiple male and female participants who collectively engage in the five Ms.

In the first of these, the initiation of a new member of the *kula*, the novice is brought to a very secret place where the circle of *tāntrikas* gathers; prostitutes (*veśyās*) are brought in to serve as sexual partners; meat, fish, and wine are consumed; the guru engages in sexual union with the prostitutes; and the rite is to proceed for three days.[23]

The second sexual rite, *yoni pūjā*, typically involves one male worshipping the *yoni* of one female. First, the adept obtains a woman who is "wanton" and ideally menstruating; he leads her to the ritual space and gives her a narcotic drink (probably *bhaṅg*, a liquid marijuana beverage); he places her on his thigh and honors her *yoni*, which should be unshaven; he anoints her *yoni* with sandal paste and gives her wine to drink; he paints a half-moon on her forehead with vermillion; he kisses her cheeks and massages her beasts; and she in turn anoints his penis with sandal pate and saffron. The central part of the rite, then, is sexual union and the production of the sexual fluids, the *yoni tattva* or *tattva uttama*, the "supreme essence." And these combined fluids can then be used either as a *tilaka* mark on the forehead in daily ritual or mixed with wine and consumed orally.[24]

Finally, the *cakra pūjā* is a more elaborate rite involving a number of male and female couples for the ritual partaking of the five Ms. At Kāmākhyā, *cakra pūjās* have traditionally been held on auspicious days such as the vernal equinox, with *yogis* and *yoginīs* sitting paired in a circle to perform the rite.[25] The number of participants varies, though some texts call for a minimum of eight, with the number of males and females always equal. Members of all social classes and castes may participate, caste laws being dissolved in the space of the *cakra*; indeed, "for the duration of the formation of the Cakra, all men in the circle are considered as Śiva and all women as Devī."[26] The *cakra pūjā*, in turn, has various names and forms, such as *kaula cakra*, *yoginī cakra*, and *bhairavī cakra*, many of which are still performed in various guises to this day in Assam.[27]

All these varieties of sexual ritual, however, do involve some common elements: first, in all of them, the female body and specifically the *yoni* is identified with the great *yoni pīṭha* and supreme place of desire,

Kāmarūpa; and second, the act of sexual union is equated with the offering of sacrifice (*yajña* or *bali*).

The bodily pīṭhas and the secret Kāmākhyā

As the esoteric counterpart to the offering of blood sacrifice in the geographic locus of Kāmarūpa, Tantric ritual is based on a kind of interior, esoteric landscape, in which the *pīṭhas* are mapped onto the bodies of the male and female practitioners. Here the "form of desire" (*kāmarūpa*) and the place called desire (*kāmākhyā*) refer not simply to the actual *yoni pīṭha* in Assam but metaphorically to the *yoni* of the female partner, which is itself "the abode of the Goddess, a center of transformative sexual energy, also identified as the subtle 'mouth of the Yoginī.' "[28] Perhaps the greatest single ode to the *yoni* is the *Yoni Tantra*, a sixteenth-century text from the Cooch Behar region immediately adjacent to Kāmarūpa and closely connected to the worship of Kāmākhyā.[29] The seat of the *yoni* is described here as the birthplace of all things, the origin of all the gods, and more sacred that all the *pīṭhas* on earth:

> Hari, Hara, and all the gods, the agents of the creation, maintenance and destruction of the universe, are all born from the *yoni* . . . [30]
>
> By simply seeing the *yoni*, he obtains the fruit of ten million holy sites.[31]

According to another sixteenth-century work, the *Kaulāvalīnirṇaya*, the *pīṭha* of Kāmarūpa is in fact twofold, visible and secret (*vyakta* and *gupta*). The former is the triangular tract of land that makes up the physical region of Assam, while the latter, "the secret Kāmarūpa, lies in each and every household. The secret one brings the best of adepts much greater merit than the visible one."[32] This secret Kāmarūpa is none other than the *yoni* of the female partner or human *śakti*, and worship there is equal to pilgrimage and worship at the great *pīṭha* of Kāmākhyā itself: "Worshipping one's wife in her *yoni* region is equal to [worshipping] the greatest of all pīṭhas, Kāmarūpa, the great seat of the *kula*"; indeed, "If worship is done here by an adept even once, then, having abandoned all other *pīṭhas*, the goddess will dwell within his own body."[33]

Likewise, the *Kulacūḍāmaṇi Tantra* declares that the body of the female partner is directly equivalent to the region of Kāmarūpa. By entering her *yoni*, the male practitioner is immediately transported to the great *yoni pīṭha* itself: "At the time when the influence of sleep [is strong], the adept enters the *yoni* temple of Kāmākhyā in Kāmarūpa by means of the nighttime ritual."[34] The body of the female partner is thus transformed into a vast interior landscape containing not just the *pīṭha* of Kāmākhyā but also the other major *pīṭhas*, which are located in the thighs, in the breaths, and at the top of the head. At each of these *pīṭhas*, one should also offer an internal sacrifice to the goddess in her various forms:

> He should invoke the goddess and infuse her throughout [the *śakti's*] body. . . . After he has recited the *mantra* 100,000 times, he should enter Uḍḍiyāna [the thighs]. Having worshiped the goddess called Yoganidrā in that *pīṭha*, he should offer sacrifice [*yajet*]. He should perform 100,000 repetitions of the *mantra* of his own chosen deity in a state of concentration. Having gone to Kāmarūpa [the *yoni*], he should then sacrifice to Kātyāyanī. At night, he should perform 100,000 repetitions of the *mantra* and first sacrifice to Kāmākhyā. Going to Jālandhara, [he should sacrifice] to Pūrṇeśī. There, too, he should repeat the *mantra* 100,000 times with concentration. Then having gone to Pūrṇagiri [the top of the head], he should sacrifice to Caṇḍī and then repeat the *mantra*. Upon entering Kāmarūpa [the vagina] he should first sacrifice to Kāmākhyā and then to the great goddess Dikkaravāsinī at the edges [of the vulva].[35]

In short, the worship of the body of the female partner (the human *śakti*) represents a striking inversion or reversal of the myth of Satī that we saw in Chapter 1. In the Satī myth, it is the goddess or divine Śakti who is sacrificed and dismembered to create the *śākta pīṭhas* here on earth. But in the Tantric rite, the goddess Śakti is symbolically *re-membered* and *reintegrated*—again, through a sacrificial act—and the *pīṭhas* are reconnected in the interior landscape of the female body or human *śakti*. But this is also, at the same time, a remarkable inversion or perhaps double-inversion of the Puruṣa myth from the *Ṛg Veda*: rather than a *male* body sacrificially dismembered to create the universe, it is now a *female* body that is sacrificially re-membered to reintegrate the universe.

Finally, still other texts take the metaphor of the interior Kāmarūpa even further, by identifying these internal seats of power with the *cakras,* the "wheels" or energy centers that are believed to lie along the axis of the spine. Typically, Tantric yogic texts describe a series of six (though sometimes four or five) *cakras,* which are imagined as multi-petaled lotuses that extend from the base of the spine, to the genitals, to the navel, to the heart, to the throat, to the eyebrows. A seventh, supreme, thousand-petaled lotus is said to lie at the top of the skull, as the seat of Lord Śiva. According to texts like the *Gorakṣa Śataka* (twelfth to thirteenth centuries), however, there is another secret *cakra* that lies between the first two *cakras,* that is, between the anus and the genitals (the *mūlādhāra* and *svādhiṣṭhāna cakras*). This secret *cakra* is Kāmarūpa or the place of the *yoni* (*yonisthāna*), which is "flashing like forks of lightning, like molten gold."[36] It is the secret place of enjoyment where Śiva and Śakti unite: "Between the two cakras, the *mūlādhāra* and the *svādhiṣṭhāna,* is the *yonisthāna* spoken of as the image of desire. It is the four-fingered space between the anus and the root of the male organ, described as two fingers-breadth from each of them. It is further characterized as the place of Śiva-Śakti, the place of enjoyment, and as Kāmarūpa."[37] Thus, within the human body itself there lies a secret *pīṭha* in which Śiva and Śakti dally in loving union, just as they do secretly on Nīlācala hill.

The secret sacrifice: Sexual union as the inner sacrificial offering

If the physical body can be imagined as the microcosmic reflection of the *śākta pīṭhas,* containing its own *yoni-pīṭha* and inner Kāmarūpa, then the physical act of sacrifice also has a microcosmic reflection within the human body: namely, the secret rite of sexual union, which serves as the esoteric counterpart to the offering of blood sacrifice. Sexual union is a key part of the "primordial sacrifice" (*ādiyāga*) or "clan sacrifice" (*kulayāga*) that makes up the core of esoteric Tantric ritual.[38] The homology between animal sacrifice and sexual union goes back at least as far as the Upaniṣads, where the male's shedding of semen into the womb of the female is directly compared to pouring the oblation into the Vedic sacrificial fire. According to the *Bṛhadāranyaka Upaniṣad,* sexual union is itself a Soma sacrifice, first performed by the creator, Prajāpati, with the first woman as his sacrificial altar:

> So he created woman and, after creating her, had intercourse with her. A man, therefore, should have intercourse with a woman. Prajāpati stretched out from himself the elongated stone for pressing Soma and impregnated her with it. Her vulva is the sacrificial ground; her pubic hair is the sacred grass; her labia majora are the Soma-press; and her labia minora are the fire blazing at the center. A man who engages in sexual intercourse with this knowledge obtains as great a world as a man who performs a Soma sacrifice.[39]

This homology recurs throughout later Tantric texts, where there is a general parallel between "bloody sacrifice and sexual rites, eros and thanatos."[40] As the *Kulārṇava Tantra* proclaims, "There is no sacrifice [*yajña*] greater than *kula* worship."[41] The ritual consumption of the five Ms is the great sacrifice (*yāga*), directly comparable to the consumption of the Soma beverage in the Vedic ritual: "Taking intoxicants like fish, meat, wine, etc. at any time other than the time of sacrifice is said to be defiling, O Beloved. Just as *brāhmaṇs* drink Soma during the performance [of sacrifice], so too, the drinking of wine is done on the proper occasion, providing both enjoyment and liberation."[42]

But in keeping with the tradition dating back to the Upaniṣads, the fifth *tattva* of sexual union in particular is imagined as the ultimate sacrificial rite. As we see in the great Tantric compendia from northeast India, such as the *Bṛhat Tantrasāra* and the *Prāṇatoṣiṇī Tantra*, sexual union is explicitly described as an analogue to the Vedic sacrifice. Here the central act is the ejaculation of semen into the vagina, which is likened to ladling the oblation onto the sacrificial fire (Fig. 18). For "sexual union is the libation; the sacred precept is the shedding of semen."[43] The adept first identifies his female partner with the goddess and himself with the god, thinking, "this one is Gaurī, and I am Śiva." He then inserts his *liṅgam* into the *yoni*, which is again called the *yoni pīṭha*, while reciting: "I sacrifice [*juhomi*]" into the "fire of the Self, which is radiant with the oblation of *dharma* and *adharma*." Then finally, reciting the *mantra*, " 'I sacrifice into the fire that is full of the bodily fluids of *dharma* and *adharma*,' he should release his semen."[44]

The secret sacrifice in the Yoni Tantra and Kāmākhyā Tantra

However, the link between sexual rites and blood sacrifice is especially clear in the literature from Assam and adjacent areas, where animal sacrifice in both Vedic and tribal forms has been widely practiced up to the present. The link is twofold, at once literal and symbolic. On the one hand, the rite of sexual union is very often preceded and/or accompanied by the offering of animal sacrifice; on the other hand, the rite of sexual union is frequently compared to offering of libations to the sacrificial fire and the ritual consumption of sacrificial offerings, very often using language and imagery taken directly from Vedic ritual texts.[45]

One of the clearest examples of these connections between sacrifice and sexual union is found in the *Yoni Tantra*—arguably the most sexually explicit of all *tantras*. Throughout the text, the *Yoni Tantra* states that the rite of sexual union should be accompanied by the offering of animal sacrifice (*bali*), and that the sexual rite and the sacrificial rite are two sides of the same worship of the goddess.[46] The *Yoni Tantra* also makes it clear that the female partner should ideally be menstruating (*rajasvalābhagam*, as does the *Kāmākhyā Tantra*[47]) and the final aim is the production of the female sexual fluids (*yonitattva*). In short, like the sacrificial ritual, the sexual rite centers on the *flow and circulation of blood* from both animal offerings and the body of the *śakti*:

> He should insert the *liṅgam* into the *yoni* and thrust vigorously. Thrusting in this way, he obtains the supreme essence. The adept should worship the goddess in the form of the *yoni*, which contains the entire world, with this essence. On the night of the new moon, he should go to a crossroads, a cremation ground or a desolate place and make a sacrificial offering [*bali*] of cooked fish and rice prepared with milk; then he becomes fully accomplished like the god of wealth . . . By offering animal sacrifice [*sāmiṣānnaṃ balim*], in an empty house or [his own] house, the son of Kālikā becomes liberated together with the ten million *kulas*. By reciting and reading [the *mantra*], by seeing and touching the vulva of a menstruating woman, the adept becomes the Lord of Yoga.[48]

> Having honored the great *yoni* with [sacrifices of] goats, sheep, human beings, antelopes, mongooses, buffaloes, cows, jackals, lions, horses and tortoises, he should worship in a devotional mood . . . Offering with the *yonitattva*, he never again returns to this earth.[49]

Here we see that the worship of the *yoni* (ideally, a menstruating *yoni*) and the act of sexual union are repeatedly linked to the offering of blood sacrifice. Again, these sacrifices include a wide array of often highly un-Vedic, wild, and impure animals, such as fish, mongoose, buffalo, jackal, lion, and tortoise. And, as we saw in chapter 2, such offerings probably reflect less any Vedic tradition that the local indigenous sacrificial practices of pre-Hindu Koch Bihar and Assam.

The most powerful sacrifice, however, is not animal flesh, but rather the offering and oral consumption of the male and female sexual fluids. According to the *Kāmākhyā Tantra,* these sexual fluids are the "clan fluid" (*kula dravya*) or "essence of the clan" (*kulātmikā*), which is the key to material and spiritual liberation.[50] Yet as the *Yoni Tantra* explains, the combined semen and menstrual blood (*yonitattva*), also represent the ultimate sacrifice (*bali*) and the supreme food offering (*naivedyam*), which in turn brings the greatest spiritual and material rewards:

> He should make an offering [*bali*] with his own semen and the menstrual blood and recite the *mantra.* At the beginning of the night he should make an offering of cooked fish, a fowl's egg, mouse flesh, buffalo-flesh, human flesh, wine, meat, and flour cakes . . . Meditating on the goddess, he should worship the goddess, who is in the form of the *śakti.* That man will attain the four aims of life: duty, wealth, pleasure and liberation. At night the sacrifice [*bali*] of wine and meat should be offered by adepts. With great effort, he should penetrate the *yoni,* having first caressed her breasts. The goddess herself is in the form of the *śakti,* if the intercourse is performed in the inverse position [*viparītarata*]. Then that man lives happily together with the ten million *kulas,* by washing the *yoni* and washing the *liṅga.* He should worship the great *yoni* and make an offering, according to the ritual injunction. He should divide that water into three parts, and offer one to the *śakti.* Then the wise one, the best of adepts, should mix the other two parts with wine and drink it, O goddess. He should please the supreme woman with garments, jewelry and perfume. He should worship the Vidyā [goddess] in that *yoni,* according to the ritual injunction. With the vulva and penis, with the washing of the vulva, with the uttering of the word "vulva" [*bhaga*], and with the nectar of the vulva and penis, the best of adepts should make a food offering [*naivedyam*].[51]

As J.A. Schoterman points out in his edition of the *Yoni Tantra,* the offering and consumption of the sexual fluids (the *yonitattva* or *kula dravya*) is a Tantric analogue of the consumption of the Soma beverage in the Vedic sacrificial rite. Just as the Soma-juice was mixed with milk or water, so too, the *yonitattva* is mixed with wine or with water: "In the Tantric conception the Vedic Soma-juice mixed with milk or water has been equalized with *Yonitattva*, the union of seminal and ovarian fluid .... Just as the pure Soma juice is mixed with milk or water, likewise the Sādhaka mixes—again—the *Yonitattva* with wine or water ... the Vedic drinking of the Soma has been transformed into a yogic practice connected with the *Yonitattva*."[52]

The remnants of desire: Sexual fluids and sacrificial leftovers

In addition to these general comparisons to the sacrificial ritual, many *tantras* also refer to the sexual fluids using even more specific terminology drawn from the Vedic sacrifice. One of the most interesting of these is the concept of the "remnant" or "leftover" (*ucchiṣṭa* or *śeṣa*) used in many *tantras* to refer to the combined sexual fluids after they have been offered into the "sacrificial fire" of the female *yoni*.[53] As the *Kāmākhyā Tantra* describes the ritual, the "remnants" of the sexual fluids offered to the *yoni* must be collected from the female body and consumed orally in order for the power of the sacrifice to be realized: "The remnants of the *śakti* [*śakty-ucchiṣṭa*] should be consumed; otherwise, one goes to hell. What one offers to the *śakti*, O Goddess, is offered to the gods."[54] Likewise, the *Bṛhat Tantrasāra* declares that the combined sexual fluids or *kula dravya* is the most awesome and dangerous of substances. As the *ucchiṣṭa* or sacrificial leftover, it is the very essence of this secret offering and ritual meal:

> With the sacrificial elements, the semen, unbroken grains of rice, perfume, flowers, O Deveśī, he should worship the goddess in the vagina ... With incense, lamps and various food offerings, the *kula* adept should honor her in various ways, and then he should [consume] the remnants [*ucchiṣṭa*] himself.[55]

The term *ucchiṣṭa* has a number of complex meanings, most of them quite negative and tied to profound impurity. These include: "left, rejected, stale, spit out of the mouth (as remnants of food) ... one who has not washed his hands and mouth and therefore is considered impure, impure, that which is spit out, leavings, fragments remainder (especially of a sacrifice or food)."[56] As Charles Malamoud has shown, *ucchiṣṭa* (or *śeṣa)* is technical term used in the Vedic sacrifice to refer to that portion of the victim that is "left over" once all the offerings have been made. Like leftovers generally in India, it is considered impure and polluting; but at the same time, it is also considered to be the powerful "seed" that gives birth to the next sacrifice: "Power is . . . derived from forces that are contaminating; these forces belong to the violent substratum of chaos out of which the world has emerged . . . The sacrifice produces new life—the divine seed—from the disintegration of a previous existence . . . It is the impure remainder of the sacrifice that gives birth to the new life produced from death."[57] The same aura of dangerous power surrounds the leftover of the Tantric rite or sexual sacrifice. If consumed outside the ritual, it will send one to the most terrible of hells: "apart from the time of worship, one must never touch a naked *śakti.* And apart from the period of worship, the nectar must never be drunk by adepts. Touching it, their lives are lost, and drinking it, they would go to hell."[58] But once placed in a sacrificial vessel and consecrate, the *kula dravya* is transformed into divine nectar, *amṛta.* By consuming this nectar, the *tāntrika* will enjoy supreme bliss and fulfillment of all worldly and other-worldly desires.

> Then with great effort, he must obtain the precious *kula* nectar. For with that divine nectar, all [the gods] are pleased. Whatever the wise man desires, he will immediately attain . . . Having purified the *kula* substance, which has the nature of Śiva and Śakti, and having placed this nectar of life, which is of the nature of the supreme, ultimate reality, in a sacrificial vessel, [he attains] the eternally blameless state free of all distinctions.[59]

Here we see perhaps the clearest example of Tantra's use of the "power at the margins," that is, the ritual transformation of substances that are normally considered impure, dangerous, and destructive. The otherwise polluting substances that overflow the boundaries of the body and social body are now transmuted into the ultimate source of material power and spiritual realization.

Kuṇḍalinī yoga and the inner sacrifice

Finally, this sacrifice of sexual union has yet another layer of internalization: namely, the internal ritual of *kuṇḍalinī yoga,* whereby the adept awakens the inner fire of the serpent power (*kuṇḍalinī śakti*) believed to lie within every human body. In the Tantric view of the body, every human being contains a microcosmic embodiment of the goddess Śakti, who lies within all of us in the form of the crooked one (*kubjikā*) or coiled one (*kuṇḍalī* or *kuṇḍalinī*), imagined as a serpent at the base of the spine. In most ordinary human beings, this coiled serpent power is asleep and unconscious. According to Debendranāth Bhaṭṭācārya, a modern Śākta from Assam, the serpent power normally lies slumbering "like a sleeping baby" in the lowest *cakra*, which is none other than the "mother's *yoni*" (*mātṛ-yoni*). Through the techniques of *kuṇḍalinī yoga*, this serpent power is awakened and raised upward through the higher *cakras* until the Śakti energy reunites with the Śiva in the thousand-petaled lotus at the top of the head. Here, in the crown *cakra*, Śiva and Śakti unite in an internalized orgasm of transcendental bliss:

> When the adept awakens the *kuṇḍalinī śakti* and raises it from the *mūlādhāra cakra* (the mother's *yoni*), the *kuṇḍalinī śakti* blissfully plays in each of the other *cakras*; when it rises from the *ājñā cakra* to the lotus of the *sahasrāra*, he is united with the supreme Self (he has sexual union [*maithuna*]).[60]

This union of Śiva and Śakti in the thousand-petaled lotus at the crown, then, is a kind of transcendent mirror of their union in the lower *cakra* of Kāmarūpa, the secret "place of desire" that lies hidden between the anus and genitals.

Again, however, this internalized sexual union is still understood and described as a form of sacrifice. This is an offering to the inner fire, the burning power of the goddess who lies inside us all. According to the seventeenth- to eighteenth-century Assamese text, the *Yoginī Tantra*, this union of Śiva and Śakti through *kuṇḍalinī yoga* is the true sacrifice, the true killing of animal victims, the true offering of wine, and the true sexual union:

> The *yogi* drinks the supreme nectar that flows from the union of the seed with the Kuṇḍalī . . . This is known as the great drinking or *kula yoga*, O great goddess. Having slain the beast of "sin and merit" with the sword of knowledge, O Śāmbhavī, he should lead the mind to the Supreme Self; this is known as the "meat" of leading. Having united all his senses with his mind, he should join them to the Self; that *yogi* is a "fish eater" and is free of his bonds, O Beloved. One should unite the infinite universe with the Supreme Brahman. The union of the Self

> with the Supreme Śakti is considered [the true sexual union], not the sexual union with semen. These practices should be kept very secret.[61]

In sum, as Agehananda Bharati explains in his classic work, *The Tantric Tradition*, the fundamental symbolism of *kuṇḍalinī yoga* remains that of the sacrifice, the very old Indian paradigm of offering sacred fluids into the fire altar:

> As the *sādhaka* is about to drink the *surā* (which is the *madya*, liquor . . .) he says, "I sacrifice (*juhomi*)." As he does so he mentally draws the coiled-up energy of the *kula* (*kulakuṇḍalinī*) from her seat in the basic *cakra*; this time, however, he does not draw her up into the thousand-petalled lotus in the yogic cranium but instead he brings her into the tip of his tongue and seats her there, and at this moment he drinks the beverage from its bowl, and as he drinks he impresses the thought on his mind that it is not he himself who is drinking but the *kulakuṇḍalinī* now seated on the top of his tongue to whom he is offering the liquid as a libation.[62]

Here we see the logical extension of the "interiorization of the sacrifice" that was already at work in the Upaniṣad's "sacrifice of yoga." But it has also taken on some radical new meanings in the context of Tantric ritual and the worship of the goddess as power.

Sexual transgression and ritual impurity in Tantric sādhanā

Like the offerings of blood sacrifice to the goddess, however, the secret sacrifice of sexual union also contains a series of profound ritual transgressions and deliberate uses of impurity. As Marglin notes, in Hindu traditions generally, sexual intercourse itself "is considered polluting," insofar as it involves the spilling of bodily fluids that cross the boundaries of the physical body and social body. Above all, it must be kept strictly separate from sacred spaces like temples that cannot be defiled by the flow of bodily fluids: "sexual intercourse in the temple is prohibited and would pollute the temple just like the shedding of blood, spitting and all other crossing of the boundaries of the body would."[63]

Yet Tantric sexual union not only accepts the inherent impurity of sexual union but in fact exaggerates and exploits it as a source of tremendous power. Tantric *maithuna* is by no means a conventional act of sexual union between married partners of compatible casts aimed at producing a child; rather, it is an explicitly transgressive rite that deliberately inverts normal laws surrounding sexual relations. Thus, both the *Yoni* and *Kāmākhyā Tantras* call explicitly for union with a woman who is menstruating—a highly impure act, "much abhorred in Hindu society"[64] and considered "one of the greatest sins."[65] Classical Indian law books such as the *Gautama Dharma Sūtra* and *Vasiṣṭha Dharma Sūtra* are quite clear that sexual intercourse with a menstruating woman is a highly polluting act that requires arduous penance to purify.[66] As we have seen above, sexual union with a menstruating woman is associated with all manner of negative outcomes, including the birth of the cursed demon king, Naraka who was conceived during Earth's menstrual flow.[67] The *Brahmavaivarta Purāṇa* likewise contains several cautionary tales about children born of women during the menstrual period, who are therefore inherently unclean (*aśauca*), degraded, and tainted by the sin of menstruation (*ṛtu-doṣata*). Thus, a *kṣatriya* conceived by a menstruating woman was valorous but was doomed to become a robber because of the sin of his birth; and the *mlecchas* or non-Hindu barbarians themselves were born from a *kṣatriya's* seed planted into the womb of a *śudra* woman who was menstruating.[68]

But again, as we saw in Chapter 2, the impurity of menstruation is also tied to the auspicious power of the goddess. Thus the *Yoni Tantra* even refers to the goddess herself by the highly unexpected title of "Caṇḍālī."[69] As Schoterman notes, the term *caṇḍālī* here seems to have a profound double meaning. In one sense, the *caṇḍāla* is traditionally considered "one of the lowest groups of Hindu society, their occupation being the execution of criminals and the transportation of the corpses of persons who do not have relatives"; and this is probably related to the fact that "especially women living on the fringe of society were chosen as śakti in Tantric rituals." Yet at the same time, the term *caṇḍālī* can also be used to designate "a woman on the first day of her menses—a fact of importance in the Yonitantra," given its strong emphasis on intercourse with a menstruating partner.[70]

According to the *Kāmākhyā Tantra*, however, the preferred partner is not just a woman who is menstruating (*ṛtuyuktalatā*), but also a prostitute (*veśyā* or *veśyālatā*) or the wife of another man (*parastrī* or *parakīyā*).[71] These three—the menstruating woman, the prostitute, and the wife of another—are the ultimate source of power for the adept in sexual union:

> Having approached the *yoni* of another man's wife in particular, the wise man should make offerings. He should consider worship there, O goddess, as comparable to the *yoni* of a prostitute ... With a woman in her menstrual period, he will attain manifold pleasures. Instantly, he will attain powers that are difficult even for the gods. Therefore, O goddess, the *yoni* practice is said to be the greatest of all.[72]

The systematic violation of class boundaries is in fact a key part of the most powerful Tantric rites. According to the *Yoginī Tantra,* the traditional rule for sexual relations—including many forms of Tantric union—is to remain within one's own social class: "*Brāhmaṇ* women for *brāhmaṇs*, *kṣatriya* women for *kṣatriyas*, *vaiśya* women for *vaiśya*s, O Deveṣī—that is the traditional rule in sexual union."[73] But for the most radical, left-hand *tāntrika*, who follows the path of the *avadhūta* or "one who has shaken off worldly life," all things are permissible. Any foods, any beverages, and relations with any caste are allowed for the Tantric hero who has left class and purity behind:

> Edible food and wine of all kinds are for him, O Sambhavī. Meat and fish are his, O Goddess, as are all things in the water, on the earth or in the air ... Apart from his mother's *yoni*, he has intercourse with all *yonis* ...
>
> O Śivā! Among all stages of life, all castes, all *yogis* and in all places, one should make no distinctions. Bliss is itself the nature of the Ultimate Reality (*brahmaṇ*). And that is located within the body ...[74]

Likewise, the sexual position of the male and female partners should be inverted, upside down, and transgressive. The *Yoni Tantra* and other texts call not just for sexual union in the ordinary position of the male on top of the female; rather, they suggest the position known as *viparīta-rata*, which Sir Monier-Williams translates as "inverted sexual intercourse," with the female on top of the male. The term *viparīta* has a wide range of (almost entirely negative) meanings, including: "turned round, reversed, inverted ... acting in a contrary manner .... perverse, wrong, contrary to rule ... unfavorable, false, untrue, a perverse or unchaste woman."[75] In sum, it is intercourse in the inverted, perverted, or contrary position—a position that is depicted quite clearly and repeatedly on the tenth- to twelfth-century Madana-Kāmadeva temple north of Kāmākhyā, a remarkable Pāla-era temple filled with erotica and known as the "Khajuraho of Assam" (Fig. 19).

Finally, the aim of this inverted sexual union is not the production of child, but rather, the production of the powerful *yonitattva* and the *kula dravya,* the combined male and female sexual fluids that are consumed orally as the "leftovers" (*ucchiṣṭa*) of the Tantric sacrifice. Again, classical Hindu law books such as the *Gautama Dharma Sūtra* state quite explicitly that the consumption of any bodily fluids and especially sexual fluids is extremely polluting, comparable to consuming impure animals such as predators or pigs.[76] Yet for the Tantric rite, the consumption of the sexual fluids is the ultimate source of material power and spiritual liberation.

In sum, the sexual rite is clearly built—much like the public rite of animal sacrifice—on the systematic inversion of social laws and the deliberate trafficking in the "power at the margins." In tabular form, these inversions could be outlined as follows:

	Conventional sexual union	***Tantric maithuna***
Female partner	One's own wife, not menstruating	Menstruating woman, prostitute, or wife of another
Class relations	*Brāhmaṇs* for *brāhmaṇs*, etc.	Intercourse with all *yonis*
Sexual position	Male on top	Inverse union (*viparīta-rati*)
Goal	Production of a child	Production of *yonitattva* and oral consumption of sexual fluids

From sacrificial transgression to "unlimited transgression"

Perhaps even more clearly than the sacrificial offerings of buffaloes and other impure animals, sexual rites work by a very clear logic of ritual transgression and the systematic inversion of traditional laws of purity and caste. In this sense, Tantric sexual rites do seem to confirm

Bataille's key insight that blood sacrifice, violence, and sexual transgression all share a common link: they each involve a kind of "organized explosion,"[77] or controlled violation of normal social and moral laws, which gives birth to a radical sense of freedom, power, and liberating ecstasy: "The external violence of the sacrifice reveals the internal violence of the creature, seen as loss of blood and ejaculations."[78] For they each work by breaking down the walls of isolation that separate individual beings, bursting through the limits of the finite, discontinuous ego and opening the self up the limitless expanse of the infinite:

> The embrace restores us . . . to the totality in which man has his share *by losing himself*. For an embrace is not just a fall into the animal muck, but the anticipation of death . . . The totality reached . . . is reached only at the price of a sacrifice: eroticism reaches it precisely inasmuch as love is a kind of immolation.[79]

Thus the ultimate or "infinite transgression," for Bataille, is not simply the release of power through bloodshed or sexual union; rather, it is the transgression of the very boundaries of the self through mystical experience, the complete dissolution of the finite ego into a state of "divine continuity": "In the region where the autonomy of the subject breaks away from all restraints, the categories of good and evil, pleasure and pain, are infinitely surpassed . . . On this scale, the chain releases of atomic energy are nothing."[80] In this sense, the final aim of transgression is not simply the attainment of worldly power or occult abilities; rather, it is the shattering of all worldly dualities that opens up a space of unlimited affirmation, the space of the divine. As Foucault suggests in his essay on transgression,

> Transgression opens onto a scintillating and constantly affirmed world, a world without shadow or twilight, without that serpentine "no" that bites into fruits and lodges their contradictions at their core. It is the solar inversion of satanic denial. It was originally linked to the divine, or rather from this limit marked by the sacred it opens the space where the divine functions.[81]

This explosion of the finite self through violent and erotic transgression does indeed seem to characterize the ultimate aim of the Tantric rite. Like the offering of blood sacrifice, the rites of *yoni pūjā* and *maithuna* also promise to bring all manner of supernatural powers and worldly benefits. According to the *Yoni Tantra*, it was by worship of the *yoni* and the *yonitattva* that the Pāṇḍavas were victorious in battle, Śiva conquered death and destroyed Tripura, and Rāma defeated Rāvana and his family.[82] In sum, "If one obtains the *yonitattva* and enters into battle, he will conquer all his enemies and be victorious, O Durgā, without doubt."[83] However, the goal of Tantric transgression ultimately goes much further than mere worldly power or success in battle. As Sanderson concludes, the goal of Tantric transgression is nothing short of a kind of "fearless omnipotence, of unfettered super-agency through the controlled assimilation of their lawless power in occult manipulations of impurity":

> This inhibition, which preserve that path of purity and barred his entrance into the path of power, was to be obliterated through the experience of a violent, duality-devouring expansion of consciousness beyond the narrow confines of orthodox control into the domain of excluded possibilities by gratifying with wine, meat and . . . caste-free intercourse."[84]

Thus the *tāntrika* has shattered not just the boundaries of social class and laws of purity, but ultimately the limits of the human condition itself, destroying all dualities in a state of unifying bliss. As one contemporary Śākta, Debendranāth Bhaṭṭācārya, describes the state of liberation: "The *kula yogi* is free and plays like a child . . . Though he is wise, he is called madman"; indeed,

> He makes no distinction between filth and sandal paste; his conduct is the same toward an enemy as toward his own son; in his mind a cremation ground is equal to a palace; and gold and straw are considered the same . . . How can the individual who knows the Supreme Reality make any distinction between praise and reproach, victory and defeat, wealth and poverty, violence and love?[85]

Such a being has transcended any sense of disgust or fear; to him semen and menstrual blood are pure[86]; he can eat any animal flesh and drink any wine without fear of pollution. Thus, Matsyendranātha's key Tantric text, the *Kaulajñāna Nirṇaya*, describes the state of ultimate liberation as one in which all dualities between pure and impure, merit and sin, sacred ritual and defiling pollution has been radically dissolved:

> [the *yogī*] always perceives sweet smells and bad smells without duality. Just as a lotus petal in water is not stained, so too, the *yogī* is not stained by merit or sin, O Sureśvarī. The sin of killing a *brāhmaṇ,* etc, and the fruit of an Aśvamedha sacrifice; bathing in all the sacred waters and contact with *mlecchas*—the *yogī* surely does not perceive any [distinction] between these actions.[87]

Having exploded all the dualities of limited human world, the true *yogī* has thus become equal to the gods themselves. According to the *Akulavīra Tantra,* also said to have been revealed to Matsyendranātha in Assam,

> He is Brahmā, he is Hari, he is Rudra, and he is Īśvara. He is Śiva, he is Paramadeva, he is Soma as well as Agni . . . He is an Arhant and even Buddha. He is himself the goddess and the god; he is the disciple and the guru. He is himself meditation and the one who meditates, and he is himself everywhere the deity [meditated upon].[88]

Here we see that the ultimate transgression is the overstepping of the very boundary between human and divine.

Conclusions: Capillary flows and overflows of power

In its structure, symbolism, and goals, then, the sexual rite is best understood less as a matter of sensual ecstasy than as the esoteric counterpart to the sacrificial ritual—a ritual that is, again, centered on the circulation of power through the circulation of bodily fluids and above all blood. In this case, it is the blood flowing from the goddess' human embodiment, the female partner or *śakti,* which is first offered to the goddess and then consumed orally as the esoteric counterpart to the sacrificial rite. And again, its goal is precisely the unleashing of the tremendous power of the goddess that lies within both the individual body and the social body, a power normally contained by manifold social taboos, but released through the systematic transgression of those prohibitions in Tantric ritual.

However, what we see historically in the Tantric traditions of Assam (and throughout India) is a progressive "interiorization" of the sacrificial paradigm. We see a gradual movement inward from the heavy focus on blood sacrifice in the *Kālikā Purāṇa* (tenth to eleventh centuries), to a strong focus on the sexual sacrifice in the *Kāmākhyā* and *Yoni Tantras* (sixteenth century), to a largely internalized sexual rite and sacrificial offering in the form of *kuṇḍalinī yoga* in the *Yoginī Tantra* (seventeenth to eighteenth centuries). As White notes, this more internalized and symbolic interpretation of Tantric sacrifice is part of a broader trend seen throughout South Asia during the later medieval period, as "the *homa* fire sacrifice rituals of early tantrism, which often involved the offering of human and animal blood . . . became sublimated into yogic practice."[89] At least in the case of Assam, this probably reflects the loss of royal patronage of the great sacrificial rites after the decline of the Pāla dynasty; but, as we will see in Chapter 6, it also likely reflects the critique of both animal sacrifice and sexual rites that followed in the wake of the popular devotional revival led by Śaṅkaradeva in the sixteenth century. Facing both a chaotic political climate and intense critique from the devotional reformers, the secret sacrifice appears to have retreated increasingly inward. This interiorization of the sacrifice is, again, at once a continuation of the sort of interiorization we see as early as the Upaniṣads; but it also combines these Vedic paradigms with profoundly non-Vedic and explicitly transgressive elements that aim not to contain but to unleash the tremendous power of the goddess.

To this day, however, Assam remains quite infamous in the Indian popular imagination as the locus *par excellence* of secret sexual rites.[90] One of the most modern remarkable accounts comes from the popular Bengali novelist, Samaresh Bose, who published what is alleged to have been his own first-hand observation of a *cakra pūjā* performed at Kāmākhyā. His account reads like mixture of British Orientalist fantasies, Bollywood films, and American pornography, as he describes an "unexpected and unbelievable" scene surrounded by howling jackals and grinning skulls. Apparently, Bose had never witnessed a sexual encounter quite as intense as this one:

> The Goddesses or Shaktis reached out and conferred their blessings. The Yogis then lifted them and placed them on their own laps and held them tightly to their hearts . . . [T]hey gave themselves up to the abandon of erotic foreplay; men started addressing their women as goddesses, such as Devi, Deveshi, and Shivani.
>
> After the foreplay had gone on for some time the men uttered some mantras as they started lovemaking. The so far still air began to be filled with moans, groans and deep breathing. Then there were moments

> of stillness followed by the deep and prolonged letting out of breath. After the breath was let out the intensity of lovemaking became more frenzied. . . . This would end with both laughing and becoming active again. (I was married by then, but had no idea that sexual intercourse could be like this.) . . .
>
> The whole thing seemed to me so incredible that I experienced none of the normal reactions that an individual would feel when he or she saw anyone making love, though they were masters of the myriads of techniques of lovemaking.
>
> The men often between bouts of rigorous lovemaking became still and controlled their breath. The women often had their feet wrapped around the men's waists . . . Jagat was shaking all over and either laughing or crying. Her two hands and legs were around Yogeshvar's neck and she had taken almost the shape of a circle. Yogeshvar was holding her tight with his hands. Pranatosh Baba and Pabitri Ma seemed to be permanently stuck to each other and were rolling all over the ground in a peculiar manner. Only strange inarticulate noises could be heard from them. This must be the moment of total bliss.[91]

How much (if not all) of Bose's narrative is imaginary may never be known. But it does provide telling evidence of the lingering power of Kāmākhyā as the supreme "place of desire" and locus of divine transgression in the popular imagination to this day.

Chapter Five

WHAT ABOUT THE WOMAN? GENDER POLITICS AND THE INTERPRETATION OF WOMEN IN TANTRA

What about the woman? That's the most embarrassing question you can ask any Tantric.

—Agehananda Bharati, "Making sense out of Tantrism and Tantrics" (1976)[1]

Women are gods, women are life, women, indeed, are jewels. One should always have intercourse with women, whether one's own wife or otherwise. What I have told you is the secret of all the *tantras*.

—*Yoni Tantra* (YT 7.16–17)

Since their first encounter with Tantra, Western observers have been particularly troubled by—and at times quite obsessed with—the question of women's roles in Tantric ritual. Indeed, if Tantra in general has long served as a kind of empty mirror onto which Western authors have projected their own deepest anxieties, fears, and sexual fantasies, then women in Tantra have served as a special kind of mirror onto which we have often projected our most acute anxieties about gender roles and the shifting balance of power between the sexes over the last two hundred years. Much of the horror, shock, and scandal expressed by early Orientalists and Christian missionaries, for example, focused on the role of women in Tantric ritual and the obscene indecency of female partners in sexual rites. For the Baptist missionary, Rev. William Ward writing in 1817, Tantric rites involve an obscene worship of the naked female body in which the men "behave towards this female in a manner which decency forbids to be mentioned."[2] Conversely, most of the contemporary, popular and New Age literature has celebrated Tantra as a "cult of the feminine" in which woman is the "Erotic Champion," offering a much-needed source of power, liberation, and freedom for contemporary women.[3]

Much of the modern scholarship on women in Tantra has likewise tended to fall into one of two rather simplistic binary positions.[4] Throughout the early twentieth century, many European and Indian scholars alike hailed Tantra as a kind of Cult of the Divine Female; as Mircea Eliade put it in his classic work on *Yoga*, Tantra is "religious rediscovery of the mystery of woman ... Woman incarnates both the mystery of creation and the mystery of Being, of everything that *is*, that becomes and dies and is reborn."[5] Likewise, the Marxist-leaning Indian scholar, N.N. Bhattacharyya, praised Tantra as an ancient, matriarchal, sex-based religion centered on worship of "the Female Principle" who in turn "stood for the oppressed peoples, symbolizing all the liberating potentialities in the class divided, patriarchal and authoritarian social set up of India."[6]

On the other side, more skeptical writers have described Tantra as a primarily masculine affair, in which women are used largely as passive objects and sources of raw power for the benefit of male practitioners. As we see throughout modern scholarship,

> [I]t would ... be wide of the mark to state that it acted as a liberating force which aimed at the improvement of the social status of women ... The social inferiority of woman is even a necessary presupposition for the liberating antinomianism of Tantric *sādhanā*.[7]

> Women ... are made subordinate to and dependent upon males and their ritual role is ... limited to being a partner for male adepts.[8]

> The feminine partner is used as a means to an end which is experienced by the *yogin* himself.[9]

> [T]he vast majority of the "living" Yoginīs of South Asia are poor marginalized women whose sexuality is idealized and glorified in words even as it is exploited in practice.[10]

Since the early 1990s, however, many feminist-leaning authors have tried to recover Tantra as a positive celebration of female power and sexuality. As Miranda Shaw has argued, Tantric sexuality is in fact liberating for women and "offers not a mode of exploitation but of complementarity and mutuality . . . Tantric texts encourage a sense of reliance on women as a source of spiritual power."[11] Indeed, Madhu Khanna even proclaims the motto: "Tantra is dharma for women!"[12] More recently, Loriliai Biernacki has offered a somewhat more nuanced feminist argument. Focusing on a small group of late texts from northeast India, Biernacki argues, first, that there is a broad diversity of representations of women in Tantra, and, second, that even texts written by male authors may also offer more positive representations of women as "venerable, powerful persons" with possibilities for guruship and other authoritative roles.[13]

Yet ironically, there has been virtually no effort to acknowledge the many different forms of feminism—both Western and Indian—or to sort out how different strands of feminist thought (liberal, radical, second-wave, third-wave, post-feminist, etc.) might approach a Tantric tradition. For example, the volume *Is the Goddess a Feminist?* never engages the plurality and complexity of contemporary feminism (or "feminisms," as some prefer to describe the "diversity of motivation, method and experience of modern feminists").[14] Much of the contemporary scholarship seems to assume either a kind of generic, homogenous "feminist" approach or one rooted in rather out-dated feminist theory from the 1970s and 1980s.[15] Indeed, by no means all contemporary feminists agree that Tantra is positive or empowering for women. June Campbell, for example, actually served as the secret consort (*songyam*) to a male lama in Tantric Buddhist sexual rites and reached the very opposite conclusion as had Shaw about the role of women. Using sophisticated feminist theory of her own, Campbell argues that women are not so much empowered or liberated by Tantric ritual as they are used to reinforce the power and status of a deeply patriarchal religio-political system.[16]

Yet all of these common views of women in Tantra, it seems to me, are problematic. For they all tend to assume a rather naive binary of oppressive domination versus liberating empowerment, and they all assume a fairly simplistic concept of human agency that is imagined to be either passively determined by structures of power or radically free and autonomous.[17] More often than not, moreover, they tell us a great deal more about the particular biases and political agendas of the individual scholar (conservative, liberal feminist, post-feminist, Marxist, etc.) than they do about any actual religious tradition.

My own view is that the role of women in Tantra is far more complex than a simple binary of empowerment or exploitation. First, not only is the complex body of traditions we call "Tantra" itself radically diverse and heterogeneous,[18] but more important, even within a single tradition there are multiple possible roles for women. In the Assamese tradition, for example, women often serve as ritual prostitutes (*veśyā*) whose role is little more than to provide a willing *yoni* and a source of sexual fluids for the male adept. But they can also be revered and worshipped as incarnations of the goddess in her prepubescent form (*kumārī*); they can become Tantric disciples and adepts (*yoginī*, *sādhakā*); and in some cases they can even become gurus and spiritual teachers themselves (Figs. 20–21).[19] Using insights from Deleuze, Guattari, and Butler, therefore, I will argue for a more complex view of agency and of gender/power relations. Far from a simple matter of empowerment or exploitation, agency involves a complex negotiation between the limitations imposed by structures of power and the available spaces for subversion and transformation of those structures. In the case of Tantra, women's sexuality is ritually and discursively constructed in ways that are often extremely essentialized and heteronormative (i.e., woman is the *yoni*, the bearer of menstrual blood, and the counterpart to the male *liṅgam*). Yet at the same time, the very fact that she is identified with the tremendous power of the goddess also opens *new room to maneuver* and a *space to renegotiate the dynamics of power:* it offers the possibility that she could in fact assume power in a more active way by herself becoming the leader of a spiritual lineage.

The cult of true yoni-hood: Reverence for the female body and sexual organ

One of the things that has most attracted many contemporary Western readers—including many feminists—to Tantra is its apparent celebration of femininity and the female body. On the whole, "Tantrism seems to be inspired by a genuine awe for the female as the seat of reproduction, the source of all life."[20] Indeed, it is difficult not to detect a certain amount of what Gayatri Spivak calls "womb envy," or the recognition of the womb as a powerful place of production,[21] throughout these male-authored Tantric texts.

This is particularly evident at the great *yoni pīṭha* of Kāmākhyā. Not only is this considered the supreme locus of the goddess' sexual organ and her annual menstruation, but it is also a major center of the performance of *kumārī pūjā*, or the worship of preadolescent girls as embodiments of the goddess' creative power. According to the seventeenth-century Assamese text, the *Yoginī Tantra*, every human *kumārī* embodies all the Mahāvidyā goddesses with all their divine powers, and therefore, "when just one girl is worshiped, all the [goddesses] are worshiped."[22] There is, moreover, no distinction of caste in *kumārī pūjā*; virgins of even the lowest, most impure families—including prostitutes (*veśyā*)—should be worshipped as incarnations of the goddess.[23] Thus, in the rite of *kumārī pūjā*, the virgin is literally "placed on a pedestal" and revered as the living embodiment of the goddess' tremendous power. As Madhu Khanna notes, "The young girl is represented as a powerful mother goddess. . . . The young girl is made to sit on a special pedestal (*pīṭha*) like the image and offered either five or sixteen ritual offerings."[24]

The *Yoginī Tantra* also narrates the mythic origins of *kumārī pūjā*, which link the virgin to both tremendous power and destructive potential. The goddess first assumed the form of a virgin in order to destroy a terrible demon named Keśī, who had overrun the earth and could not be defeated by Viṣṇu, Śiva, or any of the male gods. Taking the form of an innocent and beautiful young *kumārī*, the goddess appeared to the demon and was soon invited to his house. When the demon offered her something to eat, she took the opportunity to devour everything in his house and city, including the demon himself. Thenceforth, all the gods and sages began to worship the goddess in the form of virgins.[25]

As Marglin notes, the *kumārī* embodies the power of *raja* or menstrual blood in its fullest state, before the female has lost any of her creative energy. As such, she is considered both tremendously powerful and potentially dangerous, associated with the goddess in her most formidable and martial forms: "Virginity is associated with heat and danger deriving from that force or power residing in the accumulated *raja* of the virgin. The goddess Durgā is also called the virgin (*kumārī* or *kanyā*) goddess."[26] As we see in the *Yoginī Tantra* narrative, the virgin represents the tremendous and voracious power of the female in its primordial form—a power at once creative and destructive, beautiful and yet voracious. The *kumārī* is, in other words, *śakti* in its rawest state, before the flow of desire has begun.

Women, fire, and other dangerous things

The same association of women with both tremendous power and destructive potentiality runs throughout Assamese Śākta and Tantric literature. Thus, the *Kālikā Purāṇa* contains several fascinating taxonomies of powerful but dangerous things associated with women and with the goddess. For example,

> Whenever one sees a pot of wine, a woman dressed in red, a lion, a corpse, a red lotus, a tiger together with an elephant, a guru or a king he should bow his head to Mahāmāyā. Whenever he has contact with the menstrual blood of his devoted wife, he should meditate on Caṇḍikā.[27]

> Having seen a vessel full of liquor or a woman in a red garment, or the [severed] head of a man, he should meditate upon the goddess Tripurā Bhairavī.[28]

Many other non-Assamese texts contain similar lists of powerful, dangerous, impure, and yet auspicious things associated with women and the goddess. According to the *Kulacūḍāmaṇi Tantra*, one should pay homage to the goddess upon seeing a graveyard, a corpse, a black flower, a red dress, a king, a prince, a buffalo, an image of Mahiṣamardinī, a vessel of wine, fish, meat, or a *kula* woman.[29] Likewise, the *Kaulāvalīnirṇaya* says that one should honor the goddess upon seeing raw meat, a jar of intoxicating liquor, girls playing, a cremation ground, a group of women, or a woman wearing red clothes.[30]

As cognitive scientists like George Lakoff have shown, taxonomies like these that contain series such as "women, fire and dangerous things" tell us a great deal how both the mind and culture work.[31] Indeed, they reveal the ways that various groups classify their world and construct a meaningful universe and cultural reality. However, as historians of religion like Bruce Lincoln have shown, such taxonomic systems also tell us a great deal about hierarchies of power, political structures and gender relations within a social order.[32] If we analyze the chain of associations in the class of things associated with the goddess, for example, we find the following qualities all tend to be repeatedly linked together: femininity, intoxication, impurity, power, death, redness, sexuality, and blood. If we were to then ask what all these qualities have in common, it would seem that they all center on a triad of powerful but dangerous forces, namely, sexuality, violence, and femininity, all of which are symbolized by redness and blood. The female, in sum, is imagined as a key link in a taxonomic chain that connects bloodshed and death with impurity and sexual fluids, signaling an immense but profoundly dangerous source of power. And much of the aim of Tantric ritual, as Sanderson notes, is precisely to "unleash the feminine, thereby unleashing her power," as one enters into relations with "dangerous female forces which populate the domain of excluded possibilities that hem about the path of purity."[33]

This reverence for the tremendous but dangerous power of female sexuality runs throughout the Tantric texts of the northeast region. The *Yoni Tantra*, for example, praises the *yoni* as the source of all creation, the divine organ that gives birth to all the gods and all the elements of the cosmos: "Hari, Hara, and all the gods, the agents of the creation, maintenance and destruction of the universe, are all born from the *yoni*."[34] And women, insofar as they embody the creative power of the goddess' *yoni*, should be honored as one would honor the goddess herself. Thus we find repeated instructions not to insult women or strike them but instead to pay homage to them: "One should never show anger to a maiden or a woman, O Queen of the gods . . . One should diligently worship a maiden who belongs to the *kula*."[35] Likewise, the *Yoni Tantra* proclaims,

> One should have no hatred toward women, especially in the worship of women. Wherever he is, the adept should go to a woman, touch her, and see her . . . Women are gods, women are life, women, indeed, are jewels. One should always have intercourse with women, whether one's own wife or otherwise. What I have told you is the secret of all the *tantras*.[36]

Because all women are embodiments of the goddess' creative power, a woman of any caste or class can serve as a partner in Tantric ritual. Any girl from a prostitute or washer-woman to a *brāhmaṇ* is suitable, provided she is skillful, lustful, and free of disgust or shame:

> A dancer, a *kāpālikā* [member of the "skull-bearer" Śaivite sect], a prostitute, a washer-woman, a barber's daughter, a *brāhmaṇ* girl, a daughter of a *śūdra*, a cowherd girl, and a daughter of a garland-maker—these are praised as the nine kinds of maiden. Otherwise, any maiden who is artful and has lustful eyes. Apart from his mother's

> *yoni*, one should enter all *yonis*. He should have intercourse with any *yoni* between the ages of 12 and 60.[37]

We should note here that, apart from the *brāhmaṇ* girl, most of these female partners come from very low and often quite impure and/or transgressive castes; and many of them deal with impure bodily "leftovers" or "leavings," such as skulls (*kāpālikās*), sexual fluids (prostitutes), dirt (washerwomen), and hair-clippings (barbers). As her very name (*rajakī*) suggests, the washerwoman is inherently tied to impurity, since she deals with dirty and soiled garments, including those soiled with *rajas* or menstrual blood.[38] Other Assamese texts like the *Kāmākhyā Tantra* call specifically for prostitutes (*veśya*) as ritual partners.[39] And still others like the *Śrī Kāmākhyā Guhya Siddhi* associate the eight Tantric Mātṛkā goddesses with eight kinds of low-caste women, including prostitutes, wine-dealers, and ditch-diggers, signaling the "suitability of such low caste women in Kaula practice."[40] Although some later texts from the northeast call for sexual union only with one's own wife (*svakīyā*),[41] the *tantras* known to be from Assam and Cooch Behar clearly prefer low-class and impure partners—a preference closely tied to the logic of transgression at work in Tantric ritual, as we have seen in the previous chapters.

As the embodiment of divine, feminine, creative power, the *yoni* is thus the supreme object of worship, and *yoni pūjā* is the central ritual described in texts like the *Yoni Tantra*. The female partner is to be seated (or placed on a *pīṭha* or pedestal in some texts[42]) and offered a narcotic beverage (*vijayā*). Then her sexual organ should be honored as the goddess herself:

> Having brought the beautiful, young, wanton woman, who is free of disgust or shame, having placed his own beloved or that of another, well-adorned, in the circle, and having first offered her *vijayā*, he should worship her, full of devotion. Having seated her to his left, he should worship her unshaved *yoni*. In the hollow of the *yoni*, he should offer sandalwood and beautiful flowers.[43]

In sum, just as the great *yoni pīṭha* of Kāmākhyā is worshipped as the matrix of the universe and the supreme pedestal of power, so too, the individual *yoni* here is worshipped as the matrix of procreation and the seat or pedestal (*pīṭha*) of the supreme essence of menstrual blood.

Gender un-troubled: Feminist readings and re-readings of Tantric sex

Yet if it is true that many *tantras* repeatedly praise women and the female body, it is by no means obvious that they can be read as "feminist" texts in any modern sense of term. The female is revered and honored here, not primarily because of her intellectual abilities or personal virtues, but because of her possession of and identity with her sexual organ. Texts like the *Yoni Tantra* and *Kāmākhyā Tantra* are quite clear as to why women are to be revered: it is because they have *yonis* —indeed, because *they are yonis*. Throughout the *Yoni Tantra*, for example, the word *yoni* is used both to signify the female sexual organ *and* to signify the female herself.[44] As Biernacki herself admits in an endnote, "That the word for female sex organ at times also just refers to the woman as a being suggests that woman's identity is intricately intertwined with, and constructed upon, the notion of her sex organ."[45] It does not appear to make much difference who the woman is or to which caste she belongs (since any from a prostitute to a *brāhmaṇ* will do, and in some ways the lower the class the better), because her primary virtue is her identity with the *yoni* or *bhaga* and her ability to produce the prized "flower of the *yoni*" (*yoni-puṣpa*) or menstrual blood:

> Without the vulva, O Great Lady, everything would be futile. Simply by the worship of the *yoni*, one could obtain the fruit of all religious practices.[46]

> I know of no worship equal to worship of the *yoni*. By kissing and embracing the *yoni*, one attains the wish-fulfilling tree. By seeing [it] he becomes the lord of all adepts, by touching [it] he can infatuate all beings.[47]

> If one makes a mark on one's forehead with the *yoni-puṣpa*, then, with this red mark, O goddess, he goes to Durgā's heavenly realm.[48]

As June McDaniel observes, texts like the *Kāmākhyā Tantra* are primarily concerned not with the fate of the female partner or the benefits she might achieve from the worship of her *yoni*, but with the manifold supernatural powers to be obtained by the male practitioner: "The effects of this practice on the female *tantrika* is not mentioned," and overall, the primary goal appears to be the "enrichment of the male *tantrikas*."[49] Moreover, as Davidson points out, virtually all of the known Hindu and Buddhist Tantric texts—including even those Buddhist *tantras* ostensibly written by women—describe the sexual ritual from the male perspective and focus exclusively on the male sexual position. Out of the hundreds of Tantric manuals and lineages, living and dead, we have uncovered "not a single text or lineage that preserves instructions about yogic or sexual practices that relate to women's position."[50]

Indeed, if we were really to employ contemporary feminist analysis in a critical way, we would have to say that most of Tantric philosophy and practice is founded on a very clear—even exaggerated and extreme—form of gender essentialism. The celebration of the female sexual organ and menstruation may seem attractive from the standpoint of some feminist movements popular during the 1960s and 1970s, such as so-called second-wave feminism and radical feminism.[51] But it seems quite problematic from the standpoint of any feminist theory written since the 1980s, with the rise of third-wave feminism, post-feminism, and the widely influential work of authors like Elizabeth Spelman, Judith Butler, Gayatri Spivak, and many others.[52] As Alison Stone observes, feminist theory since the 1980s has seen a widespread debate over the essentialism and universalism assumed by most second-wave feminists, that is, the idea that there is some core essence of womanhood that is common to all women everywhere:

> The central target of anti-essentialist critiques was the belief ... that there are shared characteristics common to all women, which unify them as a group. Anti-essentialists of the third wave repeatedly argued that such universalizing claims about women are always false and function oppressively to normalise particular socially and culturally privileged forms of feminine experience.[53]

By assuming that certain forms of women's experience are universal, essentialist views inevitably tend to privilege certain forms of femininity as the norm; ironically, they "thereby end up replicating between women the very patterns of oppression and exclusion that feminism should contest."[54] Above all, most contemporary feminists would probably find the equation of the female with her *yoni* deeply problematic and hardly very empowering. As Butler notes, summarizing many other feminist arguments, "The identification of women with 'sex' . . . is a conflation of the category of women with the ostensibly sexualized features of their bodies and, hence, a refusal to grant freedom and autonomy to women."[55]

At the same time, most of Tantric ritual is also founded on an extreme and exaggerated form of heteronormativity, that is, the assumption that the male–female heterosexual binary is fundamental, universal, and even eternal. Throughout the Assamese literature (and virtually all Tantric literature), male and female, *liṅgam* and *yoni*, are celebrated as the embodiments of the divine male and female principles, and this binary is in turn hypostatized and inscribed into the very fabric of the universe: "Mahāmāyā is in the form of the vagina, and the eternal Śiva is in the form of the penis. Merely by worshipping those two, one achieves liberation while still alive, without doubt."[56] The divine love-play of Śiva and Śakti generates the entire cosmos and, in turn, Tantric ritual reenacts this divine play in order to generate the male and female sexual fluids that are the ultimate source of power. As lord Śiva explains to the goddess in the *Kāmākhyā Tantra*,

> Listen, O goddess, I am telling you the great secret knowledge. I am semen, and you are indeed blood. The whole world consists of these two. But just as the whole pure body is born of semen and blood, even so that essence goes forth in the body of the child.[57]

This would appear to be the very epitome of what Butler calls the "heterosexual matrix for conceptualizing gender and desire," that is, the larger cultural framework that determines how sexuality will be constructed in a social order governed by normative male–female relationships: "Gender norms . . . operate by requiring the embodiment of certain ideals of femininity and masculinity, ones that are almost always related to the idealization of the heterosexual bond."[58] Throughout texts like the *Yoni* and *Kāmākhyā Tantras*, male and female are consistently identified with their genitalia (*liṅgam* and *yoni*), and this binary is conceived as a metaphysical, divine, transcendent relationship that produces and structures the entire cosmos, from the very origin of the universe down to the individual human body.

If we were to follow Butler's critique, then, Tantric ritual would seem to be an extreme example of the *performative* nature of gender and sex itself. As Butler suggests, neither gender nor sex is a "natural," inherent quality of our physical existence; rather, these are both the effect of a "*ritualized production*,"[59] a repetitive performance of gender norms that over time produce the illusion of a pre-given, "natural" femininity and masculinity: "As a sedimented effect of a reiterative or ritual practice, sex acquires its naturalized effect .... The repetitive nature of gender performance makes sex appear stable and natural."[60] Tantric ritual would seem to take this ritualized gender performance to its furthest extreme. In Butler's terms, the repeated worship of the female partner as the goddess and *yoni*, combined with the performance of male–female sexual union as the human reflection of Śiva and Śakti, makes "maleness," "femaleness," and the heterosexual bond appear not just natural and stable, but in fact divine, immutable, and inherent in the very fabric of reality.

The yoni on a pedestal and the cult of true Śakti-hood

Finally and perhaps most obviously, the fact that highly esoteric, male-authored texts speak reverently of the female body can hardly be taken uncritically as evidence that women had actual power in the public sphere. After all, the discourse of "reverence and honor" for women has long been used by patriarchal regimes as a means of praising those aspects of femininity that serve men's needs (especially reproduction and domesticity) while limiting women's access to power in the public domain. Placing women on pedestals and honoring their reproductive abilities is one of the oldest and most recurring tropes in patriarchal discourse. This was the basic logic, for example, of the "Cult of True Womanhood" in the nineteenth century. Throughout the nineteenth-century American literature, as Norma Broude observes, women were considered to have a "superiority confined entirely to the moral and spiritual realm" and were thus "placed on a pedestal that effectively barred them not only from equal citizenship but also from... any real voice in the public realm."[61] A century later, this was much the same logic used by leaders of the Christian right in the late twentieth century, as we see in Jerry Falwell's famous critique of the Equal Rights Amendment:

> I believe that women deserve more than equal rights. And, in families and in nations where the Bible is believed, Christian women are honored above men. Only in places where the Bible is believed and

> practiced do women receive more than equal rights. Men and women have differing strengths.[62]

Historically, it would seem, reverence for the female body and its reproductive powers has no necessary or direct connection to any actual empowerment of women in the larger social sphere. As Samjukta Gupta notes in the case of Hindu Śākta traditions and the identification of women with the goddess, "the fact that certain sections of Hindu society worship the Goddess as the active creatrix and even as the saving godhead did not radically change women's position in the Hindu social structure."[63]

Last and not least, however, there is also the problem of the extreme secrecy of Tantra in general and of women's roles in particular. The Assamese *tantras*, like most Tantric texts, warn repeatedly about the need for absolute secrecy, above all in the case of esoteric sexual rites such as the *yoni pūjā* or *cakra pūjā*. These rites must be performed only in the most remote places and never revealed to noninitiates: "This secret teaching is the supreme, great emission. It must be kept extremely secret [*gopanīyaṃ gopanīyaṃ, gopanīyaṃ*], with great effort, just like the secrecy of sexual intercourse or the region of the breast; just like the secrecy of the *yoni*, so too, this supreme initiation [must be kept secret]."[64] Indeed, if someone accidentally comes upon an adept performing the rite of *yoni pūjā*, he should pretend to be performing more mundane, non-transgressive Vaiṣṇava rites.[65] As Dehejia observes in the case of contemporary *bhairavīs* or female sexual partners in modern Assam: "It is impossible to meet up with these bhairavīs unless an initiate oneself . . . No one on meeting a bhairavī would . . . realise she was one."[66] Thus, even if women *are* praised and celebrated in Tantric ritual, this is in most cases limited to highly esoteric contexts and rarely extends into the larger social or political sphere.

Some have argued that the intense secrecy surrounding Tantric ritual is not simply limiting to women's power, but is indeed quite exploitative of that power for largely male interests. As June Campbell reflects on her own experience as a *songyam* or secret consort in Tantric Buddhist ritual, the ideal of the complementary union between male and female in *maithuna* was profoundly tainted by the extreme secrecy and power-dynamics that surrounded her relationship:

> The imposition of secrecy . . . was a powerful weapon in keeping women from achieving any kind of integrity in themselves, for it seems

> clear that the fundamental and ancient principles of Tantric sex—the meeting together of two autonomous individuals as partners for sexual relations to promote spirituality—was tainted by the power wielded by one partner over the other.[67]

In sum, it seems difficult to find much evidence of female empowerment *merely* in the fact that Tantric texts speak reverently of women and of the female sexual organ. Many critics, such as Campbell, have concluded that the very opposite may be the case. That being said, however, it would *also* surely be far too simplistic to say that Tantric ritual is simply a matter of exploitation, manipulation, and appropriation of the female body for exclusively male interests. For the very fact that women are imagined as embodiments of the goddess' divine power *also* opens a new space of possibility within the construction of gender and some room for a *renegotiation* of power relations. Despite the extreme essentialism, heteronormativity, and secrecy at work in its ritual and discourse, Śākta Tantra does in fact open the door for at least a few women to assume actual power and communal authority.

Taking power: Śākta Tantra and the possibility of female authority

Alongside the more common roles of the *kumārī* (the virgin worshipped as the goddess) and the *śakti* (the female partner in sexual rituals), many *tantras* also hold open the possibility for one other important female role: the guru. Female gurus are mentioned in a wide array of texts, and in some cases, women are praised as not only natural spiritual leaders but as even more auspicious than male gurus. According to the *Tripurārṇava Tantra*, women are inherently gurus simply by virtue of their female nature and their identity with the supreme goddess: "There are no rules for women; all are said to be gurus. Merely by receiving an authoritative *mantra*, she is the supreme guru. She can teach by means of the authoritative *mantra* and obtain books. A man does not have such authority, for woman is the supreme deity."[68] Likewise, according to Brahmānandagiri, a sixteenth-century Śākta author from northeast India,

> Initiation from a woman is said to be auspicious, and [initiation] from a mother is said to be eight times more valuable . . . A holy woman of virtuous conduct, devoted to the guru, with her senses restrained, versed in the essential meaning of all the *tantras*, and devoted to worship is suitable to be a guru, with the exception of widows.[69]

Indeed, the *Mātṛkābheda Tantra* contains an entire hymn in praise of the female guru (the *strī-guru-stotra*) who is honored as the bearer of all knowledge, wisdom, and liberation. She is herself the great goddess incarnate, who contains all the deities within herself:

> The supreme mother is the savior from the bonds of the world. She is eternal, bestowing knowledge and liberation. Glory to her. Seated at the left side of the Lord, she is worshipped by the gods, always bestowing wisdom. Glory to her. She is the self-nature of the eternal bliss located in the great thousand-petaled lotus [in the crown *cakra* at the top of the head], the goddess bestowing the great liberation. Glory to her. She has the self-nature of Brahmā and Viṣṇu, the self-nature of the great Rudra.[70]

The Assamese Tantric texts also refer to an array of powerful *yoginīs* and spiritual teachers, such as the great *yoginīs* who revealed the Kaula path to Matsyendranātha and inspired the Yoginī Kaula tradition. As we saw in Chapter 3, the *Yoginī Tantra* also tells the story of a beautiful *yoginī* named Revatī, who was described as a wise, true *brāhmaṇ* woman, "versed in the Vedas and Āgamas, a holy woman, like a goddess."[71] Indeed, Revatī was so ravishing that she infatuated lord Śiva himself, coupled with him, and gave birth to Viśva Siṅgha, the Koch king who conquered Kāmarūpa in the sixteenth century.

Historically, there are numerous examples of real human female gurus, in addition to the ones praised in texts. Although the epigraphic and ethnographic research shows the numbers of female *tāntrikas* and gurus to be quite small in comparison to their male counterparts (between 1 and 20 per cent, by Davidson's count),[72] they clearly have existed historically and continue to exist today. One need only think of Shri Ramakrishna's powerful and assertive Tantric guru, the Bhairavī, who led him through at least four of the five Ms; or the twentieth-century Tantric saint, Madhobi Ma, "Nectar Mother"; or Tantric gurus such as Gauri Ma and Jayashri Ma in modern Bengal[73]; or, as we will see in Chapter 7, the internationally famous guru and embodiment of the goddess, Shree Maa of Kāmākhyā.[74] As Gupta suggests in her study of female holy women in India, Śākta female saints do appear to have more religious freedom and higher status than their counterparts among Vaiṣṇava women saints. And even today there are hereditary Śākta families in regions like Mithila who follow the tradition that the primary initiation be given by a woman.[75]

In my own experience in contemporary Assam, I have likewise found female Śāktas to be relatively rare, but also unusually assertive, forceful, and at times quite intimidating. On one occasion during my early research at Kāmākhyā, I was conducting interviews with a group of holy men and women seated on the steps of the temple begging for alms. One formidable-looking female Śākta from eastern Assam quickly turned the tables on me, by conducting a rather aggressive interview of her own. She immediately demanded to know who I was, why I was asking so many questions, what business I had digging into Tantra, and so on. The other, mostly male *sādhus* sitting nearby clearly respected (and, indeed, appeared rather intimidated) by her, chortling approvingly as she began to interrogate the nosy white man. When I meekly began to explain my interest in the subject, she entered into a long—and by no means unintelligent—discussion of the imbalance of power between India and America and the profound misunderstanding of Indian culture by Western tourists. Indeed, I think I heard a more accurate critique of the effects of neo-colonialism from this feisty *sādhvī* than from any number of postcolonial theorists.[76]

The ambivalence of agency: Subversion of gender norms from within the structures of power

So how do we explain this seeming tension between the highly essentialized, heteronormative, secretive, and not particularly empowering image of women in Tantric ritual and the powerful image of female gurus in Tantric texts and living traditions? Here I would suggest that we need to deploy a more nuanced model of agency that avoids the simplistic binarism of empowerment vs. exploitation, radical freedom vs. passive determinism. As theorists like Deleuze and Butler have argued, agency is best understood not as a simple matter of domination versus resistance, passive, fixed identity versus pure, autonomous freedom; rather agency is "crucially *ambivalent*" involving "both potential for freedom through differentiation and diversification, and limitations on that potential."[77] As Butler suggests, gender roles are neither a product of pure free choice nor an essential fixed identity; instead, they are the result of *ritualized, stylized performative acts* that are repeated over and over, giving the illusion of a "natural" gendered identity. However, the very fact that they must be repeated, ritually performed and re-performed *also* means that there are always "gaps or fissures" revealing that which escapes or exceeds the norm; the constant reiteration of gender norms also opens the space for subversion, destabilization, and transformation.[78] As Eugene Holland comments, summarizing this point in both Deleuze and Butler,

> Gender norms which are purported to express essential identities are in fact the effect of recurrent acts that constitute them as such. Gender roles are neither the expression of fixed of identities nor the result of pure free choice: they stem from the imposition and incorporation of norms in repeated actions and behavior, and have no other ulterior reality than such repetition. However, the constitution of (a sense of) identity by repetition . . . is always also subject to variations on that repetition . . . What repetition may actually produce . . . is not just repetition of the same (enforcement of norms) but difference: variation, divergence, deviation, even subversion of norms.[79]

What this means, though, is that there is no agency or resistance that exists somehow beyond relations of power; there is no agency outside of power, since the subject is herself a product of relations of power and of the ritualized repetition of gender norms. Any subversion or transformation of gender roles can therefore only occur *within and through* the existing relations of power: "there is no subverting of a norm without inhabiting that norm . . . the norm that forms the subject is also the one that is subject to revision or alteration or critique."[80] Hence, agency is always possible but always "vexed," that is, emerging from within the mire and the limitations imposed by the existing relations of power.

This sort of ambivalent agency and the possibility for the subversion of gender norms can be seen in many examples of female leadership in other religious traditions. As Grace Jantzen has argued in her study of female Christian mystics of late medieval Europe, women were consistently imagined as humble, passive, and lowly throughout medieval discourse. Yet paradoxically, this construction or femininity also opened the possibility for at least some women to *use* that "lowliness and humility" as the basis on which to claim divine experience and spiritual authority. Even if only in rare cases, some women were able to turn their humility into evidence of their openness to the Spirit and thus a potential source of spiritual power:

> if such lowliness is gender-related, then by a paradoxical twist women are especially privileged, at an advantage as candidates for exaltation. Of course, this would actually occur only extremely rarely; in practical terms most women's lot would not be improved at all. Nevertheless, exceptional women could claim authority and special privilege on the basis of a vision directly vouchsafe by God.[81]

Likewise, the fact that women were imagined to be inherently more physical, sensual, and emotional than men also opened the possibility for a new kind of mystical experience and spiritual authority, one rooted in a highly erotic, sensual, and embodied mysticism. Thus we find medieval women mystics like Hildegard of Bingen, Hadewijch of Antwerp, Julian of Norwich and others who were able to transform their imagined weakness, physicality, and sensuality as women into a source of spiritual authority—one that in some cases even became a social and political "subversion of male authority."[82]

A similar kind of paradoxical gender dynamic has been observed in the case of nineteenth-century Spiritualism in the USA. As Ann Braude argues in *Radical Spirits*, women in nineteenth-century America were consistently imagined and discursively constructed as passive, innocent, and childlike; yet, ironically, their alleged "passivity" and simplicity also rendered women more "receptive" to communications from spirits and thereby opened the possibility for women to speak publicly with a new kind of divine authority.[83] Indeed, it gave them an opportunity to assume a quite active voice and even to become leaders of religious movements in their own right: "more women stepped beyond conventional female roles because of Spiritualism than they would have without it. In mediumship, .. Spiritualism held up a model of women's unlimited capacity for autonomous action."[84]

A similar gender dynamic, I would suggest, is at work in many Hindu Tantric traditions, though with obvious differences of time, place, and cultural context. Tantric ritual, we have seen, is highly essentialized and heteronormative, even exaggeratedly so. And sexual rites are largely described from the male point of view, primarily for the benefit of the male practitioner. Yet at the same time, the fact remains that women are imagined as embodiments of *śakti*, at once "feared and revered"[85] as receptacles of divine creative energy and strength. As two contemporary female devotees put it in an interview in 2000,

> In every house of Kāmrūp we find Devī, our mother goddess . . . they consider every woman a Devī, and it follows that the energy in every house is existing . . . That is where *śakti* comes in, because you feel in every woman that much more special, you feel that special divine force is kind of encompassed in me because I am a woman, so it's in me and it's up to me to tap and link it into that force . . . I am a chip of that energy.

> I am Devī. I am Śiva, I am everything, I am so powerful like mother goddess. I have to do *pūjā* for myself, I have to love myself.[86]

Historically, this identification of the female with the goddess as strength has also opened a space for at least *some* women to assume that power in a more direct way: they have had the opportunity—even if relatively rare—to become spiritual authorities, gurus, and leaders of Tantric lineages.

This more complex sort of female agency is perhaps not unlike what Gayatri Spivak calls a kind of "strategic essentialism," that is, a "strategic use of a positivist essentialism" for some larger social interest.[87] In some cases, it is advantageous for oppressed and marginalized groups to "essentialize" themselves and bring forward their group identity in a simplified way in order to achieve certain goals. In the case of Hindu Tantra, we might say that Śākta women have been able to use their highly essentialized status as *śaktis* and embodiments of the goddess' power in a strategic manner, that is, as a means to achieve a more concrete kind of authority in living Tantric communities. As such, they may not have created the foundation for a movement of radical women's liberation, but they *have* been able to open a unique *space or gap within* the dominant relations of power.

Conclusions: The alchemy of sex and gender

In sum, the case of Assamese Tantra challenges us to think about both agency and women's roles in a far more complex way than the usual binary of liberating agency versus deterministic exploitation. Instead, it forces us to recognize that women are often discursively and ritually constructed in ways that are highly essentialized and seemingly quite problematic from the standpoint of much of contemporary feminist theory. Yet at the same time, it also reveals the ways in which Tantric women can and historically have found new room to maneuver and new spaces for agency even *within* a highly essentialized, heteronormative, and male-dominated system.

As saw in Chapter 1, the Tantric concept of *śakti* or power is both fundamentally gendered and inherently performative. That is to say, power is intimately tied to constructions of masculinity and femininity and to relations between the sexes. And, as Butler's suggests, these constructions are by no means fixed essences but rather *effects* that must be *performed and continuously re-performed* through "acts, gestures, enactments," and other forms of social discourse.[88] In the case of Kāmākhyā, these performative enactments include the recitation of mythic narratives, the daily performance of animal sacrifices, the secret Tantric sexual rites, and the large public festivals that together bind the goddess and her devotees in a complex network of power and gender relations.

Going a step further than either Foucault or Butler, however, we might also say that *power itself* is "gendered" and "performed" in this tradition. Metaphysically and metaphorically, power here is largely imagined as feminine: it is the creative *śakti* of the goddess that flows through and sustains the universe with her life-giving blood. But institutionally and politically, power is largely conceived, constructed, and performed as masculine: it is the ritual authority of the priests who perform her rituals and the royal power of the kings who rule her land. In fact, one of the things that Kāmākhyā's rituals do, I would argue, is transform the *spiritual* power of the goddess into the *physical* power of the male kings and priests. Through a kind of *sexo-religio-political alchemy*, the feminine energy of the *yoni* is transmuted into the masculine authority of the *brāhmaṇ* and the *rāja*.

Of course, as Butler suggests, there are always opportunities for subversive forms of performance and "new possibilities of agency" that might transform the dominant relations of power.[89] In the case of Assamese Tantra, the fact that women are identified with the goddess and her power has meant that at least some women have historically been able to use that power for more tangible forms of authority, as ritual experts, authorities, and gurus in their own right. For the most part, it is true, their power has always been on the periphery and at the margins of the institutional worship of Kāmākhyā, which has historically been and still remains the domain of the hundreds of red-clad priests who run the central temple complex. Yet it still remains to this day a possibility inherent in the discourse and ritual practice of a tradition centered on the tremendous, creative-destructive energy of the goddess as power.

Chapter Six

THE POWER OF GOD IN A DARK VALLEY: REFORM, COLONIALISM, AND THE DECLINE OF TANTRA IN SOUTH ASIA

> Engaged in worship with women, wine and meat [*strī-madya-māṃsa-sevā*], alas, they perish! Alas, they perish! Their lives are futile. They don't understand the deeper meaning of the Vedas.
>
> —Śaṅkaradeva, *Kīrttana-ghoṣa* (sixteenth century)[1]

> The temples of Kāmākhyā leave a disagreeable impression—an impression of dark evil haunts of lust and bloodshed, akin to madness and unrelieved by any grace or vigour of art. . . . All the buildings, and especially the modern temple of Kālī . . . testify to the atrophy and paralysis produced by erotic forms of religion.
>
> —Sir Charles Eliot, *Hinduism and Buddhism* (1921)[2]

> O that the power of God might be displayed in this dark valley.
>
> —Rev. Miles Bronson (1843)[3]

But if Tantra was intimately tied to kingship and political power in South Asia, why did it so quickly decline in the modern period? If the worship of the goddess as Śakti or power was so widely patronized by Assam's rulers like the Pāla, Koch, Chutiya, Jaintia, and Ahom kings, why did it gradually disintegrate and fragment, leaving the goddess increasingly removed from the center of political power?

In many parts of India, the decline of Tantra as a major religious and political force began with the spread of Islam, particularly into key strongholds of Tantric philosophy such as Kashmir and the northwest.[4] In the case of Assam and the northeast region, however, the reasons of the decline of Tantra were complex and closely related to the changing social and political fortunes of the region from the sixteenth century to the present. For the most part, Assam was not much affected by the spread of Islam, since the Ahom kings were remarkably successful at beating back Muslim incursions into the region.[5] While it is popular and convenient to blame the decline of everything in India on the British, the critique of Tantra in northeast long predated the coming of the British colonial authorities—who were in fact rather late in coming to Assam—and in fact was already well underway from the sixteenth century onward. The neo-Vaiṣṇava reform movement led by Śaṅkaradeva in the sixteenth century was in many ways just as critical of Śākta Tantra as the British colonizers and Christian missionaries would be two centuries later; and it prefigured many of the Orientalist attacks on idolatry, sacrifice, and sexual licentiousness.

However, Tantra in Assam did become a special object of attack by the British Orientalists, colonial authorities, and Christian missionaries of the nineteenth and twentieth centuries. Indeed, if Tantra as a whole was widely viewed as the most extreme and perverse aspect of the "Indian mind"—as the "extreme Orient" and "India's Darkest Heart"[6]—then the Tantric traditions of Assam were viewed as the *most extreme extremity of the Orient*, the *darkest core of India's dark heart itself.* For British colonial authorities, who began to rule the area in 1826 after the First Burmese War and incorporated it into British-administered Bengal in 1838, Assam represented a troublesome region that was extremely frustrating and often dangerous to govern.[7] Throughout British discourse, Assam appears as a land of backward tribes, treacherous jungle, and even the sacrifice of British subjects. Above all, Assamese Tantra and the worship of Kāmākhyā, as Sir Charles Eliot put it, seemed like a dark evil cult of blood lust and black magic, reeking of perversion and madness.[8]

For the Christian missionaries conversely, the northeast represented an unexpected promise. Above all for the American Baptist missionaries working in the region, this most extreme realm of barbarism, idolatry, and spiritual darkness in Asia was a "dark valley" that might, however, be penetrated by missionary zeal and so open the entire expanse of remote Asia to the guiding light of Christ. But in both cases, Assam and the northeast region as a whole represented the most extreme, most exotic realm within the already exotic and eroticized realm of India itself. And it was, therefore, the most in need of conquering, regulating, controlling, and redeeming.

In this sense, the colonial and missionary critiques of Assamese Tantra very clearly reflect, and indeed epitomize, the gendered and sexualized nature of imperial power. As Anne McClintock, Ann Laura Stoler, and others have noted, imperial discourse consistently tends to imagine the colonized subject as not simply racialized (dark and primitive), but also as sexualized (feminine, hyper-erotic, and seductive); and this in turn helps reaffirm the image of the colonizer as masculine, rational, and self-controlled in its judicious exercise of benevolent power.[9] As the "dark valley," on the eastern-most, thickly forested fringe of the empire, Assam was widely imagined to be the most quintessentially feminine, sexual, and seductive aspect of the dark Orient itself. As such, it provided clear evidence of the need for both strong, muscular rule and the purifying light of Jesus.

Together, these combined forces of indigenous Hindu critiques, colonial assaults, and Christian missionary attacks led to the progressive de-centering of Tantra and Śākta Hinduism as a major political force in Assam. But as we will see in the following chapter, they would by no means end its power or influence in the popular culture of Assam today.

The critique of Śākta Tantra by Vaiṣṇava reformers: From "gruesome rites" and "innumerable gods" to devotional love of one god

The first major challenge to Śākta Tantra in Assam began with the rise of the immensely popular and influential devotional revival led by the charismatic reformer, Śaṅkaradeva (1449–1569). Born in what is now the Nowgong district of Assam, Śaṅkaradeva came from a staunch Śākta family, with an image of the goddess Caṇḍī as the object of worship in his father's house; but Śaṅkaradeva came to reject Śāktism and its bloody worship of the goddess.[10] While on pilgrimage at the great Jagannāth temple in Puri, Śaṅkaradeva received his great spiritual illumination and then returned to Assam to preach the devotional love of Viṣṇu, above all in the form of his *avatāra*, Kṛṣṇa. Much like the devotional revivals led by Kabir in north India and Śrī Caitanya in Bengal, Śaṅkaradeva's movement spread rapidly throughout the northeast region in large part because of its simple, direct message of devotional love (*bhakti*) of God in a personal form and its accessibility to individuals of any class or caste.

Śaṅkaradeva was quite critical of what he saw as the idolatry and bloody ritualism of the time—and above all, left-hand Śākta Tantra, with its "gruesome rites" and "worship of innumerable gods and goddesses for worldly benefits."[11] From Śaṅkaradeva's perspective, "Society was moth-eaten from within . . . The land was infested with teachers of Vāmācāra Tantra with their philosophy of sex and plate. Amongst religious rites the most spectacular were bloody sacrifices . . . to deafening drums, night vigils in virgin worship and lewd dances of temple women."[12] Thus in his *Kīrttanaghoṣa*, Śaṅkaradeva suggested that God had in fact become incarnate in the form of the Buddha in order to confuse the wicked with "the left-hand scriptures" (*vāmānaya śāstra*), and that God would finally return at the end of the age in the form of Kalkī in order to destroy the left-hand heretics and establish the Truth.[13] Śaṅkaradeva's closest disciple and successor, Mādhava (1489–1596) was also originally a Śākta and defended the practice of blood sacrifice in a famous debate with Śaṅkaradeva, before finally conceding and converting to the Vaiṣṇava faith.

Initially, Śaṅkaradeva's reformist movement and his critique of Śākta ritualism drew intense hostility from the *brāhmaṇs* of the region, who complained to the Ahom kings. Mādhava was imprisoned and another disciple was beheaded, while Śaṅkaradeva was forced to flee from place to place to avoid persecution. After leaving Assam to visit various holy sites, Śaṅkaradeva returned to the Koch kingdom, where he was initially met with hostility by king Naranārāyaṇa, who arrested and tortured two of his disciples. However, the saint presented himself at the king's court and persuaded him by the profundity of his learning and the depth of his faith.[14] Finally, Śaṅkaradeva settled in the town of Bheladonga in Cooch Behar, where he died at the age of 120. The saint left behind a massive body of literature, including numerous poetic works, such as his magnum opus *Kīrttanaghoṣa*, treatises on *bhakti*, translations of the *Bhāgavata Purāṇa* and *Rāmāyaṇa*, as well as numerous dramas and songs.

Śaṅkaradeva's devotional faith is often referred to simply as *ekaśaraṇa nāma-dharma*, meaning the religion of worship of the one true God (Viṣṇu, particularly in his incarnation as Kṛṣṇa) through recitation of his name (*nāma*). As Śaṅkaradeva put it in his *Bhaktiratnākara*, "There is only one religious duty, the worship of this god.

There is only one *mantra*, the name of this god."[15] All other deities are seen as mere manifestations of Viṣṇu, meaning that the worship of any other god or goddesses is useless. In contrast to Bengali Vaiṣṇavism, Śaṅkaradeva's *bhakti* does not involve the worship of Kṛṣṇa's female consort, Rādhā—most likely because of his fierce rejection of Śāktism and the focus on the female aspect of the divine. Moreover, in contrast to other *bhakti* traditions, it focuses primarily on the *dāsya* attitude, that is, the role of the devotee as a "slave" (rather than a friend, mother, or lover) of God. In place of elaborate ritual, sacrifice, or esoteric rites, Śaṅkaradeva's devotional worship focuses primarily on the remembrance of God's name through chanting, prayer, and devotional singing (*kīrtan*). All other rites and practices, including "*tantra, mantra . . . yajña*," and so forth are utterly surpassed by the devotional remembrance of Hari's name.[16] Indeed, Śaṅkaradeva has particular scorn for the left-hand Tantric worship with "women, wine and meat" (*strī-madya-māṃsa sevā*), an ignorant and futile practice that only leads sinful fools to their own destruction.[17]

In this most degenerate cosmic age, the Kali Yuga, when human beings are frail and weak, sacrifices are useless, and singing the name is the simplest, most direct, most appropriate form of worship: "[The same result that was attained] in Kṛta age by meditation on Viṣṇu, in the Tretā age by worship with sacrifices, and in the Dvāpara age by rituals [is attained] in the Kali age by singing the name of Hari."[18]

Śaṅkaradeva's neo-Vaiṣṇavism does, however, place great emphasis on the importance of the guru or teacher as the one who shows the way to salvation. Indeed, the novice should see the guru as god and respect him as such: "God and guru are one, different only in body."[19] Initiation therefore means taking shelter under the guru and surrendering oneself to God, to the guru, and the name. Unlike other forms of Hinduism in the region at the time, the faith was open to men of all castes, and Śaṅkaradeva was famous for giving initiation to indigenous peoples, untouchables, and Muslims without hesitation. For true devotional love of God, caste, class, and scriptural knowledge are irrelevant, and even the lowest of untouchables is considered equal to the highest priest of sacrifice and makes the supreme sacrificial offering when he sings Kṛṣṇa's name:

> Even a *caṇḍāla*, as soon as he takes Hari's name, becomes the true priest of sacrifice.[20]

A *caṇḍāla* who has Hari's name on his tongue is considered the most honorable . . . One who has Hari's name on his lips performs all austerities, sacrifices, and offerings of gifts. He is considered a twice-born knower of the Vedas.[21]

If one knows the words of Kṛṣṇa, why does he need to be a *brāhmaṇ* by birth? Let him simply remember Hari day and night. Devotion does not care if he has a caste or not.[22]

Here we see that Śaṅkaradeva adopted a fundamentally different attitude toward purity and impurity that represents a striking break with the Śākta Tantric path. Rather than unleashing and channeling the power of the impure through polluting substances and violations of caste in Tantric ritual, Śaṅkaradeva rejects the very categories of "pure" and "impure" altogether. From the *bhakti* perspective, an untouchable who is devoted to Hari is more pure than a priest and even "purifies the threefold world," while a *brāhmaṇ* who is not devoted to God is worse than a *caṇḍāla*.[23]

Quite significantly, however, Śaṅkaradeva's attitude toward women was a bit more complex and ambivalent. On the one hand, he opened the door for women to receive initiation and positions of authority, and his own grand-daughter-in-law became the head of a major *satra*.[24] Yet on the other hand, he also warned of the dangers of female sexuality, advising his followers "not to entangle themselves in the dangerous web of women," since their sexual power has the potential to "intoxicate man" and "close his better senses."[25] As Śankaradeva described the potential perils of female sexuality:

In the world of illusion, the terrible illusion of woman [*ghora nārī māyā*] is the most despised. Even the heart of a great, perfected sage is captured by her sidelong glance. Her sight destroys prayer, penance and yoga. Knowing this, the wise avoid the company of women.[26]

Again, this is probably in part a response to the Assamese Śākta tradition, with its celebration of female sexuality and the power of sexual union. Indeed, Śaṅkaradeva appears to have defined his path sharply in contrast to Śākta Tantra, and above all the worship of the *yoni*, by offering women a place as spiritual authorities while warning against their dangerous power as sexual beings.

Finally, Śaṅkaradeva and his followers also introduced new kinds of Vaiṣṇava institutions that reshaped not just the religious but also the social life and communal organization of the northeast region. The two main structures he introduced were the *satras*, or monastic centers, and *nām-ghars*, or chanting houses. The *satras* basically consist of a guru (the *satrādhikār* or head of the monastery) and those disciples initiated by him, and these serve as centers of learning and study for Vaiṣṇava monks throughout the northeast. Under the Ahom kings, the *satras* received generous patronage and became powerful bodies with an established place in society. Although this patronage ended with the advent of British rule, there are still today more than 650 *satras* in the Assam valley, such as the famous *satras* on the great river island of Majuli in eastern Assam. The *nām-ghars*, meanwhile, have played a central role in the village life of Assam and serve as essentially the "religious congregation" of many local communities. The chanting houses represent an integrated association of households who combine for the purposes of "maintaining a local centre of devotional worship."[27] As the neo-Vaiṣṇava movement spread rapidly across Assam, the *nām-ghars* effectively became the basic structural unit of rural society in much of the region. This is a large part of the reason that the state remains predominantly Vaiṣṇava to this day and Śaṅkaradeva's devotional revival continues to inform both the religious and the social fabric of Assamese culture.

Not surprisingly, given its tremendous influence on Assamese culture and religious life, Śaṅkaradeva's reform movement also helped reshape and reform Tantra in the region, as well. As Mishra observes, the transgressive left-hand worship once performed at Kāmākhyā temple gradually dropped away and was replaced by more symbolic, right hand worship at roughly the same time that Śaṅkaradeva's powerful movement became dominant in the region:

> There must have been a period during which *vamacara* system of worship was in vogue in the temple. But now, this system is dispensed with. And the priest performs the puja being accompanied by the symbolic presence of a woman companion in the form of a red flower to his left side. ..this change over to a new system is not an isolated phenomenon. The reformative attitude is evident in Tantric literatures like the *Saktisangama* and the *Mahanirvana*. Incidentally, this reformative period in the Tantras coincides with the time of Sankaradev, the great

neo-Vaisnavite reformer of Assam. This adoption of a new system of worship at Kamakhya may have been influenced by his preachings.[28]

As we will see in Chapter 7, left-hand rites and the darker side of Tantra as the path of power never fully died out in Assam but remains part of the religious fabric of the region to this day. Yet the temple of Kāmākhyā itself has been largely purified of the transgressive left-hand rites and transformed into a "sweeter" devotional center of popular worship.

The extreme orient: British critiques of Tantra and the justification for colonial rule

If the critique of Śākta Tantra began with Śaṅkaradeva's devotional revival, it reached its most elaborate and at times almost comical form in the writings of British colonial authorities in the late nineteenth and early twentieth centuries. Due to the remoteness of Assam, its dense, jungle topography, and its huge diversity of indigenous tribes, languages and cultures, the British came relatively late to the region. And when they did, they commented endlessly on the decadent, corrupt, morally depraved nature of both the land and its peoples, which they saw as the most extreme example of the decadence and depravity characteristics of India as a whole. Indeed, the consistent, ever-repeated refrain in the British writings on Assam is that this is the most extreme, most exotic, dangerous, and bizarre part of the extreme Orient itself—a land of dense jungle, crude tribes, primitive superstition, epitome of all the darkest and most dangerous tendencies in the Indian mind.

One of the more entertaining accounts of a British explorer in Assam is that of the botanist F. Kingdon Ward, *Plant Hunting at the Edge of the World.* Ward describes in vivid detail what he calls the "backward provinces" of the northeast, which are separated from civilization by mountains and jungle and contain a "veritable Tower of Babel" of different primitive tribes languages, religions, traditions: "Burma and Assam have surprisingly little to do with India, either in geological or historical time; and not much to do with it in space. They are the backwaters of the great human migratory streams. Their population, eddying between the cold tablelands of innermost Asia and the fertile plains bordering the Indian Ocean, have drawn into their vortex the flotsam and jetsam of both." And the peoples of this extreme land are equally barbaric and strange: "It is a desolate region thinly inhabited by numerous tribes caught up in the web of hills, speaking different languages, having different customs and traditions."[29]

This account of the extreme Orient of Assam is repeated throughout British writing from the late nineteenth and early twentieth centuries, such as T.T. Cooper's narrative of his travels in the northeast hills of 1873. Cooper explains that before his travels in India, he had once had an exceptionally low opinion of the "Oriental character"; as he once put it, "mosquitoes and niggers were created solely for the annoyance of Europeans." But as a result of his travels in South Asia, his opinion of the Oriental character had risen to one slightly less disparaging (though no less condescending). Like most Orientals, he suggests, the Indian character is weak, superstitious, effete, and cruel. Yet under the proper guidance of just British rule, it can become peaceful and contented:

> Everywhere superstitious, more or less ignorant and extremely sensitive to the slightest wrong; when roused by real or fancied injustice, or an insult to their religious prejudices, turbulent, and cruel in the extreme; but where governed with justice and properly protected, always peace-loving, industrious, law-abiding and contented. Nowhere in the East will this opinion receive stronger confirmation than in British India.[30]

Lying as it does on the outermost, jungly fringe of India, Assam represents the most extreme example of the Oriental character. Assam itself is for Cooper a dark, mysterious, and dangerous place, "a wilderness of swampy forest, breeding deadly miasma, and teeming with wild beasts and reptiles."[31] And its people are equally dark and savage. By the British era, he writes, the Assamese had lost whatever former energy and civilization they might have had, descending into a "lethargic existence" and "listless apathy," with little moral standards and largely addicted to opiates: "The laxity of morals amongst the people is conspicuous, and this, coupled with the vice of an inordinate use of opium, constitutes one of the greatest drawbacks to industry and progress."[32]

However, perhaps the most influential and widely read British account of the region was Sir Edward Albert Gait's *History of Assam*, published in 1905 and soon made the standard text on the northeast. Gait comments repeatedly on the Assamese peoples' weakness, flaccidity, passivity, and femininity, with their "internal tendency towards disintegration," which he attributes to the warm, wet climate of the far northeast: "The soil of the Brahmaputra valley is fertile, but its climate is damp and relaxing, so that . . . there is a strong tendency towards physical and moral deterioration. Any race that had been long resident there . . . would gradually become soft and luxurious."[33]

Above all, British authors were particularly fascinated and horrified by the practice of animal sacrifice, which was repeatedly identified as one of the clearest signs of the degenerate and barbaric character of the Assamese. Thus Cooper provides a grisly description of a Mishmee yak sacrifice that reads much like an account of a Dionysian *sporagmos*, with raw bloody flesh hacked and torn apart by the frenzied savages; and he closes his description by noting that human beings, including two Christian missionaries had been sacrificially dismembered in exactly the same way:

> The slaughter is always performed with great ceremony. The animal, with a halter round its neck, is held by a slave, while the men of the house with drawn knives forma circle round it, the women and children standing in a group at a respectful distance from the men. Then, amidst a solemn silence the chief . . . steps forward with his large Thibetan knife, and calmly surveying the animal for a few minutes, with a sudden tiger-like spring, delivers a frightful cut on its loins, apparently paralyzing it. The chief then retires, and all the men rush in with horrible yells, hack and hew at the wretched beast until it falls with piteous groans, and long before life is extinct lumps of the quivering flesh are cut off and thrown to the women and children, who scramble for the warm bloody pieces, and, amidst frantic shouts of delight, carry them, to the house, where they are boiled for the feast, The ceremony is a ghastly spectacle, and sickened me, especially when Chowsam informed me that prisoners are killed in this way, and that the unfortunate missionaries, Crick and Bourie, had been surrounded and hacked to death in a similar manner.[34]

All of these colonial attitudes toward the Orient—the critique of its weakness, femininity, sexuality, and violence—came together in the British descriptions of Tantra in Assam. Throughout nineteenth- and twentieth-century British writings, Assam is repeatedly singled out as the original heartland and homeland of Tantra, and Tantra in turn is singled out as the clearest example of all the hyper-sexuality and savagery that lies in the deepest recesses of the Oriental mind itself. As Sir Charles Eliot explained in his widely read work, *Hinduism and Buddhism* (1921), the Śākta Tantric tradition of Assam really embodies the bizarre contradictions in Hinduism as a whole—its weird mixture of elaborate philosophical speculation with sensuality, black magic, and violent ritual:

> The strange inconsistencies of Śāktism are of the kind which are characteristic of Hinduism as a whole, but the contrasts are more violent and the monstrosities more conspicuous than elsewhere; wild legends and metaphysics are mixed together, and the peace that passes all understanding is to be obtained by orgies and offerings of blood.[35]

With its complex mix of indigenous tribal ritual and Śākta Hinduism, Kāmākhyā temple was thus widely regarded as the very epitome and epicenter of this bizarre Tantric monstrosity. As Sir Charles James Lyall wrote in his report on "The Province of Assam," for the British *Journal of the Society of the Arts* in 1903:

> The celebrity of the temple of Kamakhya at Gauhati, and its importance as a centre of that bloody and sensual form of worship of Śiva and his Consort called *Tantrik*, are beyond question. The renown of this *Tirtha* is spread not only throughout Assam but also in Bengal and the chief scriptures in the latter province reckon Kamakhya in Kamrup as their most notable holy place. What we know of the religion of the Hinduised aboriginals shows that it conformed generally to this sanguinary type. Human sacrifice was common.[36]

Quite significantly, Lyall notes that the practice of human sacrifice to the dreaded Kālī led directly to the British Government confiscating portions of the northeast region. Allegedly, in 1832, two British subjects were seized inside the British territory of Sylhet by a band of Jaintias and dragged off to be sacrificed to the dark goddess Kālī. The two subjects apparently escaped, however, and the British authorities sternly warned the Jaintia king, Rām Siṅgh, to prevent such an incident in the future. Just a few months later however, four more British subjects were said to have been kidnapped and three of them actually sacrificed by the rāja of Gobha, one of the chieftains under the Jaintia king and allegedly acting under the orders of Rām Siṅgh.[37] According to Lyall's account, it was largely because of this outrageous violation of human decency and basic civility that the British were forced to seize and take command of this large territory:

> Jaintia, a country covering nearly 600 square miles and stretching from the neighborhood of Sylhet town to the Cachar frontier, remained independent under a ruler of Khasi lineage until 1835, when . . . it was confiscated in consequence of a human sacrifice performed by the Raja, who immolated three British subjects kidnapped from the Nowgong district, on the northern side of the Jaintia hills, as victims to Kali.[38]

Indeed, the British authorities repeatedly used the example of the barbarism, idolatry, and sexual perversion of Śākta Tantra to justify the need for British rule in the northeast. Thus in 1873, T.T. Cooper spoke disparagingly of the depraved and immoral character of the Assamese, their superstitious idolatry and addiction to opium, and looked forward to the day when sensible British rule would apply its gentle but firm hand to control this degenerate people: "I earnestly hope the day may soon arrive when the Government, having gained complete control and supervision of the people, may be able by some means to stamp out the vice."[39] Likewise, writing in the years after the British had taken control of the region, Sir Edward Gait praised the Empire as the only power that could save this region from its own degenerate decay and moral malaise, thus rescuing it from being overrun by some still worse barbarian race:

> The history of the Ahoms shows how a brave and vigorous race may decay in the "sleepy hollow" of the Brahmaputra valley; and it was only the intervention of the British that prevented them from being blotted out by fresh hordes of invaders.[40]

Thus the British "civilizing mission" found perhaps its greatest rationale in the extreme Orient of Assam and the exotic rites of Kāmākhyā and her Tantric devotees.

American missionaries in Assam: The doorway to the souls of Asia

Unlike much of the rest of India, however, Assam and the northeast states were "colonized" not so much by the power of the British Raj directly as by the power of the American Baptist and other missionaries who began preaching in the region in the early nineteenth century. Because of the huge diversity of ethnic groups and cultures in Assam, the British East India Company actually had a good deal of trouble administering the region and so turned to the Christian missionaries for aid. Their initial invitation to the British Baptists in Serampore was passed along to their American counterparts in the hopes of buttressing "the efforts of the handful of colonial administrators in 'elevating the character' of the people of this new territory."[41] And the American Baptists, in turn, took up the challenge in large part because they saw Assam as a key point of entry into the vast and previously inaccessible parts of Southeast and Central Asia that lay beyond the mountainous boundaries of the region. Assam was thus "envisaged as the doorway to an estimated 170 million people in Asia."[42] Indeed, the missions became the medium for a kind of "indirect rule" in the northeast hills, an area where any revenues from taxation could hardly meet even the bare administrative costs of direct colonial rule.[43] Ironically, one of the early centers of the American missionary activity in the far northeast of Assam was Sadiya, which was seen as the key gateway to the larger Asia beyond Assam.[44] As we saw in previous chapters, Sadiya was also the locus of the infamous Tāmreśvarī temple, long known for the performance of human sacrifices and the worship of the goddess in her most terrible form as the "eater of raw flesh."

Under the British colonial regime, many Hindu institutions—above all, Śākta Tantra—lost the royal patronage they had enjoyed for centuries. This provided a clear opportunity for the American missionaries to offer Christianity as an attractive alternative in the religious market, promising both spiritual and material advantages to converts. As Sanjib Baruah comments,

> Colonial rule quickly brought about a sea-change in Assam's cultural universe. The new world of ideas and material goods the missionaries brought to the hill people—western education, modern health care and so on—was bound to make differentiation from the Assamese a more attractive road to collective social mobility.[45]

On the whole, however, the missionaries had a more optimistic—though arguably also more condescending—view of the Assamese than had the British colonial authorities. Overall, the Assamese were consistently portrayed in missionary accounts as "extremely indolent and lacking in enterprise," and yet also "simple-minded, good-natured and law-abiding people;" though "dirty and bloodthirsty," the hills tribes were also said to possess a "purity of life truthfulness and hospitality."[46] According to one nineteenth-century American Baptist missionary account, "As a class [the Assamese] are idolaters . . . Thus the twin sisters, ignorance and superstition, have held almost undisputed sway—mutually rivaling each other in competing the degradation of the mass of the people."[47] But despite their ignorance and superstition, the Assamese had great potential to be converted to the guiding light of Christ. Indeed, many missionaries considered the widespread presence of non-Hindu tribal religions in the region actually to be a good thing, since it at least prevented the populace from falling into the much worse "destructive vortex of Hinduism," particularly in its bloody and sexual Śākta Tantric forms. As the missionary Sydney Endle wrote in 1911, "Their religion stands in very marked, not to say violent, contrast with the teaching of the Faith in Christ,"[48] whereas at least the tribal rituals saved the people from falling into the worst form of pseudo-religious perversion:

> These Kachari festivals . . . have their good side in that they help to keep the people to some extent beyond the influence of the destructive vortex of Hinduism, in which their simple primitive virtues might otherwise be so readily engulfed, and the adoption of which . . . is invariably accompanied by a grave and deep-seated deterioration in conduct and character.[49]

In sum, it became the task of the missionaries to "humanize" the peoples of the northeast, to "regenerate" them and so "redeem them from their utter backwardness." [50] As the Baptist writer, Anna Canada Swain, described the heroic efforts of young Christian missionaries in this dense and dangerous land in her 1935 book, *Youth Unafraid:*

> To this very rural country abounding in great fertile plains and rugged mountains, in tropical jungles filled with all kinds of game and tribes untouched by civilization, came a little group of earnest consecrated youth.[51]

The missionaries were quite clear about the fact that they worked hand in hand with the British colonial government to "civilize" this dark valley; indeed, they were the spiritual light that worked harmoniously together with the martial power of the British authorities to settle this dangerous, superstitious, and bloodthirsty land: "Backed and protected by the British administration these missionaries converted the tribes to Christianity in large numbers and reclaimed them to civilization."[52] Thus, they worked together with the British government to put a stop to head-hunting among tribes such as the Nagas, which had "profoundly changed the mode of life of all the tribes in the administered area."[53] But at the same time, the missionaries also forbade most other traditional practices such as drinking wine and celebrating indigenous ceremonies; "Christian Garos discarded earlier practices of propitiating by sacrifices the spirits and demons . . . replacing traditional music for Christian hymns . . . and sacrifices for foreign medicines."[54]

In one astonishingly honest letter from 1852, Rev. Miles Bronson cheerfully describes the rapid decline of traditional rituals, Hindu priests, and temples once they had lost royal patronage and come under British rule. He joyously prays, moreover, that God might hasten their collapse to make way for the spread of Christianity:

> I feel rejoiced to find that full two thirds of the priesthood are in trouble. They were formerly upheld and honored by the Assamese kings, but now they are on a footing with other subjects. Their incomes and their influence are decreasing, their places of worship tumbling down, their slaves all liberated, dissensions are springing up among them. If they oppress, they are liable to be brought up and punished in the magistrate's court, and they know not what to do. I verily believe that God will ere long remove this great impediment to the spread of the gospel out of the way, and therefore do I rejoice. May God help us to do something to hasten their downfall![55]

Indeed, *even after* the end of colonial rule and the decision to leave India, many British authorities argued for holding onto the northeast hills areas in order to "save" the tribal populations from falling back into the destructive vortex of Hinduism with all its sensuality and bloodshed. As Colonel J.C. Wedgewood wrote in the case of the Nagas, most of whom had converted to Christianity: "they must not be converted from good Nagas or whatever they are into bad Hindus."[56]

It is perhaps a testimony to this sentiment that American Christian missionaries still continue today to work aggressively in the northeast in order to win new converts from this dark valley. While riding the Brahmaputra Express from Kolkata to Guwahati in January 2000, in fact, I happened to sit next to a middle-aged white American missionary and his wife from Texas (or rather, I was intentionally seated next to them, since the three of us were the only white people on the train). When the missionary asked what I was doing in India and learned that I had studied Sanskrit, Bangla, and Assamese, he expressed amazement that I had bothered to learn some of their "tribal dialects." When I asked him what he was doing there, he explained that he was there to help bring the Word of God from the "wealthiest nation on earth, America," to these poor, simple, tribal peoples who had lived so long under the cloud of superstition. To demonstrate his point, he pulled out a steel, folding multi-tool that had knives, screw-drivers, clippers, and so on all built into one collapsing unit; he proudly showed it to the Indian passenger sitting in the opposite seat, a 30-ish, well-dressed man, who, as I had learned earlier, was a computer engineer. Displaying the multi-tool, the missionary declared, "See, this is made in America, the richest nation on earth, the greatest country in the world. No—now, don't touch it! You could get hurt."[57] The young Indian passenger yawned with a bored expression.

I moved to another compartment and wished the missionary well on his journey.

Conclusions: The conversion of the northeast and the decline of Tantra

Together, the three forces of *bhakti* reforms, British colonization, and Christian missionary activity have largely undermined the political power of Tantra in Assam over the last several hundred years. Still today, on the local village level, Vaiṣṇava *bhakti* remains the dominant religious and social structure in Assam, organizing much of rural society through its network of *satras* and *nām-ghars*. The Hindu kings of the region, with their blood sacrifices to the goddess, were progressively replaced by rational, masculine imperial authority. Meanwhile, the majority of the hill tribes of the northeast states converted to Christianity, which today comprises about 86 per cent of the population of Mizoram, 67 per cent of Nagaland, and 47 per cent of Meghalaya.[58]

Indeed, if the northeast was long imagined to be the most extreme eastern fringe of the extreme Orient, and if the Tantric worship of Kāmākhyā was imagined to be the worst example of all that was wrong with the Indian mind, then it was the northeast Śākta tradition that was most in need of reform, colonization, and religious conversion. Tantra, in short, provided the clearest evidence and greatest justification for the need for strong imperial rule, supported by the healthy moral influence of Christianity. Without the royal patronage they had enjoyed for centuries, the Śākta Tantric traditions gradually declined as a major political power and retreated more and more to the margins of Assam's social and cultural life. Indeed, today, even the majority of Indian historians appear to have internalized these negative images of Assamese Tantra coming down from Vaiṣṇava, British, and Christian sources. Throughout even the most respectable Indian scholarship, we see Assam regularly associated with narratives of shocking sexual perversity, barbarous rites, evil magic, and chicanery in the guise of religion. For example:

> In the name of religion . . . all sorts of atrocities were committed at the altar of the Devī temple [Kāmākhyā] . . . Above all, Tantricism collected and emphasized what is in fact superficial, trivial and even bad in Indian religion. It completely ignored its higher sides.[59]

> An atmosphere of mystery shrouded the whole country inasmuch as Kamarupa became known to the outside world as a land of black art and necromancy . . . Superstitions held the uncouth in very firm grip and made them easy victims of malicious gods and rapacious magicmen.[60]

Demonized by Vaiṣṇava reformers, British colonial authorities, Christian missionaries, and Indian scholars alike, much of Tantra has become reduced in the popular imagination to black magic, occultism, and chicanery. As White observes, "many Hindus in India today deny the relevance of Tantra to their tradition, past or present, identifying what they call '*tantra mantra*' as so much mumbo-jumbo."[61] And Assam in particular is widely regarded as the land *par excellence* of the darker side of *tantra mantra*.

Yet as we will see in the following chapter, the power of Tantra and the energy of the goddess as Śakti have never been easy to eradicate from the region, and they survive to this day in a variety of new, often revised forms.

Chapter Seven

THE POWER OF THE GODDESS IN A POSTCOLONIAL AGE: TRANSFORMATIONS OF TANTRA IN THE TWENTIETH AND TWENTY-FIRST CENTURIES

> You have very, very powerful female mendicants who exist even now . . . Even today the Devī comes into women . . . We have actual physical women . . . who conduct and lead entire cults of people. So in that sense the Devī is still alive.
>
> —A contemporary female devotee, Assam (2001)[1]

> How strange it was to worship in America! . . . Traveling from community to community, we were dismayed to find so many religious businesses filled with so few spiritual people!
>
> —Swami Satyananda Saraswati, *Shree Maa: The Life of a Saint* (1997)[2]

> If you think sexual and spiritual bliss can't be found in today's fast-paced world, you haven't experienced *Urban Tantra*. . . . No matter what your gender, sexual preference or erotic tastes, *Urban Tantra* will expand your notions about pleasure and open you up to new heights of intimacy and sexual fulfillment.
>
> —Barbara Carrellas, *Urban Tantra* (2007)[3]

In the wake of the new challenges posed by the rival powers of the *bhakti* revival, the spread of Islam, Christian missionary activities, and colonial rule, Tantra largely declined in most of South Asia as a major social and political force. With the exceptions of Tibet, Nepal, and Bhutan, Tantra was displaced as a tradition tied to royal patronage in South Asia and has since survived largely on the margins of power, in rural areas, in tribal communities, and in more remote regions such as the northeast states and the far south of India. Today, Tantra in India is indeed still very much alive, but in a rather different form than it had been prior to British colonial rule. No longer tied to royal patronage or the power of the king, Tantra and the Tantric concepts of *kāma* and *śakti* have been transformed and redefined in a number of critical ways.

In the case of Assam, we can see at least three key transformations over the last 200 years. First, there is what I would call the *institutionalization and exotericization of Tantra.* Today, the worship of the goddess Kāmākhyā is concerned not primarily with esoteric sexual rites (though these do still exist) but rather with large public festivals and *pūjās* for the thousands of pilgrims who come through on a daily basis. Second, there is the *reduction of Tantra to the level of folk medicine and mundane (and often black) magic.* As we have seen, Tantra has all along been partly concerned with the acquisition of magical powers (*siddhis*) and the ability to control the material world. Yet in the wake of colonization, Tantra has been increasingly reduced to these more mundane ends and often defined purely in terms of folk magic aimed not so much at radical liberation as at healing loose teeth, preventing lice, and stopping thieves.[4] Third and perhaps most interesting, there is what I would call the *globalization and universalization* of Tantra in a transnational context, as we see in the case of internationally famous gurus like Shree Maa of Kāmākhyā. Although she is herself seen as an embodiment of Kāmākhyā, Shree Maa is hardly a left-hand *tāntrikā.* Instead, she is a guru uniquely adapted to a global audience of spiritual seekers amidst a radically pluralistic, eclectic, and constantly changing spiritual marketplace.

Finally, the most extreme version of this sort of globalization and transnationalization of Tantra is the variety that we find on the shelves of every major book store in America, all over Amazon.com, and everywhere on the Internet, namely, the *Complete Idiot's Guide* version of Tantra. In its "Idiot's" incarnations, this 1500-year-old tradition has been increasingly commodified and mass marketed to an audience of spiritual consumers, where it is essentially reduced to a technique for achieving enhanced sexual pleasure. Today, when anyone with twenty dollars to spend can discover *Tantric Secrets: 7 Steps to the Best Sex of Your Life*, it would seem that the Orientalist fascination with the exotic

East is still alive and well.[5] If anything, it has assumed new and more pervasive forms adapted to what Dennis Altman calls the "new commercialization of sex" in a global order dominated by the sprawling McWorld of consumer capitalism.[6]

Yet all of these three trends, we will see, help illuminate the unique presence of Tantra in the contemporary world, as these old traditions adapt to new historical contexts, to new media landscapes, and to the strange new dilemmas of an increasingly globalized, interconnected new world. Indeed, they reveal the continuing power of Tantra in a rapidly changing era where it enjoys less political patronage but perhaps more popular support and global interest.

Kāmākhyā temple today: The exotericization and sweetening of Tantra

Like many other Tantric centers of modern India, Kāmākhyā temple has gradually evolved from a center of extreme, transgressive, and esoteric left-hand practice to a publicly accepted and quite "mainstream" aspect of religious life in modern Assam. A similar pattern of the "exotericization" and "institutionalization" of once esoteric Tantric traditions can be seen in many other examples from northeast India, particular in colonial Bengal. As Rachel McDermott has shown, the goddess Kālī underwent a significant process of "sweetening" and "softening" during the colonial period. During the eighteenth and nineteenth centuries, the once terrifying, violent, sexual and esoteric Tantric goddess was transformed into the loving, maternal goddess of popular devotional worship today: "After a fifteen hundred year career in the Sanskrit religious texts as a dangerous and blood-lusting battle queen and a Tantric deity incorporated into esoteric rituals . . . . Kālī started to develop . . . an additional dimension—that of a compassionate divine mother."[7]

Similarly, in my own work on the Kartābhajā sect of Bengal, I found that this once highly esoteric Tantric tradition underwent a profound transformation during the British colonial period. In response to the attacks from Christian missionaries, colonial authorities, and Hindu reformers, the Kartābhajās gradually shifted from a transgressive Tantric tradition into a popular devotional sect with a strong institutional hierarchy. Indeed, the most transgressive sexual rites of *parakīyā* love or sex with another man's wife became stigmatized as the "stinking fruit in the garden of love." In place of the more radical left-hand rites, the Kartābhajās progressively substituted a kind of "deodorized" devotional worship and large public festivals for a mass popular audience.[8]

Kāmākhyā has clearly undergone a similar kind of "sweetening" and "deodorization," shifting from the bloody and transgressive rites of left-hand Tantra to an increasingly popular, devotional, and right-hand form of worship. As we saw in the previous chapter, most of the left-hand rites at the temple itself have largely disappeared in the wake of Vaiṣṇava reforms, British colonial critiques and Christian missionary activity, and have slowly been replaced by right-hand forms of symbolic offerings to the goddess. As Mishra notes, "At present, *nitya pūjā* of the goddess follows *dakṣiṇācāra* method of Tāntrick worship."[9] In place of secret rites carried out by a few *tāntrikas* to the goddess in her bloodthirsty form and offerings to the *yonis* of female *śaktis*, most of Kāmākhyā's worship today consists of thousands of pilgrims coming to offer devotional worship at the *yoni pīṭha*. Offerings of goats, pigeons, fish, and buffaloes still comprise a significant part of the temple's daily routine and help perpetuate its reputation of dangerous power and bloodshed. And devotees still come seeking the *śakti* of the goddess. But they rarely come in search of Tantric *siddhis* or the dangerous powers of the *yoginīs*; instead, they seek the more practical benefits of child-bearing, health, and material well-being through the power of the goddess' maternal, loving grace.

The more transgressive left-hand rites and the literal use of the *pañcamakāras* do indeed continue to this day—though no longer in the main temple itself, but primarily on the margins of the temple complex, such as in the smaller Bhairavī temple down the steep hill several hundred feet below the main temple.[10] Left-hand rites also continue to be practiced throughout the less urban areas of central and eastern Assam, though much less visible than they might have been a few hundred years ago. Between 2000 and 2008, I have interviewed hundreds of Śāktas in Assam, Meghalaya, and Tripura, who confirm that the left-hand traditions are indeed alive and well in the northeast region, even if less central to major Śākta centers like Kāmākhyā. As one Śākta from eastern Assam told me, "*vāmācāra* has always been a secret practice, a hidden path. Nowadays it is very secret. This has always been a path for few to follow. Now it is for very, very few."[11]

Today, Kāmākhyā temple remains vibrant with a wide array of major celebration and festivals that attract thousands of pilgrims; and throughout these popular devotional celebrations, we can still detect lingering elements of both Tantric and pre-Hindu tribal traditions. Without engaging in an extensive discussion of all of the many *pūjās* celebrated here, I will just mention a few of the more important and interesting ones. As in Bengal and other parts of India, the festival of Durgā Pūjā in the autumn month of Āśvina is one of the largest celebrations at Kāmākhyā, and it retains many older Tantric elements. Blood sacrifice, for example, remains a central part of the massive, 16-day celebration, as pigeons, goats, and ducks are offered in all the goddess temples on Kāmākhyā hill, while buffaloes are offered at the main temple. Perhaps most interesting is the fact that the *pūjā* also involves the sacrifice of a human replica or "mock-man" made of wheat dough[12]—a ritual that is very likely the vestigial remainder of the human sacrifices described in the *Kālikā Purāṇa*, those offered by Assam's past kings, and perhaps also those offered by various indigenous peoples. *Kumārī-pūjā*, the worship of virgins as embodiments of the goddess' power in its most potent, potential form, is also a key part of Durgā Pūjā, and 1 to 16 virgins are successively honored on each of the 16 days of the festival.[13]

A second major festival that contains many older and non-Hindu elements is the worship of the snake goddess, Manasā, held in Śravana month (July–August). Also known as Viṣahārī, the "remover of poison," Manasā has traditionally been worshipped throughout the northeast during times of disease and epidemic. However, at Kāmākhyā, the worship of Manasā is not done in the central chamber of the temple but rather in the outer *nāṭa-mandira* part of the temple, which suggests that the worship of Manasā is an indigenous, non-Hindu practice that was only "grudgingly adopted into the regular religious service of the temple."[14] Worship of snake gods is well known among the indigenous peoples of the northeast, such as the Rabhas and Khasis. The Khasis are well known for their worship of the snake deity U Thlen, allegedly at one time with offerings of human sacrifice. Many suspect that Manasā was thus "originally a local deity," who was only later roughly Hinduized.[15] Many folktales about the origin of Manasā Pūjā also point to its probable non-Hindu roots. According to one narrative, there was a wealthy merchant named Chand Sadagar who refused to worship the snake goddess and insisted on worshipping Śiva alone. Thus the goddess, "through wile and trickery," killed off all his sons, sank his merchant boats, and reduced him to destitution. Finally, they reached a compromise whereby the merchant would worship the snake goddess with his left hand while continuing to worship Mahādeva with his right.[16] Once again, this narrative seems to point to the negotiation between *vāma* and *dakṣiṇa,* left and right, heterodox and orthodox modes of worship in Assam.

One of the most interesting aspects of Manasā Pūjā, which also clearly points to non-Hindu influences, is the dance of the *deodhās.* The term *deodhā* or *deodhāi* has for centuries been used to refer to the tribal priests of many of the northeast tribes, such as the Ahoms, Chutiyas, and Bodo-Kacharis, and many scholars believe the dance to be is a direct carry-over from non-Hindu traditions, probably the Bodo-Kacharis, into the cycle of the temple.[17] To the rhythm of pounding drums, the *deodhās* dance in an increasingly wild and frenzied manner until they achieve a state of ritual possession called *dakat parā.* Indeed, they are believed to have become temporary incarnations of the gods themselves, the vehicles of Śiva, Viṣṇu, and Śakti in human form, and are worshipped as such by the thousands of devotees with various offerings of goat, pigeon, and duck sacrifices. During their state of possession, the *deodhās* display various supernatural powers and perform miraculous feats such as dancing on the edge of a sharp blade. The dance continuities well into the night and concludes with the *deodhās* prostrating themselves before the snake goddess and finally returning to their normal human states.[18] On the whole, Manasā Pūjā is perhaps the clearest example of a variety of indigenous, non-Hindu traditions and even quasi-shamanic elements being "Hinduized" and assimilated in complex ways into the mainstream life of the temple.

But surely the most famous and widely popular of Kāmākhyā's festivals today is Ambuvācī (*ambubachi* or *ameti* in local pronunciations), the celebration of the earth's menstruation in the summer month of Āṣāḍha, which we discussed briefly in Chapter 2. At least as it is celebrated in its present form, Ambuvācī is a clear example of the "exotericization," "softening," and "sweetening" of a Tantric tradition. Here the *yoni pīṭha* once associated with esoteric ritual and sexual sacrifices to the goddess in her most terrible forms becomes the center of a massive popular celebration attended by hundreds of thousands of devotees seeking the menstrual blood of the goddess in her most loving, maternal form.

Estimates of the numbers of pilgrims vary from 70,000 to 200,000, coming from all the northeast states as well as Bengal, Bihar, and Uttar Pradesh.[19] However, Ambuvācī is also a major pilgrimage destination for hundreds of *sādhus, yogis, tāntrikas, aghorīs, nāths, nāgas*, and other holy men and women from all over India, who set up small encampments around the temple grounds. Indeed, it is even a popular destination for many "white *sādhus*," that is, Western hippies and seekers of *nirvāṇa* (and/or cheap hashish) who often wear their hair in long dreadlocks in imitation of the Indian *sādhus*.[20] Finally, like most festivals in India, Ambuvācī also gives birth to a huge, teeming and prosperous marketplace, as small merchants, peddlers, and vendors from all over northeast India come to sell their various wares.[21]

Of the hundreds of thousands of devotees who attend the festival, few come seeking the terrifying power of a wild, impure, and transgressive left-hand goddess; rather, they seek the more maternal grace of a loving goddess who will hear her children in time of need. Instead of the oral consumption of menstrual blood in secret Tantric rites dedicated to the wild and impure goddess, thousands of pilgrims now come to receive the small pieces of cloth (*aṅga-vastra*) believed to be moistened with the menstrual blood of the goddess in her loving form.[22] In fact, many priests and devotees today will deny that Kāmākhyā is ever even "impure" during her menstruation, preferring to use the more benign description that "she is just resting."[23]

Significantly, the number of female pilgrims far outnumbers that of males, which clearly reflects the festival's association with fertility, reproduction, and childbearing. As one devotee put it in 2000, Kāmākhyā is "your mother, your Mā, Amma, your mommy . . . Any moment she helps you, any time she helps you. She gives birth, eating, feeding."[24] The majority of the women I interviewed at Ambuvācī had come in hopes of either bearing children, bearing a son, healing a sick child, or receiving some other domestic aid.[25] As one female pilgrim from western Assam explained to me, "Kāmākhyā is our mother, and when we cry out to her, she hears us and helps us. She is a powerful mother, and she gives us her powerful aid."[26] However, the deeper symbolism of blood and the creative energy of Śakti is still pervasive at the festival, as the temple is dominated by all things red – red flowers, red vermillion, red-clad priests and Śāktas, all bearing the sign of the goddess' flowing power.[27]

One remarkable female devotee interviewed in 2000 narrates that she first dedicated herself to mother Kāmākhyā during the onset of her own puberty. Her first menstruation happened to coincide with the goddess' menstrual celebration, and to this day she still performs her *pūjā* using the red cloth that her mother gave her during that first

Ambuvācī. As she put it, "this is my Śakti. I forget everything. All troubles, all problems in my life."[28]

Perhaps not surprisingly, Ambuvācī has also been rediscovered and celebrated by many contemporary feminists, both Western and Indian. According to Janet Chawla, writing for Women's Feature Services, Ambuvācī represents a rare but empowering image of women's creative abilities, one that is much needed in a world still dominated by negative representations of the female body:

> The Ambubachi worship of the simultaneous phenomena of monsoon rain and menstrual bleeding may reveal an important contribution to global cultural representation of the female body. Kamakhya seems to question both the dominant religious legacies of the pollution inherent in female bodily processes . . . Ambubachi Mela provides a sacred space for empowering images of the female body—a space where the maternal and erotic aspects of women's lives are encoded and celebrated as divine.[29]

Again, as we discussed in Chapter 5, we might wonder how "empowering" it actually is for women to celebrate their identity with the sexual organ, menstrual blood, reproduction, and the earth. But nonetheless, this is clear evidence of the fact that the power of the goddess has persisted into the twenty-first century and taken on ever-new meanings in a postcolonial and now transnational context.

In sum, in its popularized forms today, Ambuvācī Melā continues but also transforms many older Tantric ideas surrounding the potency of menstrual blood and the circulation of the goddess' power through the circulation of bodily fluids. Today, the oral consumption of menstrual blood in esoteric ritual has been replaced by the public act of handing out symbolic pieces of red cloth, but the underlying meaning remains much the same. Though it now flows in new directions, the power of the goddess continues to circulate between the goddess and her devotees, just as the blood of buffalos, goats, and pigeons continues to flow over stones of her temple floor.

The jewel of desire: Magic, occult power, and worldly desire in popular Tantra

With its loss of royal patronage in the face of its new rival powers like the Vaiṣṇava reformers and Christian missionaries, Śākta Tantra underwent yet another transformation from roughly the sixteenth century onward. While worship at the great Kāmākhyā temple became increasingly sweetened, devotionalized, and de-odorized for a new massive popular audience, Tantra also took on a rather different form in the more marginal and remote parts of Assam. Today, in fact, Tantra in the northeast and in most parts of India is primarily associated not with steamy sexual rituals but rather with black magic and occult power. Ironically, while we in America and Europe have redefined Tantra to mean sexual ecstasy and nookie nirvana, most Indians today associate Tantra with the dark forces of magic and the manipulation of occult power for personal gain. While every American bookstore now has thousands of titles on the scintillating secrets of Tantric sex, nearly every corner bookstand and train-station newspaper vendor has several dozen little books for sale on the secrets of Tantric magic, the use of Tantric spells to control others and win lovers, the power of Tantra to find wealth and become successful in business.

As one contemporary author, Tāntrika Śrī Kāmadeu Pujārī, observes, the knowledge of *mantras, yantras*, and traditional plant medicines is forgotten and usually disdained by most educated Indians today. Yet it still survives and is well known to many folk exorcists (*ojās*) and village folk of rural northeast India.[30] Today on the street corners of Guwahati and Kolkata, or outside Kāmākhyā temple, one can find countless books on the subject of "*tantra-mantra*," mostly containing spells and uses of various plants, roots, and animals for health, material prosperity, and/or malevolent magic. A variety of texts go by the name of *Kāmarūpī Tantrasāra, Kāmākhyā Tantrasāra, Ādi o Āsal Kāmākṣyā Tantrasāra* ("the original and true essence of Kāmākhyā *tantra*), and *Kāmarūpīyā Tantramantra āru Ouṣadh* ("the *tantra, mantra* and medicine of Kāmarūpa).[31] Most of these are quite wonderfully illustrated with vivid color covers, typically portraying sinister *tāntrikas* raising ghouls or subduing victims to be offered as human sacrifices in cremation grounds littered with skulls while powerful goddesses lurk eerily in the background (Fig. 22). To this day, Kāmākhyā has a sinister reputation for the continued practice of the Tantric rite of *śava sādhanā*, the use of a fresh human corpse as a source of tremendous esoteric power. As Dehejia notes, "in the town of Kāmākhyā people rarely leave a corpse uncremated overnight for fear of losing it to tantric practitioners."[32]

Most of these contemporary popular texts appear to be derived from much older texts on occult powers, and in particular from a once-famous text called the *Kāmaratna Tantra* or "jewel of desire." The *Kāmaratna* seems to have been a remarkably popular and widely distributed text that has appeared in different incarnations all over India, ascribed to many different authors—such as Śrīnātha, Pārvatīputra, Nityanātha, Nāgabhaṭṭa, and Siddhanātha—and translated into numerous regional languages.[33] In 1913 an Assamese manuscript written on strips of bark was found in North Guwahati in the home of the Na-Gosain family, who trace their lineage traced back to the gurus of the Ahom kings.[34] Estimated to be at least 300 years old, the text covers a remarkable array of subjects, beginning with the infamous acts of Tantric magic, namely, subjugation (*vaśīkaraṇa*), attraction (*ākarṣaṇa*), immobilization (*stambhana*), enchantment (*mohana*), and eradication (*uccāṭana*; interestingly enough, this particular text does not include the sixth act of killing, *māraṇa*, though almost every one of the other thousands of similar texts on popular Tantra does). Thus we find spells for everything from the subjugation of young damsels (*bālā vaśīkaraṇa*), women (*strī vaśīkaraṇa*), and husbands (*pati vaśīkaraṇa*),[35] to controlling elephants and tigers, preventing fire, killing lice, removing household pests, winning games of dice, discovering buried treasure, and curing animal, fish, and insect bites.[36]

A large portion of the text does deal with sexual matters—but quite notably, almost nothing at all to do with either the sexual act itself or with sexual pleasure. Instead, its focus is on the far more practical matters of helping barren women to conceive, preventing miscarriage, causing abortion, curing pain in the womb, and curing labor pain.[37] Indeed, it even contains advice for removing vaginal hair and removing bad smell from the vagina (*yoni sugandhakaraṇa*).[38]

Some portions of the text read almost like a contemporary e-mail ad for Viagra or genital-enhancement. Thus, we find recipes for increasing sexual potency (try the juice from the root of the silk-cotton tree mixed with sugar, or the eggs of a house spider ground with honey and applied to the navel[39]); for increasing penis size (try applying the paste of a long pepper mixed with salt, milk, and sugar[40]); or for the development of breasts (try mixing cardamom, the root of a pomegranate tree and white mustard seeds roasted in a fire and plastered on the breasts for eight days[41]). Notably, the text also explains how to both cause and stop a woman's menstrual flow:

> If a woman drinks pigeon excrement mixed with honey, she will menstruate.[42]

> If she plasters the vagina with a paste made by grinding husked rice with the outer cover of a bulb of a water lily, the menstrual flow will stop.[43]

Again, a primary focus here is on the flow of desire and power through the flow of blood.

Almost nothing in this text, however, has anything to do with the more racy and titillating materials that most of us today associate with the label "Tantra." And yet, this is arguably the most influential and widely used form of Tantra in India today and largely what most Indians understand by the term in common parlance. Tantra, for most South Asians today, usually means either: a) dangerous black magic, or b) practical *mantras* and magical techniques used to achieve extremely this-worldly ends—namely, how to run a comfortable household, how to deal with friends, relatives and enemies, and how to procreate. I have been collecting popular Tantric texts for about 20 years and now have a sizable library of the genre in Bangla, Assamese, and Hindi, ranging in titles from *Sarva Manokāmana Siddhi Tantramantra* ("*tantras* and *mantras* for the attainment of all one's heart's desires"), *Sāontālī Vaśīkaraṇa Tantra* ("the *tantra* of subjugation belonging to the Sāontāls," an eastern tribal people known for magic), *Bṛhat Yantra-Mantra Vidhāna Rahasya* ("the secret of performing great *mantras* and *yantras*"), and so on.[44] In all of these, enhanced sexual pleasure and the art of "nookie nirvana" is completely irrelevant. This is perhaps the most telling difference between contemporary Western and contemporary Indian reappropriations of Tantra for a modern age: while the former seeks a form of ecstatic, liberating sexual experience for a happy consumer culture, the latter seeks a form of more mundane getting-by amidst a difficult world full of poverty, disease, and financial peril.

Yet this too, of course, may change as India becomes increasingly affluent, and the USA appears to be more and more a late-stage empire in rapid decline.[45] Soon it may be the Americans seeking financial aid from the Tantric goddess and Indians seeking their own sensual *nirvāṇas*.

Shree Maa of Kāmākhyā: The goddess of desire in the land of great illusion

While Tantra has largely declined as a political force in South Asia, it has assumed a variety of remarkable new forms in the late twentieth and twenty-first centuries, amidst the new transnational flows of people, ideas information. One of the most striking examples of the new transmutations of Tantra is the internationally famous female guru, Shree Maa of Kāmākhyā (Fig. 23). While rooted in many older Śākta traditions of Assam and Bengal, Shree Maa also reflects a kind of "*bhakti*-fication" of Kāmākhyā, a transformation of the goddess from a powerful, often terrifying Tantric goddess, into a more sweetened, devotional figure. But she also represents the globalization of Tantra for a transnational audience of spiritual seekers.

Born in Digboi, Assam, sometime between 1938 and 1948, Shree Maa came from a wealthy family descended from the great Bengali saint and poet, Rāmprasād Sen. From an early age Shree Maa recounts having a wide array of mystical experiences, visions, and trance states. Rather significantly, several of these early visions occurred at Kāmākhyā temple during the time of Ambuvācī Melā. For example, while visiting the temple with her family on the last day of Ambuvācī and the goddess' menstruation, Shree Maa received a vision of a blinding, bright light that knocked her unconscious amidst the pouring rain: "When I woke up I saw a bunch of sadhus were drying my cloth. Then Mother told me that now I could be free. I could go anywhere." Her own (human) mother became very angry with her, thinking she was just a silly child playing games. In response Shree Maa picked up an axe and hit herself repeatedly on the head with it. When they saw the child completely unscathed after repeated blows with an axe, her mother and family bowed down and praised her as a divine being.[46]

Elsewhere Shree Maa recounts another, still more remarkable trip to Kāmākhyā for the goddess' annual menstruation. Here she met a mysterious woman chewing a mouthful of betel nut, with red saliva flowing out of her mouth. In a very odd but symbolically loaded gesture, the strange woman put her red-stained mouth in Shree Maa's lap, and as she laughed and laughed, Shree Maa suddenly recognized that she was the goddess herself in human form:

> There was a big festival celebrating Mother Kamakhya's menstrual period and for three days the temple was closed . . . [O]ne day a dark skinned lady came to the homa. She had curly hair and was chewing betel nut, and red saliva was coming out of her mouth. She put her head in my lap, and she was laughing. My whole cloth became soaked, colored with the red water from her mouth and spotted with oil. She looked at me, and laughed and laughed. . . . Right away I knew who

> she was. She was Mother; a form of Mother who came to test . . . The next day was the Kamakhya Temple opening, after the third day of her period.[47]

In this remarkable passage, we see a clear chain of symbolic associations, all circulating around the image of blood, redness, and fluid: the mother goddess Kāmākhyā is menstruating; a mysterious figure identified as a form of the goddess appears with red juices flowing from her mouth; and these juices from the mother are then spilled onto the lap of Shree Maa, whose clothes are turned red. From mother to mother, from womb to lap, the circulation of blood and red fluids is complete.

In keeping with the classic Tantric dictum that "to the pure, all things are pure," Shree Maa also recounts seeing the entire universe as divine and therefore seeing no distinction between clean and unclean. Like the Kaula *siddhas* before her, she saw nothing as polluting or taboo: "I saw God everywhere. I would get on my knees and eat with the dogs because they were God too."[48]

From an early age, however, Shree Maa's theology was remarkably eclectic and syncretistic, and she had no trouble incorporating visions of Jesus with those of Rāmakṛṣṇa, Kālī, or Kāmākhyā. Indeed, she reports meeting with Jesus regularly since she was in the fourth grade: "Jesus would always play with me, that was so much fun. He would talk about his life and about how he was born." Apparently, Jesus revealed to her that he was himself also a transnational and univeralistic guru, who had visited India at the age of 7 and studied Sanskrit, learned Ayurvedic medicine, and debated pundits in Benaras.[49]

After attending college, Shree Maa spent a number of years wandering in the forests around Kāmakhyā and in the foothills of the Himalayas. She also entered into an extended period of austerity and penance, living for eight years on a daily meal that consisted of nothing more than a little piece of turmeric and basil leaves washed down with sandal paste mixed with water. In 1980, she is said to have weighed a mere 60 pounds.[50]

The White Sadhu: Shree Maa meets Sahib Sadhu and comes to America

While in the holy town of Bakreshwar, West Bengal, in 1980, Shree Maa encountered a complex and fascinating American-born figure known as Swami Satyananda, also called "the White Sadhu" or "Sahib Sadhu" (Fig. 24). According to his own narrative, Satyananda had been traveling in India for many years and had studied with an Indian *sādhu* in the Himalayas who initiated him in 1971. Satyananda's primary form of worship, we should note, was the worship of the goddess Caṇḍī and the *yajña* or fire sacrifice as his primary form of *sādhanā*—thus continuing the ancient theme of sacrifice in yet another new guise in the modern era.[51]

Not long after meeting, the white *sādhu* and Shree Maa became intimate spiritual companions and began traveling together throughout India. Even then, Shree Maa had begun to adopt a universalistic spiritual vision and rather eclectic practice. During her travels with Satyananda, she carried with her a portable shrine containing images of Kṛṣṇa, Durgā, Jesus, and Mecca, embodying her faith in the oneness of all religions.[52] In the early 1980s, Shree Maa received a divine message from her spiritual master, the great Bengali saint, Shri Ramakrishna (1836–86), who instructed her to leave India and travel to America. She was, he said, to "perform worship in the West as you do in the East" in order unite East and West: "The Motherland and Fatherland must be made one."[53]

Satyananda was initially opposed to the idea of returning to America—which he decried as a land of "religious businesses" and the "land of great illusion": "You can cut my head off, but I'm not going to America. It's Mahamaya land!"[54] But the two did come to the USA and eventually settled in an ashram near Napa, California, where they have attracted a large American audience. When Linda Johnsen's widely read book *Daughters of the Goddess* was published in 1994, with Shree Maa featured prominently, on the cover, their *ashram* was flooded suddenly with visitors hoping to meet the holy Mother of Kāmākhyā.[55]

From esoteric Tantra to a universal spiritual vision for a global world

Today, in her numerous biographies, written works, Web sites, and audio recordings, Shree Maa is presented as a global guru with a transnational following and a universal spiritual message: "Shree Maa . . . travels the world to share with devotees in the delight of worship and meditation. In addition to large families across America, Europe,

South America and Asia she has uncountable devotees in places too numerous to mention."[56] Likewise, her temple, the Devi Mandir in California, is described as a cosmopolitan spiritual hub for seekers from all over the world, bringing men and women of all backgrounds and ethnicities together for worship of the goddess:

> Devi Mandir is located in a suburb of cosmopolitan San Francisco bay Area, where we serve Hindus from around the world. They come in all colors from many countries both East and West, speaking many languages, and yet they all have one thing in common: when they enter into the temple, they leave all thoughts of divisions and become simply children of God, children of the Divine Mother.[57]

This sort of universalistic spiritual vision is embodied in the Devi Mandir itself, which features a vast "Cosmic Altar" containing dozens of Hindu gods and goddesses in a kind of divine smorgasbord of images. Likewise, one of the unique forms of worship at the temple is the "Cosmic Puja," which involves "the worship of all the Divine Beings of the Universe."[58] At the same time, Shree Maa has also incorporated elements of Christianity into her cosmic worship, and the temple also features images of Jesus and the Virgin Mary in addition to the many Hindu deities. To this day, Shree Maa celebrates Christmas "with Christmas carols, prayers to Jesus and even a Christmas tree. A sculpture of Jesus that Shree Maa made with her own hands is decorated with flowers and red and blue Christmas lights."[59] Perhaps the most striking example of this religious synthesis appears in her biography, *Shree Maa: The Life of a Saint*, which features an image of Shree Maa holding a white baby against a backdrop of the Manhattan skyline with the two figures of Jesus and Shri Ramakrishna standing behind her.[60]

The teachings of Shree Maa and Swami Satyananda are essentially rooted in much older Hindu *bhakti*, Śākta, and Tantric traditions of Assam and Bengal. Although drawing her spiritual vision from the Tantric seat *par excellence*, Kāmākhyā, Shree Maa herself never claimed to have any profound knowledge of Tantra; rather, she simply claimed to be immersed in the devotional love of her spiritual master, Ramakrishna, and humbly following his inner commands. While in Puri, Shree Maa was visited by a respected guru named Swami Vishnu Deva Vairagi, who asked her: "What *sadhana* have you been doing to come to this state? What kind of *tantra* have you been practicing, you who come from Kamakhya, the seat of *tantra*?" Shree Maa's humble reply was simply, "I know no *tantra*. I know nothing of *sadhana*. I have only been listening to the order of Shree Ramakrishna all my life, and I do what I do because of his orders."[61]

Some have described Shree Maa's practice as a kind of "right-handed Tantric tradition,"[62] one rooted in Tantra but interpreting the more transgressive aspects of the tradition symbolically rather than literally. However, in an interview, Satyananda explained that he prefers to describe their practice in far more universal terms that include but far surpass the limits of Tantra alone:

> We believe in One All-Pervading, Infinite Divinity, which resides in every being of Creation, and is especially manifest in the hearts of all humanity. That this Deity inspires within seekers sincerity, joy, love and wisdom, and the highest respect for all that lives. That all bodies are temples for the holy spirit, and that the duty of man is to honor God through loving service to all created beings, and attentive devotion in the pursuit of self-realization.[63]

Here we can clearly see that the worship of the powerful goddess Kāmākhyā has been significantly revised, adapted, and universalized, no doubt as part of an effort to appeal to a broader and now largely Western audience. The fierce Tantric goddess, traditionally worshipped with blood and transgressive ritual, has been transformed into a far more benign, loving, and maternal goddess with a universal spiritual message. Tantra, as they define it, is not a matter of blood sacrifice or sexual rites; rather, "in Tantra yoga the goal is to connect with [the God and Mother Goddess'] energy through prayer, recitation of texts, mantras, singing, meditation, and rituals. Faith and devotion is an integral part of this worship."[64] Tantra, as the Swami explained in an interview, is merely a "practical application" of *mantra* and *yantra*, and "all three are present in every spiritual experience."[65] Ultimately, in its fullest sense, Tantra simply "involves making every action one performs in life as a divinely consecrated offering to God."[66] As such, Satyananda is quite critical of popularized American versions of Tantra, which focus purely on the sexual dimension and thus completely miss the deeper spiritual dimension of the tradition:

> The popular versions of Tantra which place emphasis on only one aspect of that offering, namely sexuality ... are not comprehensive

systems of spirituality, but rather attempts at accenting the sensational with a new vocabulary.[67]

Likewise, Shree Maa and Satyananda also downplay the more transgressive and impure aspects of the goddess Kāmākhyā, and above all her annual menstruation during Ambuvācī Melā. From their perspective, the menstruating goddess is by no means "impure," but simply resting in a state of meditative poise until her period of seclusion is over:

> There is never a time when the Divine Mother of the Universe is impure, so the idea that the Goddess hides during Her period is a misunderstanding. The period of menstruation is a time when women can become extremely still and silent, and get in touch with the ultimate consciousness of their feminine nature . . . There was no issue of impurity.[68]

Shree Maa and the White Sadhu also rework and redefine the Kaula Tantric path along more devotional, far less transgressive lines. Thus, they list a hierarchy of eight practices (*ācāras*) that are essentially the same list found in classic *tantras* like the widely influential like *Kulārṇava Tantra,* which lists a gradation of practices leading from orthodox Vedic rites to the most secret and transgressive Kaula rites: "Vedic worship is greater than all others. But greater than that is Vaiṣṇava worship; and greater than that is Śaiva worship; and greater than that is Dakṣiṇācāra. Greater than Dakṣiṇācāra is Vāmācāra, and greater than Vāma is Siddhānta. Greater than Siddhānta is Kaula—and there is none superior to Kaula."[69] Shree Maa's list of practices is almost identical in name, but the practices themselves are redefined in far less transgressive, more benign terms:

> Vaishnavachara which means find our inspiration. Vedicachara which means learn about that which we love. Shaivachara which means practise that which we learn about. Vamachara which means, "Beloved Behavior," perform every action in life efficiently. Dakshinachara which means, "Preferred Path," reduce our necessity to perform worldly actions. Siddhantachara which means make our behavior correspond to the activities spoken of in the scriptures . . . . Yogachara means "Behavior of Union". Kulachara means "Behavior of Excellence": whether

> sitting still in meditation or actively pursuing some objective, the attitude toward life remains the same in every circumstance.[70]

In sum, Shree Maa is a striking example of the transformation of the goddess in a global context and in an American spiritual marketplace. Far from an esoteric tradition of transgressive sexual rites or bloody sacrifices, Shree Maa's version of Tantra is a more benign message of devotional love, universal truth, and global harmony. In the process, however, she has helped popularize the goddess Kāmākhyā and Śākta Tantra for a new age and for a new global audience.

Finally, Shree Maa also reflects the complex dynamics of gender and ethnicity in a changing transnational context, as very old Śākta traditions confront the strange new world of twenty-first-century America. As we saw in Chapter 5, Śākta Tantra does in fact open new possibilities for women to achieve real power and authority that would be rare or impossible in mainstream Hindu society. By virtue of her identity with the *śakti* of the goddess, Shree Maa like other female saints can be revered as a divine being, indeed, as the goddess herself in human form. Not surprisingly, Shree Maa has been cited by some authors as a kind of "feminist" saint, who "de-centers and undoes" patriarchal hierarchies.[71] To this author, at least, it seems a bit odd to apply the term "feminist"—in any of its various connotations or interpretations—to Shree Maa (in fact, when I asked them if they would use the term themselves, Shree Maa and the Swami clearly rejected it).[72] There is little in any of Shree Maa's teachings that addresses gender relations, women's power, female agency, etc.—issues that seem profoundly uninteresting to her, and would probably even strike her as unintelligible. If anything, her perspective might be considered "*trans-feminist*," insofar as she claims to have transcended all duality whatsoever and to see all human beings and all things as one reality. As she writes on the topic of "duality,"

> I was totally beyond this world of play duality when I was in Samadhi all the time. My mind did not get pulled to the world; it was always with God. I never asked people, "What is your name? Where are you from? What do you do?" Never! Only since coming to America, I have started to ask people these questions.[73]

In this respect, perhaps Rita Gross' ideal of a kind of "androgyny" beyond gender binaries might be the closest feminist analogue we can find to Shree Maa's spiritual vision.[74]

At the same time, Shree Maa and the White Sadhu also raise truly complex and important questions about the nature of cross-cultural encounter in a postcolonial but perhaps neo-imperial global context. For they represent a unique encounter not just between male and female but also between Occident and Orient, America and India. As Wilhelm Halbfass famously argued in *India Europe*, when East and West, India and the Anglo-European cultures meet today, the meeting does not take place on a level playing field; rather, "In the modern planetary system, Eastern and Western 'cultures' can no longer meet one another as equal partners. They meet *in* a Westernized world, under conditions shaped by Western ways of thinking."[75]

In the case of Shree Maa and the White Sadhu, however, this meeting is a bit more complex. The two of them met, after all, not in "the West," but in India—though arguably in an India that had already experienced the effects of colonialism, industrialization, and transnational capitalism. However, the movement has found its true home not in India but in Napa valley, California, surrounded by the spiritual businesses and get-rich gurus of California-style Tantra. Unlike the neo-Tantric sex-gurus and gurus of the rich like Bhagwan Shree Rajneesh, Shree Maa and the White Sadhu are remarkably low-key and seem relatively uninterested in the mega-guru, mass-profit business. Indeed, despite their odd hybridity of religious styles, they appear quite resistant to the commodification and consumerism that is so rampant in American-style Tantra.

In sum, as I will argue in the conclusion to this book, the fact that the meeting between Indian and the West takes place in a largely Westernized world does not mean that the Westernized world cannot itself be transformed and critically reformed by the encounter.

Conclusions: Tantra in the age of diaspora, globalization, and transnational capitalism

Tantra and the Śakta traditions of Assam have undergone a series of profound transformations over the last several hundred years, in the wake of reform, colonization, and now the diasporic flows of people, ideas and capital in the current global context. In India itself, Tantra has been transformed in two very different directions—on the one hand, into a sweetened, softened devotional tradition for a mass audience, and, on the other hand, into a dark, marginalized tradition of occult power and black magic. As it has come to the USA through transnational gurus like Shree Maa, however, it has also been transformed in a third way, into a universal, inclusive, and broadened tradition clearly geared to a Western Christian audience. As such, these new forms of Tantra really reflect the changing shape of religion itself in the contemporary, globalized, interconnected world order, where we see ever-more complex, hybrid, and shifting forms of spiritual life. As Paul Heelas comments, "the deregulation of the religious realm combined with the cultural emphasis on freedom of choice results in intermingled, interfused, forms of religious . . . life which exist beyond the traditional church and chapel."[76]

Finally and perhaps not surprisingly, Tantra has taken on yet another new incarnation in the late twentieth and twenty-first centuries, in the context of popular culture and consumer capitalism. Like the British Orientalist discourse of a century ago, most contemporary popular literature on Tantra continues to reduce it primarily to its sexual component. Now, however, this sexual element is celebrated as a liberating spiritual alternative and marketed to a massive popular audience of spiritual consumers. As Dennis Altman suggests in *Global Sex*, the processes of globalization have involved not just rapid circulations of information, people, and ideas, but also a kind of "new commercialization of sex" and "sexual consumerism" that includes everything from sexual tourism and cybersex to a massively expanding transnational pornography industry.[77]

The Western appropriation and reinterpretation of Tantra is clearly part of this global trend. This began at least as early as the publication of Omar Garrison's *Tantra: The Yoga of Sex* in 1964 and rapidly expanded in the 1970s and 1980s with internationally famous neo-Tantric sex gurus such as Bhagwan Shree Rajneesh.[78] Today we can browse a seemingly infinite series of publications bearing titles like *Tantra between the Sheets: The Easy and Fun Guide to Mind-Blowing Sex* and *Red Hot Tantra: Erotic Secrets of Red Tantra for Intimate, Soul-to-Soul Sex and Ecstatic, Enlightened Orgasms*, which promise "truly electrifying sex" accompanied by "multiple orgasms, physical ecstasy, emotional fulfillment, waves of pleasure [and] sexual bliss."[79] Tantra's presence on the Internet is even more staggering. Indeed, a Google search run in August 2008 produced no less than 12,100,000 hits for "Tantra," by far the majority of which were promoting enhanced sexual pleasure and optimal orgasms, such as "Tantra, Karezza and Sacred Sex," "Tantra, the Path of Love," "Tantra for Women," "Church of Tantra, "GayTantra.com," "TantricMassage.com," and, of course, "Tantra.com." As Tantra.com proudly declares, Tantra should be embraced as "the science of ecstasy and the art of conscious loving," the path that "says Yes! to life," where "pleasure vision and ecstasy are celebrated rather than repressed."[80]

One of my personal favorites in this genre is *Urban Tantra: Sacred Sex for the Twenty-first Century*. This "Urbanized Tantra" offers "a fresh, new inclusive, smart, hip, bold, and very fun version of Tantra," including "full body energy orgasms, which [are] like chakra enemas, shamanic journeys, and religious experiences all rolled into one."[81] The forward to the book by "post-porn-modernist" performance artist, Annie Sprinkle, concludes with the following "Urban Tantra Mantra":

> Om shanty panty
> Ha hari hairy
> Tit pat tooshie
> Just say ya ya yaaaaaa
> Taxi sat samosa
> Va va voom voom
> Jaya juicy ju ju
> Thy cum be yum
> Oh ma ma me-ah
> Nookie nir-va-na
> Yum yum yum
> Om. Welcome home. Om.[82]

It would be difficult to think of a more perfect summary of the American appropriation of Tantra, which has been not only reduced entirely to its sexual component but also transformed into a hybrid amalgam of western erotica, eastern exotica and fragments of pop-culture. In short, as David Ramsdale writes in his popular sex-guide, *Red Hot Tantra*, "Tantra, like sandalwood incense and sitar music, is an Indian import,"[83] and like other exotic imports, it has become commodified and marketed to mass audience who care little about its original context, history, or meaning.

Indeed, the Americanized version of Tantra would seem to be the very epitome of contemporary consumer capitalist culture—a culture that is dominated, as Zygmunt Bauman observes, "by the postmodern values of novelty, of rapid . . . change, of individual enjoyment and consumer choice."[84] Yet it also reflects the free-wheeling, eclectic, and nature of late capitalist religious life. Today, instead of conquering and pillaging the physical artifacts of exotic cultures, spiritual consumers feel free to appropriate exotic religious artifacts and "raid the world drawing on whatever is felt desirable: the religious (perhaps shamanism and Christianity); the religious and the non-religious (perhaps yoga and champagne)."[85] Increasingly in late capitalist consumer culture, as Heelas suggests, religion itself tends to become "a vehicle for acts of consumption. The products on offer are powerful experiences; the venues are spiritual Disneylands."[86]

In short, it seems that the Orientalist fascination with the exotic, erotic East is alive and well in the twenty-first century. If anything, it has assumed new and even more pervasive forms in the postmodern global shopping mall of cultures. Today, however, it operates not under the aegis of direct colonial domination, but through the far more subtle but perhaps more powerful "empire of the market" and the absorption of ever more cultural and religious traditions into the network of consumer capitalism.[87]

CONCLUSIONS: TANTRA AND THE END OF IMPERIALISM: BEYOND "DEEP ORIENTALISM" AND "THIRD-WORLDISM"

> Bliss is itself the nature of ultimate reality. And it is located within the body. . .
>
> —*Yoginī Tantra* (YogT 1.6.51)

> This turning point, on a historical scale, is nothing other than the end of imperialism. The crisis of western thought is identical to the end of the era of western philosophy. . . Thus if philosophy of the future exists, it must be born outside Europe or equally born in consequence of meetings and impacts between Europe and non-Europe.
>
> —Michel Foucault[1]

In sum, the Śākta Tantric traditions of Assam represent not just some of the oldest and most important traditions of goddess worship in all of South Asia, or even the "womb of Tantra." They also offer a unique lens onto the larger development, transformation, decline, and survival of Tantra in South Asian history and now in a global context. As we have seen in the chapters of this book, Tantra in the northeast has evolved as a complex negotiation between local indigenous religions and mainstream Hindu traditions, mediated in large part by tribal kings and the *brāhmaṇs* whom they patronized. The site of Kāmākhyā has developed progressively from a key seat of power, associated primarily with divine menstruation and animal sacrifice, to an object of royal patronage and political power, to a site of esoteric sexual rites, to an object of contempt for reformers and missionaries, to a hugely popular devotional site and pilgrimage destination. Finally, as Tantric traditions have come to contemporary America and Europe, they have taken on even more new—and sometimes almost unrecognizable—forms, now adapted to the shifting dynamics of a late capitalist consumer culture.

Throughout my discussion of Śākta Tantra, I have tried not only to use but also to critically rethink certain aspects of contemporary theory, and above all contemporary concepts of desire and power. While authors like Deleuze and Foucault are extremely helpful for understanding the "flowing," "capillary" nature of *kāma* and *śakti* in Tantra, they also have clear limitations and themselves need to be rethought by way of Indian concepts. In contrast to Deleuze's often a-historical concept of desire and Foucault's rather amorphous concept of power, neither *kāma* nor *śakti* here are static or singular phenomena; instead, they are complex, shifting networks of relations that have undergone profound transformations in the changing course of South Asian history. Far from a kind of amorphous "intentionality without a subject," desire and power are very much *embodied and performed* through a variety of different human actors—from priests and kings, to gurus and *yoginīs*, from ordinary devotees to indigenous non-Hindu peoples. Finally, in contrast to the rather "gender blind" approaches of both Foucault and Deleuze, *kāma* and *śakti* here are also clearly tied to gender and to the shifting balance of power between the sexes. Through a kind of alchemy of sex and gender, Tantric ritual serves to transform the metaphysical power of the goddess into the physical power of (mostly male) priests, kings, and *tāntrikas*. But at the same time, as we saw in Chapter 5, it also opens the door for at least some women to embody their identity as *śakti* and assume leadership roles as powerful *yoginīs*, gurus, and even the goddess herself.

It is in this sense that the power of Tantra here is at least threefold: First, despite its complex, ambiguous meaning and its vast diversity of forms, Hindu Tantra is perhaps best understood as a path of desire and power, centered on the tremendous energy of the goddess that flows through the human body, the social order, and the body politic alike. This is power in its broadest sense, with a wide range of different forms in different historical contexts, a power that can be unleashed through esoteric ritual, manipulated as a source of supernatural abilities, but also harnessed in the service of kingship and political rule.

Second, I have suggested that much of the power of Tantra derives precisely from the "power at the margins," that is, the dangerous, often taboo, but extremely potent forces that lie at the boundaries of both the physical body and the social body. The power of Tantra, I believe, has less to do with sexual pleasure or the art of ecstasy than with the power derived from transgressive physical substances such as blood and sexual fluids, as well as marginal groups such as indigenous, non-Hindu traditions. Finally, however, the power of Tantra also lies in the fact that it forces us to critically rethink the political implications of our study of other cultures today in a world that is theoretically "post-colonial" but no less violently contested. It reminds us that we too, no less than those whom we wish to understand, are enmeshed in complex matrices of power amidst the waning empires of the twenty-first century.[2]

Thus, perhaps what the power of Tantra has to offer us today is precisely an example of a much more *embodied* kind of a religious tradition—a form of "corporal spirituality" that is neither an exotic fantasy nor a philosophical abstraction, but a living tradition very much embedded in the complex world of history, political struggles, and new cultural encounters.[3] It is to these last points that I devote the remainder of this conclusion.

Tantric studies as cultural critique: Provincializing America? Or mourning empire?

Moving beyond the stereotyped, exoticized image of Tantra toward a more complex understanding is therefore a twofold task: it requires that we remain critical of both the lingering Orientalist trends in our own culture and the white-washing, nationalistic tendencies in much of the contemporary Hindu discourse. We need, in short, "a critical Indology that confronts domination in both the scholarly process and the scholarly object."[4] The first part of this task requires a healthy spirit of self-reflexivity and self-criticism—what I would call, adapting George Marcus and Michael Fischer's phrase, "Tantric studies as cultural critique." As Marcus and Fischer suggest, this sort of cultural critique involves a fundamental act of defamiliarization, that is, an act of "going out to the periphery of the Euro-centric world where conditions are supposed to be most alien and profoundly revising the way we normally think about things in order to come to grips with what in European terms are exotica." In other words, one is forced to rethink one's own cultural assumptions in the face of what appears radically other or exotic. Ultimately, however, this sort of defamiliarization can also be the inspiration for deeper critique of one's own culture, as a "probe into the specific facts about a subject of criticism at home."[5] Perhaps the most useful corrective to Orientalist views of other cultures is in fact to treat our own culture as "strange and characterized by profound otherness," and so "turn the anthropological gaze onto the history of our own . . . cultural practices."[6]

The case of Tantra, and above all the case of Assam with its bloody and titillating reputation, is a quintessential example of this sort of defamiliazation by encounter with the seemingly exotic other. As I have tried to suggest, the concepts of *kāma* and *śakti* force us to rethink our own contemporary ideas of desire, power, and sexuality. But still more important, the case of Tantra also forces us to reflect critically on contemporary culture and our own obsessions with sex, violence, and power in the twenty-first century. By actually understanding what sexual rites are about in the Tantric context, we realize that they have little, if anything, to do with the "art of sexual ecstasy" or the "easy and fun way to mind blowing sex." Indeed, the contemporary fascination with "Tantric sex" has less to do with any actual South Asian tradition than with our own cultural conflicts, longings, fears, and repressed desires. As Rabih Alameddine so aptly put it, "Sex. In America an obsession. In other parts of the world a fact."[7] And yet we repeatedly project our obsessions onto the distant mirror of exotic others such as Tantra.

Today, however, this obsession with sex and with the exotic is hardly just an "American" or "western" thing. Rather, it has become part of the much vaster global consumer phenomenon that Brian McNair calls the rise of the "pornosphere" or "striptease culture"—that is, a transnational, instantly accessible, and incredibly lucrative pornographic culture industry: "the late twentieth century saw the development of a cultural environment pervaded by sexuality and its representation. Today. . . we are likely to view, discuss and think about sex with greater frequency. . . than any previous stage in history."[8] And the modern fascination with Tantra is clearly part of this larger saturation of sex in twenty-first-century consciousness.

Moving beyond Orientalism and its "culture of domination"[9] is therefore far more complex that just critiquing "the West" and its representations of exotic others. From the late eighteenth to the early twentieth centuries, the culture of domination was the fairly obvious colonial power of European imperialism. Yet in the late twentieth and early twenty-first centuries, the culture of domination is often invisible, working not so much through the brute power of military might as through the more subtle "imperialism of the market," that is, the progressive absorption of more and more of the world into the logic of consumer capitalism.[10] Indeed, when we see thousands of books for sale through global outlets such as Amazon.com with titles like *Urban Tantra, Red Hot Tantra, Tantra between the Sheets*, and *The Complete Idiot's Guide*, we are reminded that the fascination with the exotic Orient is indeed alive and well in the twenty-first century. It is no longer part of the old-fashioned form of imperialism by military conquest, but rather part of new imperial logic of cultural appropriation, absorption, and commodification within a global capitalist market.

In this sense, going beyond Orientalism is not simply a matter of "provincializing Europe," or de-centering Europe as the sovereign subject of history, as Dipesh Chakrabarty has argued.[11] Nor is it even a matter of "provincializing America," or de-centering the USA as the new global hegemon (an empire already in decline, according to many observers).[12] Going further still, it might be a matter of provincializing the "sovereign empire of the market" itself, that is de-centering the logic of late capitalism as the subject of modern history. In the present transnational world order, the old binaries of "East and West," Europe and its others no longer make much sense, as the "Oriental" regions of India and China are among the most rapidly developing capitalist economies.[13] As Bruce Lawrence notes, "East and West elide, but in a single age-old global economy that perpetuates inequality, even as resources, services and benefits of the High Tech Era flow toward Asia."[14] Today, for example, Tantra is being commodified and mass-marketed not just to American consumer audiences in California, but also to Indian consumers in places like Poona, where Osho (the guru formerly known as Bhagwan Shree Rajneesh) established a large and hugely lucrative spiritual resort in the late 1980s.[15] The commodification of Tantra, in sum, is no longer simply a European or an American or a "western" thing, but rather a global phenomenon, and indeed, perhaps the very epitome of the complex cultural logic of late capitalism.

Beyond third-worldism: Avoiding both an eroticized Orient and a sanitized "Hinduism"

However, if it is true that we need to be critical of the lingering elements of Orientalism and exoticism in contemporary discourse on Tantra, we must be no less wary of the temptation to revert to the ideal of a kind of pristine, purified, sanitized ideal of Hinduism in which the messy, transgressive aspects of Tantra somehow did not exist. As June Campbell suggests, a respectful, intelligent study of Tantra does not mean that we should retreat into an "idealization or denial of the messy aspect" of these traditions; rather, we would do these traditions real justice by taking them seriously in their problematic as well as more admirable aspects, their implications for power and gender as much as for spiritual realization or transcendence.[16] Again, "the solution is not to brown-wash the textbooks on ancient Indian history, but to write more honest books about the contradictions of all civilizations."[17] As Pollock argues, a romantic sort of "third worldism" or "traditionalism" is no more helpful for understanding India than is Orientalism. Indeed, this sort of third-worldism is only the inverse mirror of Orientalism, which attempts to censor, eradicate, or sanitize those aspects of Hinduism that the Orientalists found unsavory. Most important, however, it denies the fact that relations of power were by no means unknown in Indian prior to colonial rule or were some kind of Western import. India, of course, had its own long history of political power, gender dynamics, and class relations long before the Europeans came along:

> In rejecting Eurocentrism, we have to be particularly watchful of its mirror image, "third worldism"... This seems to be a decided danger in some of the reformulations of colonial transformation now in vogue (and of the more commonplace naive image of a spiritual, quietistic India)... [D]omination did not enter India with European colonialism. Quite the contrary, asymmetries of power—the systematic exclusion from access to material and nonmaterial resources of large sectors of the population—appears to have characterized India in particular times and places over the last three millennia.[18]

Defending other cultures against the violence of imperialism does not mean that we should sanitize them of their own history of power and domination, that we should forget that the class system existed or that women and indigenous groups were largely disempowered for most of

South Asian history. "By all means one is eager to help in the project of 'reclaiming traditions, histories, and cultural from imperialism' [Edward Said]. But can we forget that most of the traditions in question have been empires of oppression in their own right—against women, above all, but also against other domestic communities?"[19] To truly move beyond the imperialism of Orientalist discourse, we also need to be critical of the retreat into nationalism and the defense of a pristine "tradition" that is so often the flipside of imperialism. In short, we must "problematize not only the construction of a hyperreal 'Europe' as the centre of history but also analogous constructs such as 'India,' 'Hinduism' and 'the Indian mentality.' "[20]

In the case of Tantra, this means that we should be mindful of the ways in which representations of Tantra have historically fed into the politics of imperialism old and new, twenty-first-century consumer-style no less than nineteenth-century British-style. And we should take seriously many of the arguments raised by critics such as the authors of *Invading the Sacred* and use these as a valuable impetus to reflect critically on the politics of South Asia studies. But it also means that we cannot avoid looking at the dynamics of power within South Asian Tantric traditions themselves, their own gender politics, their own tensions with non-Hindu indigenous populations. As we have seen in the case of Assam, this is a tradition that is intimately tied to very real relations of power, to kingship and war, and to the complex dynamics between priests and kings, rulers and subjects, men and women. If we wish to write a more accurate history of South Asian religions, one that might move beyond the simplistic binaries of Orient and Occident and think more seriously about desire and power in the contemporary global context, these aspects of Tantra should neither be exoticized and fetishized nor whitewashed and sanitized. As King concludes, "If one rejects the isolationist premises that underpin the Orientalist's absolute distinction between East and West, the possibility of interaction, dialogue and a 'fusion of horizons' remains so long as we remain hermeneutically open-minded."[21]

The power of Tantra today: Spiritual corporality and political spirituality

In this sense, a serious critique of our representations of Tantra need not be a source of postcolonial angst. Rather, it opens the hope for a more positive transformation through our encounter with Tantra in all its rich complexity and historical diversity. For it allows us both to reimagine Tantra in new, less distorted ways *and* to reflect back on our own culture and see ourselves as "exotic" in our own way. A serious engagement with Indian concepts such as *kāma* and *śakti*, I have argued, can help us to rethink the nature of desire and power in contemporary discourse; indeed, it allows us to think of desire as something that includes but far exceeds the limits of sexual desire; and it enables us to think about power as a complex phenomenon, in which the categories of politics, religion, and sexuality are not separate but intimately intertwined and historically interrelated. Perhaps most important, a serious encounter with Tantra also forces us to think carefully about the complex, often tense and contested nature of cross-cultural understanding. In my view, this means seeing both ourselves and those whom we study as embodied, historical, politically situated beings, all of us situated very much in the flesh.

Thus, perhaps the most valuable thing we can take from Tantra today is an example of a profoundly embodied tradition that is embodied in every possible sense: through the flowing power of the goddess in the material world, through profoundly physical rituals that utilize the divine power within the human body, and through a kind of spirituality that is also historically tied to royal power and the body politic. Arguably more so than any other South Asian tradition—or indeed, any other world religion—Tantra is a religious path very much rooted in physical desire and the power of the human body, embedded and intertwined with the material world.

As such, Tantra has much in common with many contemporary attempts to outline a kind of "spiritual corporality and corporal spirituality," such as Foucault's later work. As Jeremy Carrette suggests, Foucault's later work on the body and sexuality has profound implications for the study of religion today. Like the body, sexuality, and other aspects of human experience, religion needs to be critically grounded in real historical contexts, material circumstances, and relations of power: "religious discourse is not some privileged arena free from human prejudice, but is rather constructed in and through the ambiguities of human living."[22] Tantra, it would seem, is very much what Foucault had described as a kind of embodied and material spirituality, a "religion which speaks less of a Beyond than of the transformations in this world."[23] Indeed, it is a notion of embodiment that fundamentally undoes the dualism of body and spirit, material and spiritual, religious and secular.[24]

Likewise, the Tantric body has much in common with Deleuze's more affirmative view of the body, seen not as flesh set in opposition to spirit, but rather as flesh "traversed by a powerful vitality," defined not in its wholeness or identity but "in its becoming, in its intensity, as the power to affect or be affected."[25] In Deleuze's sense, the body is not separate from but the supreme locus of the inscription of religious, cultural, and ideological concerns: "The body must be regarded as a site of social, political, cultural and geographical inscriptions, production or constitution. The body is not opposed to culture. . . it is itself a cultural, *the* cultural product."[26] Amy Hollywood has made a similar call for a more embodied understanding of mysticism as a "sensible" phenomenon, which embraces all "the messiness, multiplicity and pain—as well as. . . the pleasure, beauty and joy—of embodied subjectivity."[27]

This seems to me a close analogue to the Tantric conception of the body and of physical desire as intimately entwined with the complex terrain of religion, culture, politics, and history. Just as the body of the goddess is dismembered and incorporated into the physical landscape of the earth, incarnated in the network of holy sites or *pīṭhas*, so too, the individual human body is itself a manifestation of the goddess' power and contains its own internal network of *pīṭhas*. Just as the goddess' body and sexual organ are intimately tied to the divine body of the king and his territory, so too, the individual body is inseparable from the larger structures of the social body and body politic. And today, just as the goddess can manifest herself in a human woman such as Shree Maa of Kāmākhyā, so too, in the weird world of late capitalism, the power of Tantra can be found as much in California as in Assam, as much on the shelves of Barnes and Noble as on the street-corner bookstalls of Kolkata—albeit in radically different, at times contradictory forms.

Herein, perhaps, lies the real power of Tantra in the twenty-first century—its potential contribution to the post-imperialist philosophy that Foucault envisaged, born out of the "meetings and impacts between Europe and non-Europe." A tradition so deeply embodied, so intimately tied to social struggle and historical change, so malleable in the context of globalization and transnationalism seems uniquely relevant in the current historical moment. While the old binaries of Orient and Occident have largely dissolved, both scholars and those whom they study are still deeply enmeshed in volatile political relations and complex matrices of power. As such, we have much to learn from Tantric traditions in which the ultimate reality is located not in some transcendent other world, but rather, as the *Yoginī Tantra* put it, "within the body."

NOTES

Introduction

1 Foucault, *The History of Sexuality, Volume I: An Introduction* (New York: Vintage, 1978), pp.92–3.

2 See Hugh B. Urban, "The extreme Orient: the construction of 'Tantrism' as a category in the Orientalist imagination," *Religion* 29 (1999), pp.123–46; and Hugh B. Urban, "The cult of ecstasy: Tantrism, the new age and the spiritual logic of late capitalism," *History of Religions* 39 (2000), pp.268–304.

3 See M. Amy Braverman, "The interpretation of Gods," *University of Chicago Magazine* 97, no.2, http://magazine.uchicago.edu/0412/features/index.shtml, 2004; Paul Courtright, "Studying religion in an age of terror: Internet death threats and scholarship as a moral practice," *The Academic Exchange* (April–May 2004), http://www.emory.edu/ACAD_EXCHANGE/2004/aprmay/courtright.html (accessed April 2, 2009).

4 Krishnan Ramaswamy, Antonio de Nicolas, and Aditi Banerjee, (eds), *Invading the Sacred: An Analysis of Hinduism Studies in America* (New Delhi: Rupa and Co., 2007). See also Sarah Caldwell and Brian K. Smith, "Introduction: Who Speaks for Hinduism?" *Journal of the American Academy of Religion* 68, no.4 (2000): 705–10. This and the other articles in this special issue of the journal engage these complex problems in the study of South Asian religions.

5 Urban, *Tantra: Sex, Secrecy, Politics and Power in the Study of Religion* (Berkeley, CA: University of California Press, 2003).

6 See M. Sharma, "Religion," in H.K. Barpujari (ed.), *The Comprehensive History of Assam: Ancient Period* (Guwahati: Publication Board, Assam, 1990), p.317; Sir Charles Eliot, *Hinduism and Buddhism: An Historical Sketch* (London: E. Arnold, 1921), p.278; George Weston Briggs, *Gorakhnāth and the Kānphata Yogīs* (New York: Oxford University Press, 1938), p.166.

7 White, "Tantrism," in Lindsay Jones (ed.), *Encyclopedia of Religion* (New York: MacMillan, 2005), v.13, p.8984. On the historical origins of Tantra, see David N. Lorenzen, "Early evidence for Tantric religion," in Katherine Anne Harper and Robert L. Brown (eds), *The Roots of Tantra* (Albany, NY: SUNY Press, 2002), p.33.

8 Padoux, "What do we mean by Tantrism?" in Katherine Anne Harper and Robert L. Brown (eds), *The Roots of Tantra*, p.17.

9 Sir Monier Monier-Williams, *A Sanskrit-English Dictionary* (Oxford: Clarendon Press, 1995), p.436; Urban, *Tantra*, pp.1–43.

10 KP 58.72, 58.47–8.

11 Interviews, February 14, 2004. See also Patricia Dold, "The Mahavidyas at Kamarupa: Dynamics of transformation in Hinduism," *Religious Studies and Theology* 23, no. 1 (2004), pp.89–122.

12 Judy Kuriansky, *The Complete Idiot's Guide to Tantric Sex* (Indianapolis, IN: Alpha Books, 2002), pp.8–9. See Mark A. Michaels, *Tantra for Erotic Empowerment; The Key to Enriching your Sexual Life* (St. Paul, MN: Llewellyn Publications, 2008); Val Sampson, *Tantra between the Sheets: the Easy and Fun Guide to Mind-Blowing Sex* (Berkeley, CA: Amorata Press, 2003).

13 See Urban, *Tantra*, chapter 1 and "The extreme Orient."

14 Inden, *Imagining India* (Cambridge, MA: Blackwell, 1990), p.86. See Anne McClintock, *Imperial Leather: Gender and Sexuality in the Imperial Contest* (New York: Routledge, 1997), p.14: "Orientalism takes shape as a male power fantasy that sexualizes a feminized Orient for Western possession. . . .Sexuality as a trope for other power relations was certainly an abiding aspect of imperial power."

15 King, *Orientalism and Religion: Postcolonial Theory, India and "The Mystic East"* (New York: Routledge, 1999), p.112. As John Strachey wrote in 1888, the Indian is "feeble even to effeminacy. . . His pursuits are sedentary, his limbs delicate, his movements languid. During many ages he has been trampled upon by men of bolder and more hardy breeds" (ibid., p.113).

16 Wilson, *Religious Sects of the Hindus* (Calcutta: Susil Gupta, 1858), p.140; Monier-Williams, *Hinduism* (London: Society for Promoting Christian Knowledge, 1894), pp.122–3. Barnett quoted in John Woodroffe, *Principles of Tantra: The Tantratattva of Śrīyukta Śiva Candra Vidyārṇava Bhaṭṭācārya Mahodaya* (Madras: Ganesh and Co.,1960), pp.3–5.

17 See especially Valentine Chirol, *Indian Unrest* (London: MacMillan, 1910); George MacMunn, *The Underworld of India* (London: Jarrolds Publishing, 1933); Urban, *Tantra*, chapter 3.

18 See Urban, "Hinduism in Assam," in Knut Jacobsen (ed.), *Encyclopedia of Hinduism* (Leiden: Brill, forthcoming).

19 K.R. van Kooij, *Worship of the Goddess according to the Kālikāpurāṇa* (Leiden: E.J. Brill, 1972), p.35.

20 M.I. Borah, *Five Lectures on the History of Assam as Told by Moslem Historians*, cited in H.V. Sreenivasa Murthy, *Vaiṣṇavism of Śaṅkaradeva and Rāmānuja* (Delhi: Motilal Banarsidass, 1973), pp.39–40.

21 Bose, "The Tantrik quest," *Sunday*, January 25, 1981, http://www.shrikali.org/tantricquest.php.

22 Eliot, *Hinduism*, pp.287–9.

23 Gait, *A History of Assam* (Calcutta: Thacker Spink and Co., 1933 [1905]), p.ix.

24 Gait, *History*, pp.9, 7.

25 Lalsangkima Pachuau, *Ethnic Identity and Christianity: A Socio-Historical and Missiological Study of Christianity in Northeast India with Special Reference to Mizoram* (New York: Peter Lang, 1998), p.101.

26 Sharma, "Religion," p.317; Eliot, *Hinduism*, p.278.

27 Wilson, trans., *The Vishnu Purāṇa: A System of Hindu Mythology and Tradition* (Calcutta: Punthi Pustak, 1972 [1840]), p.lxi. Likewise, as Briggs suggested in 1938, "Her shrine in Assam seems to have been the headquarters of the

Tantric worship, the place of its origin and that from which it spread into Nepal and Tibet" (*Gorakhnāth*, p.166).

28 See Chapter 6 of this book.

29 Sircar, *The Śākta Pīṭhas* (Delhi: Motilal Banarsidas, 1973), p.15.

30 Eliade, *Yoga: Immortality and Freedom* (Princeton, NJ: Princeton University Press, 1971), p.305.

31 The few works include: Kooij, *Worship*; Hugh B. Urban, "The path of power: Impurity, kingship and sacrifice in Assamese Tantra," *Journal of the American Academy of Religion* 69, no.4 (2001), 777–816; Nihar Ranjan Mishra, *Kamakhya: A Socio-Cultural Study* (New Delhi: D.K. Printworld, 2004); Pranav Jyoti Deka, *Nīlācala Kāmākhyā: Her History and Tantra* (Guwahati: The Author, 2005); Bani Kanta Kakati, *Mother Goddess Kāmākhyā* (Guwahati: Lawyer's Book Stall, 1952).

32 Biernacki, *Renowned Goddess of Desire: Women, Sex and Speech in Tantra* (New York; Oxford University Press, 2007). While an important work, Biernacki's book examines a small group of texts from the sixteenth to eighteenth centuries. There is no convincing evidence, however, that any of these texts are from Assam. Her primary text, the *Bṛhannīla Tantra* is probably from Bengal, not Assam. See S.C. Banerji, *A Brief History of Tantra Literature* (Calcutta: Naya Prokash, 1988), p.256. The closest link to Assam is the *Yoni Tantra*, but even that was composed in Cooch Behar, west of Assam. Moreover, Biernacki chooses not to focus on the most important texts that clearly *are* known to be from Assam, such as *Kālikā Purāṇa, Kaulajñāna Nirṇaya, Yoginī Tantra*, and *Kāmākhyā Tantra*, nor does she engage any of the primary literature in Assamese.

33 See Gait, *History*, p.58; Kakati, *Mother Goddess*.

34 See the bibliography for a complete list of sources. The KP and YogT are both clearly from Assam. The KJN was said to have been revealed in Kāmarūpa (Assam). The YT is from Cooch Behar, adjacent to Assam. There is less certainty about the date or location of the KT, but given its title and heavy focus on Kāmākhyā, it seems very probable that it is from Assam. The content is so similar to the YT that it seems reasonable to date it to roughly the same period, the sixteenth century.

35 Ferguson, *Colossus: The Price of America's Empire* (New York: Penguin, 2004), p.9. See Chalmers Johnson, *Sorrows of Empire: Militarism, Secrecy and the End of the Republic* (New York: Metropolitan Books, 2004); David Harvey, *The New Imperialism* (New York: Oxford University Press, 2003).

36 Maier, "An American empire?" *Harvard Magazine* (November–December 2002), pp.28–30.

37 Martin Walker, "The Clinton Doctrine," *The New Yorker*, October 7, 1997, pp.6–8.

38 McClintock, *Imperial Leather*, p.13. As Johnson observes, "the new imperialism operates not through direct colonization but through the more subtle neocolonialism of multinational corporations" (*Sorrows of Empire*, p.30).

39 Johnson, *Sorrows*; Ferguson, *Colossus*, pp.12–13.

40 Pollock, "Deep Orientalism? Notes on Sanskrit and power beyond the raj," in Carol A. Breckenridge and Peter van der Veer (eds), *Orientalism and the Postcolonial Predicament* (Philadelphia, PA: University of Pennsylvania Press, 1993), pp.79–80.

41 Kripal, *Kālī's Child: The Mystical and the Erotic in the Life and Teachings of Ramakrishna* (Chicago: University of Chicago Press, 1998), pp.4–5, 27–9. There is a large body of literature surrounding Kripal's work. Kripal has a website that summarizes the debate and contains a useful bibliography: http://www.ruf.rice.edu/~kalischi/. See his essays "Secret talk: Sexual identity and the politics of the study of Hindu Tantrism," *Harvard Divinity Bulletin* 29, no.4 (Winter 2001), pp.14–17; and "Remembering ourselves: On some countercultural echoes of contemporary Tantric studies," *Religions of South Asia* 1, no.1 (2007), pp.11–28. For a discussion of Kripal's work in light of arguments surrounding Tantra, see Urban, *Tantra*, pp.150–3.

42 Pandita Indrani Rampersad, "Exposing academic Hinduphobia," in Krishnan Ramaswamy et al. (eds), *Invading the Sacred: An Analysis of Hinduism Studies in America* (New Delhi: Rupa and Co., 2007), p.36.

43 Sil, "Much ado about nothing," InfinityFoundation.com, March 30, 2001, http://www.infinityfoundation.com/mandala/s_rv/s_rv_sil_kali_frameset.htm (accessed April 18, 2009).

44 Braverman, "The interpretation of Gods." See also See Caldwell and Smith, "Introduction: Who Speaks for Hinduism?"

45 Malhotra, "Wendy's child syndrome," *Sulekha.com*, September 6, 2002. http://rajivmalhotra.sulekha.com/blog/post/2002/09/risa-lila-1-wendy-s-child-syndrome.htm (accessed Aprl 19, 2009).

46 Malhotra, interview, June 25, 2008.

47 Malhotra, "What is the political agenda behind American studies of South Asian Tantra," Svabhinava.org, May 27, 2004, http://www.svabhinava.org/friends/RajivMalhotra/WendyWhite-frame.html (accessed April 18, 2009). See White, *Kiss of the Yoginī: "Tantric Sex" in its South Asian Contexts* (Chicago: University of Chicago Press, 2003).

48 Bhattacharya Saxena, "The funhouse mirror of Tantric studies: a rejoinder to David Gordon White's *Kiss of the Yogini.*" *Evam* 4 nos. 1–2 (2006), pp.358–71.

49 Ramaswamy et al, *Invading the Sacred,* pp.1–2.

50 Rampersad, "Exposing academic Hinduphobia," p.71.

51 Braverman, "Interpretation of Gods."

52 Martha Nussbaum, *The Clash Within: Democracy, Religious Violence, and India's Future* (Cambridge, MA: Harvard University Press, 2007), pp.239–44.

53 Kripal, *The Serpent's Gift: Gnostic Reflections on the Study of Religion* (Chicago: University of Chicago Press, 2007), p.17. See Kripal, "Remembering ourselves."

54 Courtright, "Studying religion in an age of terror." See Nussbaum, *Clash Within*, p.258.

55 Courtright, "Silenced for hinting at an Indian oedipus," *Times Higher Education*, November 28, 2003, http://www.timeshighereducation.co.uk/story.asp?storyCode=181462şectioncode=26 (accessed April 18, 2009).

56 Interview with Wendy Doniger, December 13, 2007.

57 Doniger in Braverman, "Interpretation of Gods."

58 Doniger, interview, December 13, 2007.

59 I also made a point to interview Malhotra, Pannikar, Doniger, Kripal, Courtright, and a number of others involved in these debates.

60 King, *Orientalism*, pp.209–10.

61 Bhattacharyya, *History of the Tantric Religion: A Historical, Ritualistic and Philosophical Study* (New Delhi: Manohar, 1982), p.v.
62 Kripal, *Kālī's Child*, pp.27–8.
63 Miranda Shaw, *Passionate Enlightenment: Women in Tantric Buddhism* (Princeton, NJ: Princeton University Press, 1994), p.142.
64 White, *Kiss*, p.17.
65 Prashad, "Letter to a young American Hindu," *Passtheroti.com*, May 17, 2007, http://www.passtheroti.com/?p=487.
66 Shadia B. Drury, "There can be life beyond economics and politics," *Calgary Herald*, May 16, 1998, http://www.uregina.ca/arts/CRC/herald_belife.html: "The sovereign imperialism of the market economy... reduce[s] all of life to commodities at the mercy of market forces." See also Bryan S. Turner, *Orientalism, Postmodernism, Globalism* (New York: Routledge, 1994), p.18.
67 Malhotra, "About me," *RajivMalhotra.com*, http://rajivmalhotra.com/index.php?option=com_contenttask=viewjd=16Itemid=30 (accessed April 19, 2009).
68 Lily Shapiro, "Discourse for whom? knowledge, power, complicity and irony in the debate between American academics and Hindus," Honors Thesis, Department of Anthropology, Amherst College, 2008, p.47. See Shankar Vedantam, "Wrath over a Hindu God: U.S. scholars' writings draw threats from faithful," *Washington Post*, April 10, 2004, p.3.
69 Peter van der Veer, "The foreign hand: Orientalist discourse in sociology and communalism," in Carol A. Breckenridge and Peter van der Veer (eds), *Orientalism and the Postcolonial Predicament* (Philadelphia, PA: University of Pennsylvania Press, 1993), pp.42–3.
70 Prashad, "Letter." On the radical diversity of "Hinduism," see Robert Frykenberg, "The emergence of modern 'Hinduism' as a concept and as an institution," in Gunther D. Sontheimer (ed.), *Hinduism Reconsidered* (New Delhi: Manohar Publications, 1989), p.30.
71 King, *Orientalism*, p.213.
72 See Urban, *Tantra*, pp.29, 37; M.R. Khale (ed.), *Bāna's Kādambarī* (New Delhi: Motilal Banarsidas, 1956), pp.338–9; David Lorenzen, "A parody of the Kāpālikās in the *Mattavilāsa*," in David Gordon White, *Tantra in Practice* (Princeton, NJ: Princeton University Press, 2000), pp.86–7.
73 One of the more useful definitions is David Gordon White (ed.), *Tantra in Practice*, p.9: "Tantra is that Asian body of beliefs and practices which, working from the principle that the universe we experience is nothing other than the concrete manifestation of the divine energy of the godhead that creates and maintains that universe, seeks to ritually appropriate and channel that energy... in creative and emancipatory ways." For other useful definitions, see Douglas Brooks, *The Secret of the Three Cities: An Introduction to Hindu Śākta Tantrism* (Chicago: University Chicago Press, 1990), pp.53ff; Sanjukta Gupta, Dirk Jan Hoens, and Teun Goudriaan, *Hindu Tantrism* (Leiden: Brill, 1979), pp.7–9.
74 Biardeau in André Padoux, *Vāc: The Concept of the Word in Selected Hindu Tantras* (Albany, NY: SUNY Press, 1990), p.40.
75 Biardeau, *Hinduism: The Anthropology of a Civilization* (Paris: Flammarion, 1981), pp.149–50.

76 Monier-Williams, *Sanskrit-English Dictionary* (Oxford: Clarendon Press, 1995), p.271.
77 Wendy Doniger and Sudhir Kakar, trans., *Kamasutra: A New Complete English Translation of the Sanskrit Text* (New York: Oxford University Press, 2002), pp.xi, xiii.
78 Doniger and Kakar, trans., *Kamasutra*, p.8.
79 Flood, *The Tantric Body: The Secret Tradition of Hindu Religion* (London: I.B. Tauris, 2006), p.84.
80 KP 62.1–3.
81 KP 62.133.
82 Orzech, *Politics and Transcendent Wisdom: The Scripture of the Humane Kings in the Creation of Chinese Buddhism* (University Park, PA: Pennsylvania State University Press, 1998), p.8. See John Woodroffe, *The World as Power* (Madras: Ganesh and Co., 1974).
83 Samjukta Gupta, "The goddess, women and their rituals in Hinduism," in Mandakranta Bose (ed.), *Faces of the Feminine in Ancient, Medieval and Modern India* (New York: Oxford University Press, 2000), p.93.
84 Woodroffe, *Principles of Tantra*, v.2, p.355.
85 Padoux, "Hindu Tantrism," in Mircea Eliade (ed.), *Encyclopedia of Religion* (New York: MacMillan, 1986), v. 14. pp.274–5.
86 Caldwell, *Oh Terrifying Mother: Sexuality, Violence and the Worship of Kālī* (New York: Oxford University Press, 1999), p.188.
87 Chidester, *Patterns of Power: Religion and Politics in American Culture* (Englewood Cliffs, NJ: Prentice Hall, 1988), p.2; see Hugh B. Urban, "Politics and religion: an overview," in Lindsay Jones (ed.), *Encyclopedia of Religion* (New York: MacMillan, 2005), v.11, p.7248.
88 Gilles Deleuze, "Désir et plaisir," *Magazine littéraire* 325 (October 1994), pp.59–65. See Gilles Deleuze and Claire Parnet, *Dialogues* (New York: Columbia University Press, 1987), p.101: "Sexuality can only be thought of as one flux among others."
89 Gilles Deleuze and Félix Guattari, *Anti-Oedipus: Capitalism and Schizophrenia* (Minneapolis, MN: University of Minnesota Press, 1983), p.27. See Judith Butler, *Subjects of Desire: Hegelian Reflections in Twentieth Century France* (New York: Columbia University Press, 1987), p.205.
90 Stephen Best and Douglas Kellner, *Postmodern Theory: Critical Interrogations* (New York: Guilford Press, 1991), p.87. See Deleuze and Guattari, *Anti-Oedipus*, p.293.
91 Deleuze and Guattari, *Anti-Oedipus*, p.5; the quote is from Henry Miller, *Tropic of Cancer* (New York: Grove Press, 1994), p.258.
92 As for example when Deleuze and Guattari assert "that the social field is immediately invested by desire, that it is the historically determined product of desire, and that libido has no need of any mediation. . . in order to invade and invest the productive forces and the relations of production. *There is only desire and the social, and nothing else*" (*Anti-Oedipus*, p.29).
93 Butler, *Subjects*, pp.206, 213–15: "Desire is the locus of a precultural idea, the essence of the individual which is subsequently distorted and repressed through the imposition of anti-erotic political structures. Here Deleuze appears to undermine his original project to historicize desire" (p.215). See Best and Kellner, *Postmodern Theory*, p.106.

94 Butler, *Subjects*, pp.219, 215. See Foucault, *History of Sexuality*, pp.105–6; Foucault, *Language: Counter-Memory, Practice: Selected Essays and Interviews* (Ithaca, NY: Cornell University Press, 1977), p.215: "desire has had and continues to have a long history."

95 Foucault, *The History of Sexuality*, pp.92–3.

96 Foucault, *Power/Knowledge: Selected Interviews and Other Writings* (New York: Pantheon, 1980), p.98. See James D. Faubion (ed.), *Power: Essential Works of Foucault, 1954–1984* (New York: New Press, 2001), p.xxvii.

97 Lois McNay, *Foucault: A Critical Introduction* (New York: Continuum, 1994), p. 90.

98 Foucault, "Entretien sur la prison: le livre et sa méthod," *Magazine littéraire* 101 (June 1975), p.28.

99 Foucault, *History of Sexuality*, p.103.

100 Jantzen, *Power, Gender and Christian Mysticism* (Cambridge: Cambridge University Press, 1995), p.15. Foucault's indifference to the implications of gender has been noted by many feminist critics. See McNay, *Foucault*, p.150; Jana Sawicki, *Disciplining Foucault: Feminism, Power and the Body* (New York: Routledge, 1991), p.8.

101 Frédérique Appfel Marglin, *Wives of the God King: The Rituals of the Devadasis of Puri* (New York: Oxford University Press, 1985), p.21.

102 Padoux, "What do we mean by Tantrism," p.21.

103 Shulman, *Tamil Temple Myths: Sacrifice and Divine Marriage in the South Indian Śaiva Tradition* (Princeton, NJ: Princeton University Press, 1980), p. 347.

104 Kripal, "Remembering ourselves," p.26.

Chapter One

1 Butler, *Gender Trouble: Feminism and the Subversion of Identity* (New York: Routledge, 1990), p.97.

2 KP 62.73–5.

3 Bāṇabhaṭṭa's seventh-century fantasy tale, *Kādambarī*, mentions a strange old holy man who had a collection of *tantras*, though it is not clear what these were in this context; the first epigraphic reference to texts called *tantras* comes from a Cambodian inscription of the early ninth century. See Urban, *Tantra: Sex, Secrecy, Politics and Power in the Study of Religion* (Berkeley, CA: University of California Press, 2003), p.28; Sanjukta Gupta, Dirk Jan Hoens, and Teun Goudriaan, *Hindu Tantrism* (Leiden: Brill, 1979), pp.22–4.

4 See M.C. Joshi, "Historical and iconographic aspects of Śākta Tantrism," in Katherine Anne Harper and Robert L. Brown (eds), *The Roots of Tantra* (Albany, NY: SUNY Press, 2002), p.47.

5 Gupta et al., *Hindu Tantrism*, p.37; Sircar, *The Śākta Pīṭhas* (Delhi: Motilal Banarsidas, 1973), pp.15–16.

6 Frédérique Appfel Marglin, *Wives of the God King: The Rituals of the Devadasis of Puri* (New York: Oxford University Press, 1985), p.21.

7 The story evolved over time from the *Śatapatha Brāhmaṇa* (SB 1.7.4.1–4) to its more elaborate forms in the *Mahābhārata* (MB 12.274.36–59) and Purāṇas (KP 18.41–7). See Wendy Doniger O'Flaherty, *The Origins of Evil*

in Hindu Mythology (Berkeley, CA: University of California Press, 1976), pp.274–90; Sircar, *Śākta Pīṭhas*, pp.5–7.

8 Sarma, *An Early History of Kamarup Kamakhya* (Gauhati: Kalita Art Press, 1998), p.10.

9 Wendy Doniger O'Flaherty, *Other People's Myths* (New York: MacMillan, 1988), p.118.

10 Sircar suggests that it may lie near Bijapur in the modern state of Karnataka (*Śākta Pīṭhas*, p.14).

11 KP 18.41–7. See MBP 11.60–116, 12.30–1.

12 Wendy Doniger O'Flaherty, trans., *The Rig Veda* (New York: Penguin, 1984), pp.30–1.

13 KP 62.75–6. See MBP 11.113–16. Kubjikā, literally the "hunchbacked" or "crooked" goddess, is likely a prefiguration of the goddess as Kuṇḍalinī, who is believed to lie in the human body in the form of a coiled serpent. See White, *Kiss of the Yoginī: "Tantric Sex" in its South Asian Contexts* (Chicago: University of Chicago Press, 2003), p.82.

14 KP 39.73. See YogT 1.15.51, MBP 12.30–1, 76.19–20.

15 Nihar Ranjan Mishra, *Kamakhya: A Socio-Cultural Study* (New Delhi: D.K. Printworld, 2004), p.27.

16 Sircar, *Śākta Pīṭhas*, pp.16–17.

17 Caldwell, *Oh Terrifying Mother: Sexuality, Violence and the Worship of Kālī* (New York: Oxford University Press, 1999), p.104. See H. Brunner, G. Oberhammer, and A. Padoux (eds), *Tāntrikābhidhānakośa II* (Wien: Verlag der Österreichischen Akademie der Wissenschaften, 2004), pp.87–88.

18 Davidson, *Indian Esoteric Buddhism: A Social History of the Tantric Movement* (New York: Columbia University Press, 2002), p.207.

19 Gupta et al., *Hindu Tantrism*, p.38; Davidson, *Indian Esoteric*, pp.164–5.

20 George Weston Briggs, *Gorakhnāth and the Kānphata Yogīs* (New York: Oxford University Press, 1938), p.311; see Chapter 4 of this book.

21 KCT 7.86–87.

22 Sircar, *Śākta Pīṭhas*, p.15.

23 Ronald M. Bernier notes that parts of Kāmākhyā temple date as early as seventh to eighth centuries: *Himalayan Architecture* (Madison, NJ: Fairleigh Dickinson University Press, 1997), p.23. See also Pranav Deka, *Nīlācala Kāmākhyā: Her History and Tantra* (Guwahati: Lawyer's Book Stall, 2004), p.10.

24 HT 1.7.12.

25 Mukunda Madhava Sharma, *Inscriptions of Ancient Assam* (Gauhati: Gauhati University, 1978), p.104.

26 M. Sharma, "Religion," in H.K. Barpujari (ed.), *The Comprehensive History of Assam: Ancient Period* (Guwahati: Publication Board, Assam, 1990), p.322. See KP 62.110, 38.85, 8.43.

27 As Deka notes, "The art of stone sculpting reached its apex on the Nīlācala during the reign of the Pāla dynasty in Kāmarūpa" (*Nīlācala Kāmākhyā*, p.79). See R.D. Choudhury, *Architecture of Assam* (New Delhi: Aryan Books, 1998), p.108.

28 The figures have been dated to roughly the twelfth century by South Asian art historians Susan Huntington and Kimberly Masteller (personal communications, March–May, 2008).

29 Deka, *Nīlācala Kāmākhyā*, p.79.
30 P.C. Choudhury, *The History of the People of Assam to the Twelfth Century AD* (Gauhati: Department of Historical Research in Assam, 1966), p.241.
31 Choudhury, *The History*, p.241.
32 KP 8.40–42; 8.44–47; see KAN 9.30–34.
33 White, "Tantrism: An overview," in Lindsay Jones (ed.), *Encyclopedia of Religion* (New York: Thomson Gale, 2005), v.13, p.8984.
34 P.C. Bagchi (ed.), *The Kaulajñāna Nirṇaya and Some Minor Texts of the School of Matsyendranātha* (Calcutta: Metropolitan Printing and Publishing House, 1934), p.8.
35 Bagchi, *The Kaulajñāna Nirṇaya*, p.35.
36 Dehejia, *Yoginī Cult and Temples: A Tantric Tradition* (Delhi: National Museum, 1986), pp.11–19.
37 AVT, colophon.
38 KJN 16.7–8.
39 KJN 22.9–11, translated by White, *Kiss*, pp.213–15. See R.K. Sharma, *The Temple of the Chaunsaṭhayoginī at Bheraghat* (Delhi: Agam Prakashan, 1978), p.30: "Matsyendranātha . . . developed the Yoginī cult when he lived in the midst of women in Kāmarūpa. Every woman in Kāmarūpa was recognized as a Yoginī and hence he named this cult after them."
40 Mahendranāth Bhaṭṭācāryya, *Śrī Śrī Kāmākhyā-Tīrtha* (Guwahati: D. Bhaṭṭācāryya Press, 2000), p.25. The KP contains a full list of the 64 *yoginīs*, KP 63.37–44.
41 KP 62.90–1.
42 Dehejia, *Yoginī*, p.78; see KP 63.7–107, BNT 14.12, 14.29–46.
43 This dating was given by my colleague, Susan Huntington, an expert on Pāla-era art of northeast India.
44 Personal communications with Kimberly Masteller, January through May 2008, and Padma Kaimal, March 30, 2008. David Gordon White and Loriliai Biernacki also agreed that a Yoginī temple could have existed at Kāmākhyā (personal communications, 2008).
45 Deka, *Nīlacala Kāmākhyā*, p.79. See also Ganga Sarma, *Kamrup Kamakhya* (Guwahati: Bishnu Prakashan, 2002), p.13: "Even today one can find the beautiful images of sixty four Yoginis and eighteen images of Bhairabas. Perhaps due to. . . natural calamities, the upper the temple was ravaged and the lower was gradually submerged."
46 Rob Linrothe, "Siddhas and śrīśailam, where all wise people go," in Rob Linrothe (ed.) *Holy Madness: Portraits of Tantric Siddhas* (New York: Rubin Museum of Art, 2006), pp.133–4. The *siddha* Kṛṣṇācārya the junior is also connected with Assam. The *siddha* received a message from a *ḍākinī* who instructed him to go the place of the goddess of Kāmarūpa. There he found a chest containing a powerful drum, and whenever he played it, five hundred *siddha yogīs* and *yoginīs* appeared and became his attendants. See Debiprasad Chattopadhyaya (ed.), *Taranatha's History of Buddhism in India* (Delhi: Motilal Banarsidass, 1990), p.268.
47 Satyendranath Sarma, *Assamese Literature* (Wiesbaden: Harrassowitz, 1976), p.44. On the identity of Luī-pā and Matsyendra, see White, *The Alchemical Body: Siddha Traditions in Medieval India* (Chicago: University of Chicago Press, 1996), p.91. Many believe the *siddha* Saraha was born in Rani in the

district of Rampur, Assam. See H.K.Barpujari (ed.), *Comprehensive History of Assam: Ancient Period* (Guwahati: Publication Board of Assam, 1990), p.266.

48 S. Sasanananda, *History of Buddhism in Assam* (New Delhi: Bahri Publications, 1986), pp.161–2. See. Choudhury, *History*, p.427; Sharma, "Religion," p.342. Some Assamese scholars also believe that the *siddha* Ratnapāla, who is said to have been converted to Tantric practice by Saraha, was none other than king Ratnapāla of Assam, and that Darika-pā, the disciple of Lui-pā, may have been king Indrapāla. See Barpujari (ed.), *Comprehensive History*, p.267.

49 Linrothe, "Siddhas," pp.133–4.

50 Eliade, *Yoga: Immortality and Freedom* (Princeton, NJ: Princeton University Press, 1971), p.202.

51 Dehejia, *Yoginī*, p.1. Likewise, Gupta, Goudriaan, and Hoens argue: "Without doubt the Himalayan and Vindhyan tribes played a role of some importance as sources of exotic rituals. . . The process of formation of Tantric rituals can therefore be reasonably expected to have been localized primarily in those areas. . . which possessed a relatively strong element of non-Aryan tradition" (*Hindu Tantrism*, p.37).

52 Flood, *Tantric Body: The Secret Tradition of Hindu Religion* (London: I.B. Tauris, 2006), p.14. See John Woodroffe, *Shakti and Shākta* (New York: Dover, 1978), pp.587–89.

53 Davidson, *Indian Esoteric*, p.179.

54 Davidson, *Indian Esoteric*, p.234.

55 Davidson, *Indian Esoteric*, pp.209–10.

56 Sircar, *The Śākta Pīṭhas*, p.33.

57 Bhaṭṭācārya, *Asamat Śaktipūjā* (Guawhati: Bāṇī Prakāśa, 1977), p.9.

58 MB 2.23.19; 2.31.9–10; 2.47.12.

59 Davidson, *Indian Esoteric*, pp.211–3.

60 KP 38.100–103.

61 YogT 1.9.13–16.

62 KP 38.130.

63 KP 38.199, 38.149–50.

64 Davidson, *Indian Esoteric*, p.209.

65 Monier-Williams, *Sanskrit-English Dictionary*, p.1052.

66 KP 60.11–21. See Davidson, *Indian Esoteric*, p.321. While Davidson dismisses this as a fantasy of tribal worship, it seems likely that this may be a realistic description of indigenous festivals of Assam, many of which—such as the widely popular *bihu* festivals—involve highly erotic songs and dances that reflect indigenous fertility rites. See P. Goswami, "Hindu and tribal folklore in Assam," *Asian Folklore Studies* (1967), pp.19–27; Sharma, "Religion," p.305.

67 Mishra, *Kamakhya*, pp.15–17; Sircar, *Śākta-Pīṭhas*, p.15.

68 Mishra, *Kamakhya*, p.5. On human sacrifice, see Chapter 3 of this book.

69 Sharma, "Religion," p.319. "There is a tradition amongst the local priesthood . . . that the former worshipers were Garos and pigs were offered as sacrifices" [Bani Kanta Kakati, *Mother Goddess Kāmākhyā* (Guwahati: Lawyer's Book Stall, 1952), p.37].

70 Hamlet Bareh, *The History and Culture of the Khasi People* (Gauhati: The Author, 1967), pp.18, 37.

71 Bareh, *History*, pp.37–8.

72 According to one tale, the Garos had been attacked by wild men from the north and fled their lands. A woman among them carried an image of the goddess of fertility, Phojou. The goddess demanded to be put down on Nīlācala hill and was worshiped there with the sacrifice of a goat. See Mira Pakrasi, *Folk Tales of Assam* (New Delhi: Sterling Publishers), pp.44–5: "The goddess Phojou remained forever at the place. . . and her worship has been going on for ages. The Garos call this place. . . the sanctuary of the past. People other than Garos call it Kamakhya."
73 Patricia Dold, "The mahavidyas at Kamarupa: Dynamics of transformation in Hinduism," *Religious Studies and Theology* 23, no.1 (2004), p.96.
74 Kakati, *Mother Goddess*, p.64. See Pranab Kumar Das Gupta, *Life and Culture of Matrilineal Tribe of Meghalaya* (New Delhi: Inter-India Publications, 1984).
75 Kakati, *Mother Goddess*, p.64.
76 Kakati, *Mother Goddess*, p.16.
77 Gaṅgāprasād Baragohāiṅ, "Tāi āhomer hindudharma grahaṇ āru paravatī asamar rājnītit iyār prabhāv," in Praphulla Dās and Candan Phukan (eds), *Mahādev* (Śivsāgar: Śivrātri Udyāpan Samiti, 2006), p.11.
78 Mahendra Nāth Bhaṭṭācāryā, *Śrī Śrī Kāmākhyā-Tīrtha* (Guwahati: D. Bhaṭṭācāryya Press, 2000), p.15.
79 KP 62.142.
80 KT 3.10–16.
81 K.R. van Kooij, *Worship of the Goddess according to the Kālikāpurāṇa* (Leiden: E.J. Brill, 1972), pp.32–3.
82 KP 58.57–8. See also the description of Kāmākhyā in the MBP 77.5–7.
83 Foucault, *Power/Knowledge*, p.98; Foucault, *History of Sexuality*, p.103.
84 Lois McNay, *Foucault: A Critical Introduction* (New York: Continuum, 1994), p.105; Habermas, *The Philosophical Discourse of Modernity* (Cambridge, MA: Polity Press, 1987), p.287. As Foucault himself put it, "this enigmatic thing which we call power, which is at once visible and invisible, present and hidden, ubiquitous. . . The question of power remains a total enigma. Who exercises power?" (*Language, Counter-Memory*, p.213).
85 David Cousins Hoy (ed.), *Foucault: A Critical Reader* (New York: Basil Blackwell, 1986), p.10–11.
86 McNay, *Foucault*, p.105. As Best and Kellner comment, "power is mostly treated as an impersonal and anonymous force which is exercised apart from the actions and intentions of human subjects. Foucault methodologically brackets the question of who controls and uses power for which interests" [Stephen Best and Douglas Kellner, *Postmodern Theory: Critical Interrogations* (New York: Guilford Press, 1991), p.70].
87 I am using gender and performance here largely in the ways that Judith Butler employs them in her critique and extension of Foucault in *Gender Trouble: Feminism and the Subversion of Identity* (New York: Routledge, 1989).

Chapter Two

1 Douglas, *Purity and Danger: An Analysis of the Concepts of Pollution and Taboo* (London: Routledge, 1966), p.161.

2 Madeleine Biardeau and Charles Malamoud, *Le sacrifice dans l'Inde ancienne* (Paris: Presses universitaires de France, 1976), p.153. See Smith, *Reflections on Ritual, Resemblance and Religion* (New York: Oxford University Press, 1989), p.50; Heesterman, *The Broken World of Sacrifice: An Essay in Ancient Indian Religion* (Chicago: University of Chicago Press, 1993).

3 Davidson, *Indian Esoteric Buddhism: A Social History of the Tantric Movement* (New York: Columbia University Press, 2002), p.181. White also notes that "the *homa* fire sacrifice rituals of early tantrism... often involved the offering of human and animal blood" [White, "Tantrism: An overview," in Lindsay Jones (ed.), *Encyclopedia of Religion* (New York: Thomson Gale, 2005), p.8986).

4 The "visceral" power of redness is also noted by Patricia Dold, "The mahavidyas at Kamarupa: Dynamics of transformation in Hinduism," *Religious Studies and Theology* 23 (2004), p.102.

5 See Urban, "The Power of the impure: Transgression, violence and secrecy in Bengali Śākta Tantra and modern western magic," *Numen* 50, no.3 (2003), pp.269–308; Alexis Sanderson, "Purity and power among the brahmans of Kashmir," in Michael Carrithers, Steven Collins, and Steven Lukes (eds), *The Category of the Person* (New York: Cambridge University Press, 1985), pp.190–216. For literature on transgression, see Peter Stallybrass and Allon White, *The Politics and Poetics of Transgression* (Ithaca, NY: Cornell University Press, 1986); Michael Taussig, "Transgression," in Mark C. Taylor (ed.), *Critical Terms for Religious Studies* (Chicago: University of Chicago Press, 1998), pp.349–64.

6 Similar celebrations of the earth's menstruation take place in Orissa and Kerala. As Marglin describes the Orissan tradition: "The menses of the goddess takes place around the month of Jyeṣṭha (May–June)... The festival is celebrated for four days. The earth—pruthibī—is believed to be menstruating... During the four days of the festival the women, like the goddess, are considered to be impure (*āśauca*); they do not wear vermilion mark, oil or comb their hair, just like women during their menses" [Frédérique Appfel Marglin, *Wives of the God King: The Rituals of the Devadasis of Puri* (New York: Oxford University Press, 1985), pp.234–35]. Caldwell describes a similar cycle of menstruation in Kerala, where it is closely tied to agriculture [Caldwell, *Oh Terrifying Mother: Sexuality, Violence and the Worship of Kālī* (New York: Oxford University Press, 1999), p.115].

7 Shulman, *Tamil Temple Myths: Sacrifice and Divine Marriage in the South Indian Śaiva Tradition* (Princeton, NJ: Princeton University Press, 1980), p.347.

8 DBP 9.9.35–37; see BVP 2.9.14.

9 DBP 7.38.16–18.

10 KubT 7.56–58. The date of this text is not certain, but it is probably later than the sixteenth century.

11 Marglin, "Female sexuality in the Hindu world," in Clarissa W. Atkinson (ed.), *Immaculatę, Powerful: The Female in Sacred Image and Social Reality* (Boston, MA: Beacon Press, 1985), p.44. There is a vast literature on menstruation in India; see Narendranath Bhattacharyya, *Indian Puberty Rites* (Delhi: Munshiram Manoharlal, 1980); Susan S. Wadley, *The Powers of Tamil Women* (New York: Maxwell School of Citizenship and Public Affairs, 1980),

p.164; Urban, "Matrix of power: Tantra, kingship and sacrifice in the worship of mother goddess Kāmākhyā." *South Asia* 31, no.3 (2008), pp.500–534.

12 White, *Kiss of the Yoginī: "Tantric Sex" in its South Asian Contexts* (Chicago: University of Chicago Press, 2003), p.67. See Madhu Khanna, "The goddess-woman equation in the Tantras," in Durre S. Ahmed (ed.), *Gendering the Spirit: Women, Religion and the Post-Colonial Response* (New York: Zed Books, 2002), p.49.

13 Bhattacharyya, *Indian Puberty Rites,* p.11.

14 Marglin, "Female sexuality," pp.40–4. See Caldwell, *Oh Terrifying Mother*, p.119.

15 Patrick Olivelle, *Dharmasūtras: The Law Codes of Ancient India* (New York: Oxford University Press, 1999), pp.102–3, 108–9, 151–2, 263.

16 Olivelle, *Dharmasūtras*, p.264.

17 Khanna, "The goddess-woman equation," p.49.

18 Sarma, *Kamrup Kamakhya* (Guwahati: Bishnu Prakashan, 2002), p.23.

19 Sarma, *Kāmarūpa Kāmākhyā,* p.108.

20 See Mishra, *Kamakhya: A Socio-Cultural Study* (New Delhi: D.K. Printworld, 2004), pp.51–4; Bhaṭṭācāryya, *Śrī Śrī Kāmākhyā-Tīrtha* (Guwahati: D. Bhaṭṭācāryya Press, 2000), pp.112–13.

21 Khanna, "The goddess-woman equation," p.51. As Sanderson notes, "the monthly discharge of their inner depravity, contact with which was feared by the orthodox as the destroyer of wisdom, strength and sight, was revered by he devotee of Bhairava and Kālī as the most potent of power-substances" ("Purity and power," p.202).

22 See Dehejia, *Yoginī Cult and Temples: A Tantric Tradition* (Delhi: National Museum, 1986), p.57; Urban, "The path of power: Impurity, kingship and sacrifice in Assamese Tantra," *Journal of the American Academy of Religion* 69, no.4 (2001), and "Matrix of power."

23 KP 55.1–2; MMT 4.9–12.

24 Smith, *Reflections,* p.50.

25 Biardeau, *Stories about Posts: Vedic Variations around the Hindu Goddess* (Chicago: University of Chicago Press, 2004), p.2. See also J.C. Heesterman, *The Inner Conflict of Tradition: Essays in Ancient Indian Ritual* (Chicago: University of Chicago Press, 1985).

26 Dehejia, *Yoginī,* p.57.

27 Davidson, *Indian Esoteric,* p.181.

28 KP 31.10–15.

29 KP 35.

30 KP 74.129. See Kooij, *Worship of the Goddess according to the Kālikāpurāṇa* (Leiden: E.J. Brill, 1972), pp.28–9.

31 KP 74.130, 134–35.

32 KP 74.135–38.

33 Sanderson, "Purity and power," p.208 n.3.

34 KP 31.7.

35 Heesterman, *Broken World,* p.87.

36 Heesterman, *Inner Conflict,* p.46.

37 See Eliade, *Yoga: Immortality and Freedom* (Princeton, NJ: Princeton University Press, 1971), pp.111–13; Heesterman, *Broken World*, p.215; Biardeau and Malamoud, *Le sacrifice*, pp.57–80.
38 Heesterman, *Broken World*, p.71.
39 O'Flaherty, *Origins of Evil in Hindu Mythology* (Berkeley, CA: University of California Press, 1976), p.155. Curiously, the ŚB does describe a ritual of burying five heads—the heads of a man, horse, ox, sheep, and goat—in the five directions of the bottom layer of the fire altar (8.5.2.1). Heesterman argues that this is evidence of an older, pre-*brāhmaṇic* sacrifice based on violent beheading that was later replaced by the nonviolent ritual (*Broken World*, p.73).
40 Heesterman, *The Inner Conflict*, p.87.
41 Smith, *Reflections*, p.71.
42 Kooij, *Worship*, pp.7–8. On sacrificial themes in the *Mahābhārata*, see Alf Hiltebeitel, *The Ritual of Battle: Krishna in the Mahabharata* (Ithaca, NY: Cornell University Press, 1976).
43 See Urban, "Path of power" and "Matrix of power."
44 SB 6.2.1.1–3; 7.5.2.32.
45 According to Monier-Williams, a *gaura* is a kind of buffalo, a *gavaya* is a species of ox. The *śarabha* may originally have been a kind of goat or deer, though in later Hinduism it becomes an eight-legged mythical animal [Smith, *Classifying the Universe: The Ancient Indian Varna System and the Origins of Caste* (New York: Oxford University Press, 1994), p.279n].
46 ŚB 13.2.4.1–4.
47 Heesterman, *The Inner Conflict,* pp.87–8.
48 KP 55.3–6. It is unclear how the nine kinds of animals and eight kinds of sacrifice are being counted here. B.N. Shastri interprets the eight as follows: 1. bird, 2. tortoise, 3. alligator, 4. nine kinds of animal (namely, i. goat, ii. boar, iii. buffalo, iv. lizard, v. *śoṣa*, vi. yak, vii. spotted antelope, viii. hare, ix. lion), 5. fish, 6. blood of one's own body, 7. horses, 8. elephants (KP, p.331n). What exactly the *śoṣa* is remains unclear.
49 KP 67.3–5. The YogT lists buffaloes, tortoises, yaks, rabbits, and other wild animals (2.9.158, 2.7.170); the MMT lists many kinds of fish, buffalo, ram, bird, alligator, deer, and eggs of various animals as suitable sacrifices (4.1–6). The YT lists goats, sheep, human beings, antelopes, mongooses, buffaloes, cows, jackals, lions, horses, and tortoises (3.6). The KJN likewise states that a member of the *kula* should be willing to eat any kind of animal flesh, including dog, cat, camel, jackal, horse, tortoise, boar, heron, buffalo, fish, and so on (11.14–17).
50 Kakati, *Mother Goddess Kāmākhyā* (Guwahati: Lawyer's Book Stall, 1952), p.65. On Khasi sacrifices of birds, goats, pigs, and cows, see Gupta, *Life and Culture of Matrilineal Tribe of Meghalaya* (New Delhi: Inter-India Publications, 1984), pp.166–7.
51 Maheshwar Neog, *Early History of the Vaiṣṇava Faith and Movement in Assam* (Delhi: Motilal Banarsidass, 1980), p.80.
52 Biardeau and Malamoud, *Le sacrifice*, pp.146–7.
53 KP 67.57–8.
54 Biardeau and Malamoud, *Le sacrifice*, pp.146–7.

55 Frederick J. Simoons, *A Ceremonial Ox: The Mithan in Nature, Culture and History* (Madison, WI, University of Wisconsin Press, 1968).
56 Woodward, "Economy, polity and cosmology in the Ao Naga mithan feast," in Susan D. Russell (ed.), *Ritual, Power and Economy: Upland-Lowland Contrasts in Mainland Southeast Asia* (Evanston, IL: Northwestern Illinois University Center for Southeast Asian Studies, 1989), p.129.
57 Woodward, "Economy," p.132.
58 Woodward, "Gifts for the sky: Animal sacrifice, head hunting and power among the Naga of Burma and Assam," in Graham Harvey (ed.), *Indigenous Religions: A Companion* (New York: Cassell, 2000), p.223.
59 Heesterman, *The Inner Conflict*, pp.87–8.
60 KP 55.11–16.
61 KP 55.17–20.
62 KP 67.20–1.
63 S. Endle, *The Kacharis* (Delhi: Cosmo Publications, 1975), pp.39–41. Some Assamese scholars have also noted that the offering of victims to Kāmākhyā follows the "tribal method" of beheading. See M. Śāstrī, "Dharma āru darśan," in G. Sarma (ed.), *Asamīya Jātir Itivṛtta* (Jorhat: Assam Sahitya Sabha, 1977), p.120.
64 Beck, "The Goddess and the demon: A local south Indian festival and its wider context," *Puruṣārtha* 5 (1981), pp.131–32.
65 KP 58.17–18.
66 KP 58.22–24.
67 Kristeva, *Power of Horror: An Essay on Abjection* (New York: Columbia University Press, 1982), p.3: "These bodily fluids, this defilement, this shit are what life withstands, hardly and with difficulty, on the part of death. There, I am at the border of my condition as a living being."
68 Douglas, *Purity and Danger*, p.161.
69 Douglas, *Purity and Danger*, p.115. See Stallybrass and White, *The Politics and Poetics*, p.21.
70 Bakhtin, *Rabelais and His World* (Cambridge, MA: MIT Press, 1984).
71 Bataille, *Erotism: Death and Sensuality* (San Francisco: City Lights, 1986), p.65.
72 Bataille, *Erotism*, pp.65, 116.
73 Zimmer, "On the significance of the Tantric yoga," in Joseph Campbell (ed.), *Spiritual Disciplines: Papers from the Eranos Yearbooks* (Princeton, NJ: Princeton University Press, 1985), p.14.
74 Sanderson, "Purity and power," pp.202, 192.
75 KP 58.17–24. See KP 56.52–57.
76 KP 74.135–38.
77 KP 74.54–57.
78 Eliade, *Yoga*, p.296.
79 Brooks, *Secret of the Three Cities: An Introduction to Hindu Śākta Tantrism* (Chicago: University Chicago Press, 1990), p.92. See Sanjukta Gupta, Dirk Jan Hoens, and Teun Goudriaan, *Hindu Tantrism* (Leiden: Brill, 1979), p.159.
80 Flood, *Tantric Body: The Secret Tradition of Hindu Religion* (London: I.B. Tauris, 2006), p.10. See White, "Tantrism," p.8985.
81 KJN 14.75–6.
82 KJN 4.14–15.

83 KJN 7.20–25; Bagchi, *Kaulajñāna Nirṇaya and Some Minor Texts of the School of Matsyendranātha* (Calcutta: Metropolitan Printing and Publishing House, 1934), pp.49–50, 53–4.
84 KT 2.3–5.
85 Shulman, *Tamil Temple Myths*, p.29.

Chapter Three

1 Doniger and Kakar, trans., *Kamasutra: A New Complete English Translation of the Sanskrit Text* (New York: Oxford University Press, 2002), p.9.
2 Orzech, *Politics and Transcendent Wisdom: The Scripture of the Humane Kings in the Creation of Chinese Buddhism* (University Park, PA: Pennsylvania State University Press, 1998), p.8. See Flood, *Tantric Body: The Secret Tradition of Hindu Religion* (London: I.B. Tauris, 2006), p.11.
3 White, *Kiss of the Yoginī: "Tantric Sex" in its South Asian Contexts* (Chicago: University of Chicago Press, 2003), p.262.
4 Flood, *Tantric Body*, p.80. On the relation between the king and the goddess, especially the goddess as buffalo slayer, see Thomas B. Coburn, *Encountering the Goddess: A Translation of the Devī Māhātmya and a Study of its Interpretation* (Albany, NY: SUNY Press, 1991), p.203n; Madeline Biardeau, "Devi: The goddess in India," in Yves Bonnefoy (ed.), *Asian Mythologies* (Chicago: University of Chicago Press, 1993), pp.95–8.
5 KP 84–7.
6 The YogT describes in detail the rise of the Kochs in Assam under Viśva Siṅgha in the sixteenth century, followed by the wars between the Kochs and Ahoms and the Muslim invasion of Assam in the seventeenth century (1.13–14).
7 See Beane, *Myth, Cult and Symbols in Śākta Hinduism: A Study of the Indian Mother Goddess* (Leiden: E.J. Brill, 1977), pp.87–8; Urban, "Matrix of power: Tantra, kingship and sacrifice in the worship of mother goddess Kāmākhyā." *South Asia* 31, no.3 (2008), pp.500–534.
8 Sadashiv Ambadas Dange, *Encyclopedia of Puranic Beliefs and Practices* (New Delhi: Navrang, 1987), v.3, p.44.
9 Coburn, *Encountering*, p.203n.
10 Biardeau, *Hinduism: The Anthropology of a Civilization* (Paris: Flammarion, 1981), p.137.
11 Flood, *Tantric Body*, p.78. White notes that "[d]own to the nineteenth century, the kings of Nepal worshiped the nine Durgās at the end of the autumn festival of the Nine Nights (*navarātrī*) precisely because this was the beginning of the season of military campaigns" (*Kiss*, p.129).
12 White, *Kiss*, p.137.
13 Dehejia, *Yoginī Cult and Temples: A Tantric Tradition* (Delhi: National Museum, 1986), p.85.
14 Davidson, *Indian Esoteric Buddhism: A Social History of the Tantric Movement* (New York: Columbia University Press, 2002), p.60; Flood, *Tantric Body*, p.76.
15 Mukunda Madhava Sharma, *Inscriptions of Ancient Assam* (Gauhati: Gauhati University, 1978), pp.91, 93, 161.
16 P.C. Choudhury, *The History of the People of Assam to the Twelfth Century AD* (Gauhati: Department of Historical in Assam, 1966), p.429.

17 Sharma, "Religion," in H.K. Barpujari (ed.), *The Comprehensive History of Assam: Ancient Period* (Guwahati: Publication Board, Assam, 1990), pp.342–3.
18 K.L. Barua, *Early History of Kamarupa* (Guwahati: Lawyer's Book Stall, 1966), p.48.
19 Sharma, *Inscriptions*, pp.226–7.
20 Sharma, *Inscriptions*, p.164.
21 Sharma, *Inscriptions*, p.187. On Indrapāla's patronage of Śāktism, see Sharma, *Inscriptions*, pp.201, 206.
22 Sharma, *Inscriptions*, pp.231, 236. Elsewhere Indrapāla is praised as the "breaker of the force of the adversary," "a destroyer of kings who are not submissive," and "like the thunderbolt (of Indra) destroying arrogant kings" (*Inscriptions*, p.204).
23 Sharma, *Inscriptions*, p.231.
24 J.C. Heesterman, *The Inner Conflict of Tradition: Essays in Ancient Indian Ritual* (Chicago: University of Chicago Press, 1985), p.109. See MB 13.1126.9.
25 KP 84.40, 82.125.
26 KP 85.75–6. Elsewhere, the KP advises the king to appoint learned *brāhmaṇs* as ministers (84.102) and warns him never to "insult a *brāhmaṇ* for any reason. If a king insults *brāhmaṇs* he will suffer in this world and in the afterlife. He should not fight with them or take their wealth. At the time of ritual performance they should always be worshipped" (84.120–22).
27 Heesterman, *Inner Conflict,* p.127
28 Romila Thapar, "Sacrifice, surplus and the soul," *History of Religions* 33 (1994), p.312. White notes that later Tantric traditions continued a "symbiotic relationship between Tantric 'power brokers' and their power-wielding royal patrons" (*Kiss,* p.133).
29 KP 36.7. See Schoterman (ed.), *The Yoni Tantra* (Delhi: Manhohar, 1980), pp.30–1.
30 Barua, *Early History*, p.17.
31 KP 38.99–161.
32 Sree Dharanikanta Devsharma, *The Holy Shrine of Kamakhya* (Guwahati: The Author, 1999), pp.14–16. See Subhendugopal Bagchi, *Eminent Indian Śākta Centers in Eastern India* (Calcutta: Punthi Pustak, 1980), p.145.
33 There is one reference to Kāmeśvara (Śiva) and Mahagaurī (the Goddess) in an inscription of Indrapāla (eleventh century), which is probably a reference to Kāmākhyā.
34 Swami Satyananda Saraswati, *Shree Maa: The Life of a Saint* (Napa: Devi Mandir Publications, 1997), pp.13–14.
35 Devasarma, *Kāmākhyā Darśan* (Guwahati: Kāmākhyā Pradarśanī, n.d.), p.18.
36 Sharma, *Inscriptions*, pp.161, 91, 93.
37 H.K. Barpujari (ed.), *The Comprehensive History of Assam, Volume Two* (Guwahati: Publication Board, Assam, 1985), p.73.
38 Ray, *Transformations on the Bengal Frontier: Jalpaiguri, 1765–1948* (New York: Routledge, 2002), p.44. Many royal histories contained portraits in which Viśva Siṅgha and his mother were depicted as gods. See Mishra, *Kamakhya: A Socio-Cultural Study* (New Delhi: D.K. Printworld, 2004), p.5; N.C. Sarma (ed.), *Darrang Rajvamsavali* (Guwahati: Bani Prakash, 1973), pp.9–13, 101–113.

39 YogT 1.13.2–3.
40 YogT 1.13.16–20.
41 YogT 1.13.22–3.
42 Anwar Hussain, director, *Shri Shri Kamakhya* (1983).
43 N.N. Acharyya, *The History of Medieval Assam* (Gauhati: Dutta Baruah and Company, 1966), pp.191–2; see Guṇābhirām Baruā, *Āsām Burañjī* (Guwahati: Asam Prakāśan Parisad, 1972), pp.54–5.
44 Ray, *Transformations*, p.44. See Amantullah Khan, *Cooch Beharer Itihas* (Cooch Behar: Cooch Behar State Press, 1936), p.94.
45 In 1546, Naranārāyaṇa led an unsuccessful war against the Ahoms, which was resumed in 1562 under Chilarai; eventually, the Koches conquered the Kacharis, Manipurs, Jayantias, and Tripuris. See R.M. Nath, *History of the Koch Kingdom, 1515–1615* (Delhi: Mittal Publications, 1989), pp.50–63.
46 Nath, *History of the Koch Kingdom*, pp.58–62 and appendix.
47 Gajendra Adhikary, *A History of the Temples of Kamrup and their Management* (Guwahati: Chandra Prakash, 2001), p.38.
48 Sarma, *Kamrup Kamakhya* (Guwahati: Bishnu Prakashan, 2002), p.20.
49 Thus the Ahom king Rājeśvara Siṅgha (1751–60) was praised in a temple inscription for his "an unflinching devotion to the goddess Kāmākhyā," and for being "powerful like the brightest sun, magnanimous before the enemies like a destroying fire" (Sarma, *Kamrup Kamakhya*, pp.21–2).
50 Gait, *A History of Assam* (Calcutta: Thacker Spink and Co., 1933 [1905]), p.286.
51 Chandra Kanta Sarma, *An Early History of Kamarup Kamakhya* (Gauhati: Kalita Art Press, 1998), p.16.
52 Nirmal Kumar Basu, *Assam in the Ahom Age, 1228–1826* (Calcutta: Sanskrit Pustak Bhandar, 1970), pp.63–4; see Kashinath Tamuli Phukan, *Assam Buranji* (Calcutta, 1906), p.49.
53 Doloi, *Asamat Śaktisādhana āru Śākta-Sāhitya* (Nalbari, Assam: Padmapriya Library, 1998), p.78.
54 Basu, *Assam in the Ahom Age*, p.354.
55 Coburn, *Encountering*, p.26.
56 Biardeau, "Devi," p.95. See Heesterman, *The Inner Conflict*, p.10.
57 Barua, *Early History*, p.23.
58 Sharma, "Religion," p.307.
59 B.N. Puri, "Polity and administration," in H.K. Barpujari (ed.), *The Comprehensive History of Assam: Ancient Period* (Guwahati: Publication Board, Assam, 1990), v.I, pp.176–7.
60 Sharma, *Inscriptions*, p.186.
61 Sharma, *Inscriptions*, p.231.
62 KP 67.5–6.
63 KP 84.101.
64 KP 84.16–17.
65 KP 84.60.
66 Sarkar, in Choudhury, *The History*, p.230. As Flood comments, "These medieval kingdoms shared an ontology of divine kingship. . . The king is not merely a secular ruler but a divine king, a god incarnate, as expressed in the very term *deva* which can mean both deity and king. . . the king became the

high point of the social structure identified with the sun, with the rest of society below. Officialdom is equated with the lesser gods of the sky, and the queen is identified with the earth" (*Tantric Body*, p.77). See A.M. Hocart, *Kings and Councillors: An Essay in the Comparative Anatomy of Human Society* (Chicago: University of Chicago Press, 1970), pp.97, 183–5.

67 KP 85.13–14.

68 KP 85.79–81.

69 KP 85.21–3. Playing on the double meaning of *durgā*, the king is also to worship the goddess Durgā on the floor of his fortress (*durgā*) in order to ensure victory against his enemies (KP 84.119–20).

70 KP 85.56–61.

71 KP 67.145–151.

72 Golap Chandra Barua (ed.), *Ahom Buranji: From the Earliest Time to the End of Ahom Rule* (Guwahati: Spectrum Publications, 1985), pp.336–7.

73 Basu, *Assam in the Ahom Age*, p.224.

74 "Nepal king visits Kamakhya Temple," *India Travel Times*, June 27, 2002, http://www.indiatraveltimes.com/religion/king.html (accessed April 16, 2009). See Dold, "The Mahavidyas at Kamarupa: Dynamics of transformation in Hinduism," *Religious Studies and Theology* 23 (2004), p.117.

75 KP 67.19

76 "One goat is better than ten yaks. A single tortoise is equal to ten goats. A rabbit is better than a hundred tortoises. A boar is worth more than a thousand rabbits. A buffalo is said to be better than two thousand boars. A rhino is better than two thousand buffalos. But the fruit of a human being is equal to a thousand rhinos. A *śoṇatuṇḍa* is worth two thousand human beings. A *śvetagriva* is equal to two thousand *śoṇatuṇḍas*. And a lizard is better than a hundred *śvetagriva*s. And a human boy (*narasya kumāra*), O Goddess, is better than a hundred lizards" (YogT 2.7.157–62).

77 Beane, *Myth, Cult and Symbols*, p.59.

78 Smith, *Classifying the Universe: The Ancient Indian Varna System and the Origins of Caste* (New York: Oxford University Press, 1994), p.251. As Smith notes, "The Vedic system is ambiguous on the question of human victims. . . [I]nsofar as sacrificial victims are edible, the explicit rules against eating human flesh would seem to preclude human sacrifice. On the other hand, insofar as humans are among the five sacrificial paśus, they were eminently sacrificable" (ibid., p. 278n).

79 Heesterman, *The Broken World of Sacrifice: An Essay in Ancient Indian Religion* (Chicago: University of Chicago Press, 1993), pp.31–2.

80 See Woodward, "Gifts for the sky: Animal sacrifice, head hunting and power among the Naga of Burma and Assam," in Graham Harvey (ed.), *Indigenous Religions: A Companion* (New York: Cassell, 2000); Bikash Chandra. *Human Sacrifice and Head-Hunting in Northeastern India* (Gauhati: Lawyer's Book Stall, 1977); Mishra, *Kamakhya*, pp.5–7.

81 Briggs, *Gorakhnāth and the Kānphata Yogīs* (New York: Oxford University Press, 1938), p.169.

82 KP 67.48–50.

83 KP 67.116–18.

84 KP 67.102.

85 KP 67.69–70.

86 KP 67.76–81.
87 KP 67.82–89.
88 KP 67.106–110, 67.123ff.
89 KP 67.171–72.
90 Heesterman, *Inner Conflict*, p.109. See KP 85.75.
91 O'Flaherty, *The Origins of Evil in Hindu Mythology* (Berkeley, CA: University of California Press, 1976), p.146.
92 Heesterman, *The Inner Conflict*, pp.91.
93 Biardeau, "Devi," p.95.
94 KP 67.168.
95 KP 74.54–6; KP 58.47.
96 KP 74.68–9.
97 In February 2008, I interviewed the current priest at the temple, who repeated the narrative that human sacrifice was offered at the temple by the Jaintia kings until the nineteenth century.
98 Mishra, *Kamakhya*, p.5; see E.A. Gait, "Human sacrifices (Indian)," in James Hastings (ed.) *Encyclopedia of Religion and Ethics* (New York: Charles Scribner's Sons, 1928), p.65 and Chapter 6 below.
99 Gait, *History of Assam*, p.292.
100 Basu, *Assam in the Ahom Age*, p.237; see S.K. Bhuyan, *Assam Burañji* (Gauhati: Department of Historical and Antiquarian Studies, 1945), p.59.
101 Barua, *Ahom Buranji*, p.100.
102 Mishra, *Kamakhya*, p.5. On the Chutiyas and human sacrifice, see S.N. Sarma, *A Socio-Economic and Cultural History of Medieval Assam* (Guwahati: Pratima Devi, 1989), p.197; Barua, *Early History*, p.183; W.B. Brown, *An Outline of the Deori Chutiya Grammar* (Shillong: Assam Secretariat Printing Office, 1895), pp.vi, 75–7. The Kacharis are also said to have worshiped Kecāi Khātī with human sacrifice, again, for success in battle. See Mishra, *Kamakhya*, p.5; S.K. Bhuyan, *Kachārī Burañjī* (Guwahati: Department of Historical and Antiquarian Studies, 1984), p.xviii.
103 Barua, *Temples and Legends of Assam* (Bombay: Bharatiya Vidya Bhavan, 1965), p.87. See Gait, "Human sacrifice," v.5, p.850.
104 Barua, *Temples and Legends*, p.87.
105 Lieutenant E.T. Dalton, "Notes on the Chutiyas of upper Assam," manuscript printed in Brown, *An Outline*, p.77.
106 Seema Hussain, "Devilish devotee: A barbaric attempt at human sacrifice goes awry in Assam," *The Week*, June 29, 2003, http://www.theweek.com/23June29/events9.htm (accessed July 4, 2004). See Dold, "The mahavidyas," p.117.

Chapter Four

1 Bataille, *The Accursed Share, Volume II* (New York: Zone, 1999), p.119.
2 Monier-Williams, *Hinduism* (London: Society for Promoting Christian Knowledge, 1894), p.116.
3 Margo Anand, *The Art of Sexual Ecstasy: The Path of Sacred Sexuality for Western Lovers* (Los Angeles: Jeremy P. Tarcher, 1989).
4 BTS 695–704; PTT 554–59.

5 Bharati, "The future (if any) of Tantrism," *Loka: A Journal from the Naropa Institute* 1 (1975), pp.126–30.
6 White, *Kiss of the Yoginī: "Tantric Sex" in its South Asian Contexts* (Chicago: University of Chicago Press, 2003). See Urban, "Matrix of power: Tantra, kingship and sacrifice in the worship of mother goddess Kāmākhyā," *South Asia* 31, no.3 (2008).
7 See TA 29.6–8, 29.289–90; Lilian Silburn, *Kuṇḍalinī: Energy of the Depths* (Albany, NY: SUNY Press, 1988), pp.157–204.
8 Bharati, *The Tantric Tradition* (New York: Anchor Books, 1970), p.266. See Urban "Matrix of power"; Flood, *Tantric Body: The Secret Tradition of Hindu Religion* (London: I.B. Tauris, 2006), p.84; John R. Dupuche, *Abhinavagupta: The Kula Ritual, as Elaborated in Chapter 29 of the Tantrāloka* (Delhi: Motilal Banarsidass, 2003), pp.84ff.
9 Sarma, *Kamrup Kamakhya* (Guwahati: Bishnu Prakashan, 2002), p.6.
10 The YT is from the Koch or Cooch Behar (Koch) region, immediately adjacent to Assam and closely connected to the worship of Kāmākhyā. Given its title and intense focus on Kāmākhyā, the KT is almost certainly from Assam; and given its similarity to the YT, it is probably from roughly the same period, the sixteenth century.
11 KP 74.203–5.
12 KJN 11.11, 11.32, 3.18, 6.14.
13 White, *Kiss*, chapter 8.
14 Judith Butler, *Subjects of Desire: Hegelian Reflections in Twentieth Century France* (New York: Columbia University Press, 1987), p.213.
15 White argues that *mudrā* (literally a "seal") originally referred to "sealing" together of male and female bodies in sexual union [White, "Tantrism," in Lindsay Jones (ed.), *Encyclopedia of Religion* (New York: MacMillan, 2005), p.8986].
16 Sanjukta Gupta, Dirk Jan Hoens, and Teun Goudriaan, *Hindu Tantrism* (Leiden: Brill, 1979), p.44.
17 Kooij, *Worship of the Goddess according to the Kālikāpurāṇa* (Leiden: E.J. Brill, 1972), pp.28–9; KP 74.125–40.
18 KP 74.125–27, 140.
19 KP 74.204–5.
20 KP 74.136–8.
21 KP 81.19–23.
22 See Gupta et al., *Hindu Tantrism*, pp.36–7
23 KT 8.1–12.
24 YT 2.16–26. Schoterman (ed.), *The Yoni Tantra* (Delhi: Manhohar, 1980), pp.26–7.
25 Dehejia, *Yoginī Cult and Temples: A Tantric Tradition* (Delhi: National Museum, 1986), p.63.
26 Dehejia, *Yoginī*, p.63.
27 See Deka, *Nīlācala Kāmākhyā: Her History and Tantra* (Guwahati: Lawyer's Book Stall, 2004), pp.65–6.
28 White, *Kiss*, p.104.
29 Schoterman, *Yoni Tantra*, p.6.
30 YT 1.6.

31 YT 2.6. Likewise, the *Kāmākhyā Tantra* declares, "Worship in the region of the *yoni* brings great pleasure, O Lady of the Kula. Worship of the *yoni* is the great worship, bearing supernatural power. There is nothing equal to it. The wise man should sacrifice to the goddess there, for it is none other than the goddess... He should anoint it with fine perfumes and worship it with various offerings. There will be great pleasure, and the power of the goddess will immediately be attained" (KT 3.53–55).

32 KAN 9.30–3. "That *pītha* is said to be twofold, secret and manifest, O Great Lady. The secret one is more meritorious than the manifest one, and difficult to attain even for the best of adepts. But it is always attained by those who are skilled in the *kula* path" (YogT 1.11.55–6).

33 KAN 9.37, 9.42.

34 KCT 5.1. See Lousie M. Finn (ed.), *The Kulacūḍāmaṇi Tantra and Vāmakeśvara Tantra* (Wiesbaden: Otto Harrassowitz, 1986), p.113n.

35 KCT 6.1–8

36 Swāmī Kuvalayānanda and S.A. Shukla (eds), *Gorakṣaśatakam* (Bombay: Kaivalyadhāma S.M.Y.M Samiti, 1974), pp.10–13: "The *ādhāra* is the first *cakra*, the *svādhiṣṭhāna* is the second. Between the two is the place of the *yoni* called Kāmarūpa. In the center of the lotus called *ādhāra*, which his located at the anus and has four petals, lies the *yoni* called 'Kāma,' which is praised by sages. In this *yoni* lies a great *liṅga* facing west and shining like a jewel at the top... "

37 Briggs, *Gorakhnāth and the Kānphata Yogīs* (New York: Oxford University Press, 1938), p.313.

38 White, *Kiss*, p.106. On *antaryāga*, see S.C. Banerji, *Tantra in Bengal* (Delhi: Manohar, 1992), pp.156–8; TA 29.

39 Patrick Olivelle, *The Early Upaniṣads: Annotated Text and Translation* (New York: Oxford University Press, 1998), p.155.

40 White, *Kiss*, p.17. See Dupuche, *Abhinavagupta*, pp.84ff; TA 29.

41 KAT 10.112. See TA 28.96–111. "Just as the *brahman's* wife takes part in the Vedic ritual, so does the *dūtī* participate in the *kulācārya* practice" (Silburn, *Kuṇḍalinī*, p.179).

42 KAT 5.89–90.

43 BTS 703.

44 PTT 554.

45 See *Kāmākhyā Tantra* (KT 3.53–54, 4.33–36).

46 See YT 2.10–15, 3.16–17, 5.24–26.

47 YT 2.15, KT 4.33, 3.59. The association of menstruation, animal sacrifice and sexual union is also seen in other texts. See Jyotirlāla Dāsa (ed.), *Māyātantram: Mūla Saṃskṛta o Bāṅgānuvada Sameta* (Calcutta: Navabhārata, 1978), 12.4–7: "Having brought a menstruating woman and worshiped his chosen deity in her *yoni* at midnight, he should pray for three days... Having worshiped his chosen deity in the genitals of another's wife, the wise man should recite [the *mantra*] 108 times. Then he should worship [the goddess] 108 times using fresh flowers [i.e., menstrual blood]. Then he should worship Mahāmāyā 108 times using her menstrual blood. After that he should offer a complete oblation and recite [the *mantra*] 108 times."

48 YT 2.10–15.

49 YT 3.5–8. See also YT 3.16–17, 5.24–6. The KJN likewise associates the Tantric rite of worshiping the *yoginīs* and consuming menstrual blood with the consumption of a wide range of animal flesh: "One should take hold of a dog, a cat, a camel a jackal, and a horse, a turtle, a tortoise, a boar, a cat, a heron or a crab, shoots and pot-herbs of many various kinds, a *śeraka*, a deer, or a buffalo, as well as a rhinoceros, and various other fish, as one can obtain them. . . One should always eat these, having obtained them by whatever means. One should worship the multitude of *yoginīs* with food and drink, etc., O Beloved. Then one should perform the drinking of menstrual blood [*dhārāpāna*], if one wishes to live a long life" (KJN 11.14–19).

50 KT 9.23–4. Elsewhere the *Kāmākhyā Tantra* instructs the adept to worship the goddess, offering the "self-arisen flower" (*svayumbhūkusuma*) and "that which has arisen from the ball and the basin" (*kuṇḍagolodbhava*) (KT 3.31–2). As White has shown, the self-arisen flower is often used to refer to menstrual blood, and specifically the blood of a maiden who has not had sexual intercourse with a male [*Kiss*, pp.78–9, see Bhattacharyya, *Indian Puberty Rites* (Delhi: Munshiram Manoharlal, 1980), p.16]; the *kuṇḍagola* or *kuṇḍagolodbhava*, meanwhile can refer either to the male semen or to the female sexual fluids. In this case, because the substance is described as "white" (*śukla*), it appears to refer to the semen, so that the offering here is the combined male and female sexual fluids.

51 YT 2.16–26. Likewise the *Kāmākhyā Tantra* describes the ritual: "Having kissed and worshipped the *yoni* 108 times, the wise one should recite [the *mantra*] 108 times, with his penis placed in the *yoni*. He will attain a wealth that is fivefold what he desires and always be happy. He should always be joined with his consort, O Great Lady. Having brought the prostitute and arranged the *kula cakra*, the adept should sacrifice to the goddess in her *yoni* with a joyful mind. He should pronounce the words *bhaga liṅga* [vagina, penis] with a melodious voice" (4.33–36).

52 Schoterman, *Yoni Tantra*, p.30.

53 Finn, *Kulacūḍāmani Tantra*, p.106. As the KCT describes the rite: "Even after drinking enough to fill herself from the tips of her toes to the ends of her hair, she is still not satisfied. Then that man with a charming nature enjoys the oblation [*havis*], which is the essence of awakening. Having offered her the remnant [*śeṣa*] of his own beautiful oblation [*havis*], he should remain [in that position] and agitate [his penis] like another Kāma" (KCT 4.33–34).

54 KT 3.45. In the Orissan Śākta tradition, too, the sexual fluids are called the "leavings of Kālī or Śakti (Kālī or Śakti *ucchiṣṭa*)." As Marglin observes, "the word *ucchiṣṭa* refers to the good left-over, . . . These leavings of Kālī were the drops of female sexual fluid that were secreted from the vagina of the devadasi as a result of the movements that she performs during the dance. . . the sole meaning and purpose of this dance was the production of this sexual fluid, the fifth m, which he called the 'nectar of the kula' (*kulāmruta*)" [*Wives of the God King: The Rituals of the Devadasis of Puri* (New York: Oxford University Press, 1985), p.240].

55 BTS 703. The *Kulārṇava Tantra* also uses the term *ucchiṣṭa* to describe the secret offerings: "One should eat the leftovers [*ucchiṣṭa*] of the daughters of the Guru and Śakti and the eldest and youngest [sons] of the Guru, or of one's own eldest [son], but not of any others, O Pārvatī. He should

drink the fluid remainder of the Śakti and the edible remainders of a Vīra" (8.22–23).

56 Monier-Williams, *Sanskrit-English Dictionary* (Oxford: Clarendon Press, 1995), p.173.

57 Shulman, *Tamil Temple Myths: Sacrifice and Divine Marriage in the South Indian Śaiva Tradition* (Princeton, NJ: Princeton University Press, 1980), p.347. See Charles Malamoud, *Cooking the World: Ritual and Thought in Ancient India* (Delhi: Oxford University Press, 1996), p.21: "So long as they remain external to the hierarchical processes of the sacrifice, food scraps are objects of repulsion. But when they become the remains of a *yajña*, they become the edible food *par excellence* and play an essential role in the continuity of *dharma*."

58 BTS 704.

59 BTS 703; see KT 9.23–4.

60 Bhaṭṭācārya, *Asamat Śaktipūjā* (Guwahati: Bāṇī Prakāśa, 1977), pp.83–6.

61 YogT 1.6.69–73.

62 Bharati, *Tantric Tradition*, p.260.

63 Marglin, *Wives*, pp.89–90. See Marglin, "Power, purity and pollution: The caste system reconsidered," *Contributions to Indian Sociology* 10, no.2 (1977), pp.245–70.

64 Schoterman, *Yoni Tantra*, p.31.

65 Bhattacharyya, *Indian Puberty Rites*, p.14.

66 Olivelle, *Dharmasūtras: The Law Codes of Ancient India* (New York: Oxford University Press, 1999), pp.118, 280.

67 KP 36.7.

68 BVP 1.110.116–20.

69 YT 3.20.

70 Schoterman, *Yoni Tantra*, p.25.

71 KT 4.30, 4.33–6. Later Tantric authors insist that the partner should only be one's own wife (*svakīyā*). See Swami Nigamānanda Sarasvatī, *Tāntrik Guru vā Tantra o Sādhana Paddhati* (Calcutta: Sāradā Press, 1981 [1911]), p.189: "in the Kali age, a sexual partner who is not one's own wife is not allowed; that is the sin of adultery." On the *parakīyā-svakīyā* debate, see Urban, *The Economics of Ecstasy: Tantra, Secrecy and Power in Colonial Bengal* (New York: Oxford University Press, 2001), chapter 6.

72 KT 3.58–61.

73 YogT 1.6.37–8.

74 YogT 1.6.42–51; see YT 2.5

75 Monier-Williams, *Sanskrit-English Dictionary*, p.974. See Biernarcki, *Renowned Goddess of Desire: Women, Sex and Speech in Tantra* (New York: Oxford University Press, 2007), pp.88–9.

76 Olivelle, *Dharmasūtras*, p.117.

77 Bataille, *Erotism: Death and Sensuality* (San Francisco: City Lights, 1986), p.115.

78 Bataille, *Erotism*, p.91. See Amy Hollywood, *Sensible Ecstasy: Mysticism, Sexual Difference and the Demands of History* (Chicago: University of Chicago Press, 2002), p.38.

79 Bataille, *The Accursed Share*, v.2, p.119. "Erotic activity, by dissolving the separate beings that participate in it, reveals their fundamental continuity, like the waves of a stormy sea. In sacrifice, the victim is divested not only of clothes

but of life. . . The victim dies and the spectators share in what his death reveals. This is. . . the element of sacredness" (Bataille, *Erotism*, p.22).

80 Bataille, *The Accursed Share*, v.2, pp.183–4; see Bataille, *Erotism*, pp.39, 83.

81 Foucault, *Religion and Culture* (New York: Routledge, 1999), p.62.

82 YT 4.28, 1.8, 4.7.

83 YT 6.6–7.

84 Sanderson, "Purity and power among the brahmans of Kashmir," in Michael Carrithers, Steven Collins, and Steven Lukes (eds), *The Category of the Person* (New York: Cambridge University Press, 1985), pp.201, 199.

85 Bhaṭṭācārya, *Asamat Śaktipūjā*, pp.80–1.

86 See Daṇḍīsvāmī Damodara Āśrama (ed.), *Jñānārṇava Tantra* (Calcutta: Navabhārata, 1982), 22.30–32: "How can there be any impurity in excrement or urine? Undoubtedly, that is a false opinion. The body is born from a woman's menstrual blood. So how can that be impure, when by means of it one attains the highest state?"

87 KJN 11.27–9. "Feces [*viṣṭa*], menstrual blood [*dhārāmṛta*], semen [*śukra*], blood [*rakta*], and marrow [*majjan*] mixed together: these five means of purification [are consumed] regularly, according to the Kula doctrine" (KJN 11.11).

88 AVT 24–6.

89 White, "Tantrism," p.8986.

90 Based on my research in the area, I've found that the *pañcamakāras* are still performed in Assam (interviews with priests at the Bhairavī, Bagalāmukhī and Kāmākhyā temples, 2000–2008). Various other authors report the same. See Pandit Rajmani Tigunait, *Śakti: The Power in Tantra* (Himalayan Institute, 1998), p.172; Deka, *Nīlācala Kāmākhyā*, pp.64–7.

91 Bose, "The Tantrik Quest," *Sunday*, January 25, 1981, http://www.shrikali.org/tantricquest.php (accessed April 16, 2009).

Chapter Five

1 Bharati, "Making sense out of Tantrism and Tantrics," *Loka: A Journal from the Naropa Institute* 2 (1976), p.53.

2 Ward, *A View of the History, Literature and Religion of the Hindoos* (London: Kingsbury, Parbury and Allen, 1817), v. I, p.247.

3 André van Lysebeth, *Tantra: The Cult of the Feminine* (York Beach, ME: Samuel Weiser, 1995), p.53.

4 A point also made by Davidson, *Indian Esoteric Buddhism: A Social History of the Tantric Movement* (New York: Columbia University Press, 2002), p.97.

5 Eliade, *Yoga: Immortality and Freedom* (Princeton, NJ: Princeton University Press, 1971), pp.202–3.

6 Bhattacaryya, *History of the Śākta Religion* (New Delhi: Munshiram Manoharlal, 1974), p.165.

7 Sanjukta Gupta, Dirk Jan Hoens, and Teun Goudriaan, *Hindu Tantrism* (Leiden: Brill, 1979), p.34.

8 Douglas Brooks, *Auspicious Wisdom: The Texts and Traditions of Śrīvidyā Śākta Tantrism in South India* (Albany, NY: SUNY Press, 1992), pp.25–6.

9 David Snellgrove, *Indo-Tibetan Buddhism: Indian Buddhists and Their Tibetan Successors* (Boston, MA: Shambhalla, 1987), p.287.

10 White, *Kiss of the Yoginī: "Tantric Sex" in its South Asian Contexts* (Chicago: University of Chicago Press, 2003), pp.270–1.

11 Shaw, *Passionate Enlightenment: Women in Tantric Buddhism* (Princeton, NJ: Princeton University Press, 1994), p.11.

12 Kathleen Erndl, "Is *shakti* empowering for women?" in Alf Hiltebeitel and Kathleen Erndl (eds), *Is the Goddess a Feminist? The Politics of South Asian Goddesses* (New York: New York University Press, 2000), p.94.

13 *Biernacki, Renowned Goddess of Desire: Women, Sex and Speech in Tantra* (New York: Oxford University Press, 2007), pp.24, 143. As noted above, however, most of Biernacki's texts do not appear to be from Assam but more likely from Bengal.

14 Hiltebeitel and Erndl, *Is the Goddess a Feminist?* p.13. On feminisms, see Robyn R. Warhol and Diane Price Herndl (eds), *Feminisms: An Anthology of Literary Theory and Criticism* (New Brunswick, NJ: Rutgers University Press, 1991), p.x.

15 See Shaw, *Passionate Enlightenment*, pp.12–13, which relies primarily on feminist theory from the 1970s and 1980s. See also Biernacki, *Renowned Goddess*, p.26.

16 Campbell, *Traveller in Space: In Search of Female Identity in Tibetan Buddhism* (New York: George Braziller, 1996), pp.2–3, 106–22.

17 Davidson, *Indian Esoteric*, p.97. On the question of "what's in it for the women?" see Hugh B. Urban, *The Economics of Ecstasy: Tantra, Secrecy and Power in Colonial Bengal* (New York: Oxford University Press, 2001), pp.82–90.

18 See Urban, *Tantra: Sex, Secrecy, Politics and Power in the Study of Religion* (Berkeley, CA: University of California Press, 2003), pp.1–43.

19 June McDaniel lists five roles for women: as incarnations of the goddess; as ritual consorts; as gurus; as professional consorts; and as celibate wives and widows. "Does Tantric ritual empower women?" in Tracy Pintchman (ed.), *Women's Lives, Women's Rituals in the Hindu Tradition*, (New York: Oxford University Press, 2007), pp.159–75. See also Kathleen M. Erndl, "The goddess and women's power: A Hindu case study," in Karen L. King (ed.), *Women and Goddess Traditions: In Antiquity and Today* (Minneapolis, MN: Fortress Press, 1997), p.19.

20 Gupta et al., *Hindu Tantrism*, p.34. See *Śaktisaṅgama Tantra*, ed. Benyotosh Bhattcharyya (Baroda: Oriental Institute, 1932–78), 2.13.43–48: "Woman is the creator of the universe. The universe is her form. Woman is the foundation of the world... There is no jewel rarer than woman. There is not, nor has been, nor will be any kingdom or wealth to be compared with a woman."

21 Donna Landry and Gerald MacLean, *The Spivak Reader: Selected Works of Gayatri Chakravorty Spivak* (New York: Routledge, 1996), p.58.

22 YogT 1.12.34. See Goswami, *Kāmākhyā Temple: Past and Present* (New Delhi: A.P.H. Publishing Corporation, 1998), p.92.

23 YogT 2.17.31–32. The same text tells the story of king Viśvāmbhara who worshiped a *kumārī* born to a prostitute family named Kāñcī. During the *pūjā* she became radiant with light and gave him liberation. The place of the *pūjā* then became the holy city of Kāñcī (2.17.44–5).

24 Khanna, "The goddess-woman equation in the Tantras," in Durre S. Ahmed (ed.), *Gendering the Spirit: Women, Religion and the Post-Colonial Response* (New York: Zed Books, 2002), p.51. For documentary film of *kumārī pūjā* performed at Kāmākhyā today, see Tracy Wares, director, "Shakti: The Performance of Gender Roles at Kamakhya, Assam," video documentary for a Senior Honors Thesis, Department of Anthropology, University of California, Berkeley, 2001.

25 YogT 1.17.8–16.

26 Marglin, *Wives of the God King: The Rituals of the Devadasis of Puri* (New York: Oxford University Press, 1985), p.61.

27 KP 58.7–9.

28 KP 74.118. A similar association of women with death, sexuality, and danger is also seen throughout medieval Christian literature. See Amy Hollywood, *Sensible Ecstasy: Mysticism, Sexual Difference and the Demands of History* (Chicago: University of Chicago Press, 2002), pp.18–20.

29 KCT 4.7–14.

30 KAT 11.57ff.

31 George Lakoff, *Women, Fire and Dangerous Things: What Categories Reveal about the Mind* (Chicago: University of Chicago Press, 1987).

32 Lincoln, *Discourse and the Construction of Society: Comparative Studies in Myth, Ritual and Classification* (New York: Oxford University Press, 1989), p.137: "Taxonomy is thus not only a means for organizing information, but also. . . an instrument for the classification and manipulation of society."

33 Sanderson, "Purity and power among the brahmans of Kashmir," in Michael Carrithers, Steven Collins, and Steven Lukes (eds), *The Category of the Person* (New York: Cambridge University Press, 1985), p.202.

34 YT I.6. Likewise, the *Yoginī Tantra* proclaims, "That *yoni*-region is endowed with My splendor, and it is the place of the origin of all things" (1.15.51). See Biernacki, *Renowned Goddess*, p.57.

35 KJN 22.11-12.

36 YT 7.14–17. As the KCT declares, "If only one woman there is beheld and worshipped, then all the gods—Brahmā, Viṣṇu, and Śiva etc. have been adored. . . . If he does not worship a woman he is beset by obstacles. . . In the early morning, or at the time of taking a bath, the women of all castes are to be honored whether purified or unpurified, or even of low caste, Oh my Son!" (3.53–8).

37 YT 2.3–5.The *Prāṇatoṣiṇī Tantra* lists 26 possible female partners, whose only requirement is that they be artful: these range from a dancer or prostitute, to a butcher or hunter, to a Buddhist or even a Yavana (Greek or Muslim) (PTT p.548).

38 "The washerwoman (*rajakī*) as her name indicates is associated with menstrual blood" (Marglin, *Wives*, p.230).

39 KT 3.58–9, 8.4.

40 Dehejia, *Yoginī Cult and Temples: A Tantric Tradition* (Delhi: National Museum, 1986), p.224. See the *Śrī Kāmākhyā Guhya Siddhi* manuscript discussed by Bagchi, *Kaulajñāna Nirṇaya and Some Minor Texts of the School of Matsyendranātha* (Calcutta: Metropolitan Printing and Publishing House, 1934), p.61.

41 Biernacki cites some late texts from northeast India that call for sexual union with one's own wife (*Renowned Goddess*, pp.99–106). However, there is no

compelling evidence that these texts come from Assam. Rather, it seems more likely they these texts came from the Bengal area where debates over *svakīyā* and *parakīyā* sex were widespread during this same period. On the *svakīyā-parakīyā* debate in Bengal, see Urban, *Economics of Ecstasy*, pp.162–80. The eighteenth-century Bengali text, the *Mahānirvāṇa Tantra* also reflects this reformist trend, as do other late Bengali texts. See Svāmī Nigamānanda, *Tāntrik Guru: vā Tantra o Sādhana Padhati* (Calcutta: Sāradā Press, 1991 [1911]), p.189.

42 KCT 3.31–32.

43 YT 1.13–15.

44 YT 2.5–6, 2.21, 3.13.

45 Biernacki, *Renowned,* p.230n.2.

46 YT 7.27.

47 KT 3.56.

48 YT 5.21.

49 McDaniel, "Does Tantric ritual empower women?," pp.164, 163.

50 Davidson, *Indian Esoteric*, p.95.

51 I am thinking here of authors like Mary Daly, *Gyn/Ecology: The Metaethics of Radical Feminism* (Boston, MA: Beacon, 1990); Carol Christ (ed.), *Womanspirit Rising: A Feminist Reader in Religion* (San Francisco, CA: HarperOne, 1992).

52 See Elizabeth Spelman, *Inessential Women: Problems of Exclusion in Feminist Thought* (London: The Women's Press, 1988); Naomi Schor and Elizabeth Weed (eds.), *The Essential Difference* (Bloomington, IN: Indiana University Press, 1994); Butler, *Gender Trouble: Feminism and the Subversion of Identity* (New York: Routledge, 1990). As Spivak comments, "We must of course remind ourselves, our positivist feminist colleagues in charge of creating the discipline of women's studies, and our anxious students, that essentialism is a trap" (*The Spivak Reader*, p.68).

53 Alison Stone, "On the genealogy of women: A defense of anti-essentialism," in Stacy Gillis et al. (eds), *Third Wave Feminism: A Critical Exploration* (London: Palgrave MacMillan, 2007), p.16. Likewise, Spelman wants to "point to and undermine a tendency in dominant Western feminist thought to posit an essential 'womanness' that all women have and share in common despite the racial, class, religious, ethnic and cultural differences among us. . . The notion of a generic 'woman'. . . obscures the heterogeneity of women and cuts off examination of the significance of such heterogeneity for feminist theory and political activity" (*Inessential,* p.ix).

54 Stone, "On the genealogy of women," p.19.

55 Butler, *Gender Trouble*, p.19.

56 YT 5.25.

57 KT 7.15–16.

58 Butler, *Bodies that Matter: On the Discursive Limits of "Sex"* (New York: Routledge, 1993), p.231. See Butler, *Gender Trouble*, p.vii.

59 Butler, *Bodies*, p.95. "The materiality of sex is constructed through a ritualized repetition of norms" (p.x).

60 Butler, *Bodies*, p.10. See Ellen T. Armour and Susan M. St. Ville (eds), *Bodily Citations: Religion and Judith Butler* (New York: Columbia University Press, 2006), p.5: "rather than being an expression of (immutable) sex, gender, sex,

masculinity and femininity are learned bodily performances that masquerade as natural by invoking bodily markers (primary and secondary sex characteristics) as their signature and guarantee. Our binary sex/gender systems arises not from nature but from a social system of compulsory heterosexuality that requires desire to channel itself via these subjectivities" (p.5).

61 Norma Broude, "Mary Cassatt: Modern woman or the cult of true womanhood," *Woman's Art Journal* 21, no.2 (2000–1), p.37. For the classic work on the "cult of true womanhood," see Barbara Welter, *Dimity Convictions: The American Woman in the Nineteenth Century* (Athens: Ohio University Press, 1976).

62 Falwell, quoted in Robert Detweiler, *Uncivil Rights: American Fiction, Religion and the Public Sphere* (Bloomington, IN: Indiana University Press, 1996), p.126.

63 Gupta, "The Goddess, women and their rituals in Hinduism," in Mandakranta Bose (ed.), *Faces of the Feminine in Ancient, Medieval and Modern India* (New York: Oxford University Press, 2000), p.95.

64 KT 8. 118–19; see YT 1.4.

65 YT.7.32.

66 Dehejia, *Yoginī*, p.224n. On this point, see also McDaniel, "Does Tantric ritual empower women?"

67 Campbell, *Traveller*, p.103.

68 Śītalā Prasāda Upādhyāya (ed.), *Tripurārṇava Tantra* (Varanasi: Sampurnanand Sanskrit University, 1992), 1.196–97. See TA 29.123; Dupuche, *Abhinavagupta: The Kula Ritual, as Elaborated in Chapter 29 of the Tantrāloka* (Delhi: Motilal Banarsidass, 2003), p.132.

69 Brahmānandagiri, Rājanātha Tripāṭhī (ed.), *Śāktānandataraṅgiṇī* (Varanasi: Sampurnanand Sanskrit University, 1987), 2.31–2.

70 Tarkatīrtha, Hemantakumāra (ed.), *Mātṛkābhedatantram* (Calcutta: Navabhārata Publishers, 1978), 7.17–19.

71 YogT 1.13. 2–8.

72 Davidson, *Indian Esoteric*, p.95; see Lynn Teskey Denton, "Varieties of Hindu female asceticism," in Julia Leslie (ed.), *Roles and Rituals for Women* (Rutherford, NJ: Fairleigh Dickenson University Press, 1991), pp.211–31.

73 See McDaniel, "Does Tantric ritual empower women?" pp.159–75.

74 See Kripal, *Kālī's Child: The Mystical and the Erotic in the Life and Teachings of Ramakrishna* (Chicago: University of Chicago Press, 1998), pp.77ff; Madhu Khanna, "Parallel worlds of Madhobi Ma, 'Nectar Mother.' My encounter with a twentieth century tantric saint," in Durre S. Ahmed (ed.), *Gendering the Spirit* (New York: Zed Books, 2002), pp.137–54; Loriliai Biernacki, "Shree Maa of Kamakhya," in Karen Pechilis (ed.), *The Graceful Guru: Female Gurus in India and the United States* (New York: Oxford University Press, 2004), pp.179–202. See Chapter 7 below.

75 Gupta, "Women in the Śaiva/Śākta ethos," in Julia Leslie (ed.), *Roles and Rituals for Hindu Women* (Rutherford, NJ: Fairleigh Dickenson University Press, 1991), p.209n. See Erndl, "The goddess."

76 Interview, Kāmākhyā temple, February 10, 2000.

77 Holland, *Deleuze and Guattari's Anti-Oedipus: Introduction to Schizoanalysis* (New York: Routledge, 1999), p.120. See Armour and St. Ville, *Bodily Citations*, p.7.

78 "As a sedimented effect of a reiterative or ritual practice, sex acquires its naturalized effect, and, yet, it is also by virtue of this reiteration that gaps and fissures are opened up as the constitutive instabilities in such constructions, as that which escapes or exceeds the norm. . . This instability is the *de*constituting possibility in the very process of repetition, the power that undoes the very effects by which 'sex' is stabilized" (Butler, *Bodies*, p.10).

79 Holland, *Deleuze,* p.120.

80 Butler, Afterward to Armour and St. Ville, *Bodily Citations*, p.285. "The paradox of subjectivation is precisely that the subject who would resist such norms is itself enabled, if not produced, by such norms. Although this constitutive constraint does not foreclose the possibility of agency, it does locate agency as reiterative or rearticulatory practice, immanent to power, and not a relation of external opposition to power" (Butler, *Bodies*, p.15).

81 Jantzen, *Power, Gender and Christian Mysticism* (New York: Cambridge University Press, 1995), p.120.

82 Jantzen, *Power,* p.146.

83 Braude, *Radical Spirits: Spiritualism and Women's Rights in Nineteenth-Century America* (Bloomington, IN: Indiana University Press, 1989), p.23.

84 Braude, *Radical Spirits*, p.201.

85 YT 2.22; KCT 3.12–17. As Sanderson notes, "feared and revered, they unleashed all the awesome power of impurity, that feminine essence whose recognition and suppression . . . was enjoined on the orthodox as essential to the preservation of the social order through caste purity" ("Purity and power," p.202).

86 Interviewed in Wares, "Shakti." See also Erndl, "The goddess," p.19.

87 Spivak, *The Spivak Reader,* p.214.

88 Butler, *Gender Trouble,* pp.24, 136, 141.

89 Butler, *Gender Trouble*, pp.69, 146. See William E. Deal and Timothy K. Beal, *Theory for Religious Studies* (New York: Routledge, 2004), pp.68–9: "every social-symbolic order [is] a regulatory consolidation of power ... Such an order is established and maintained by prohibitions and repeated performances of identities within that order. Yet ... to be *constituted* within such a symbolic order is not to be *determined* by it. There is always the possibility of agency."

Chapter Six

1 Śaṅkaradeva, *Kīrttana-ghoṣa*, Maheswar Neog (ed.) (Guwahati: Lawyer's Book Stall, 1962), 3.23.

2 Eliot, *Hinduism and Buddhism, volume II: An Historical Sketch* (London: E. Arnold, 1921), p.290.

3 Bronson, in H.K. Barpujari (ed.), *American Missionaries and North-East India, 1836–1900: A Documentary Study* (Guwahati: Spectrum Publications 1986), p.205.

4 See Sircar, *Śākta Pīṭhas* (Delhi: Motilal Banarsidas, 1973), p.17.

5 Aubrey Cantlie, *The Assamese: Religion, Caste and Sect in an Indian Village* (London: Curzon, 1984), p.ix.

6 See Urban, *Tantra: Sex, Secrecy, Politics and Power in the Study of Religion* (Berkeley, CA: University of California Press, 2003), chapters 2 and 4.

7 Sanjib Baruah, *India Against Itself: Assam and the Politics of Nationality* (Philadelphia, PA: University of Pennsylvania Press, 1999), pp.21–4.
8 Eliot, *Hinduism and Buddhism, volume II*, p.290.
9 McClintock, *Imperial Leather: Gender and Sexuality in the Imperial Contest* (New York: Routledge, 1997), p.5; Stoler, *Race and the Education of Desire: Foucault's History of Sexuality and the Colonial Order of Things* (Durham, NC: Duke University Press, 1995), p.7.
10 Neog, *Early History of the Vaiṣṇava Faith and Movement in Assam* (Delhi: Motilal Banarsidass, 1980), p.85.
11 Sarma, *Assamese Literature* (Wiesbaden: Harrassowitz, 1976), p.53; see Acharyya, *The History of Medieval Assam: From the Thirteenth to the Seventeenth Centuries* (Gauhati: Dutta, Baruah and Company, 1966), pp.262–3.
12 Kakati, *Mother Goddess Kāmākhyā* (Guwahati: Lawyer's Book Stall, 1952), p.79.
13 Basu, *Assam in the Ahom Age* (Calcutta: Sanskrit Pustak Bandhar, 1970), p.229.
14 Cantlie, *The Assamese*, p.153; see Maheswar Neog, *Sankaradeva* (New Delhi: National Book Trust, 1967), p.25.
15 Cantlie, *The Assamese*, p.256.
16 Śaṅkaradeva, *Kīttana-ghoṣa*, 3.52.
17 Śaṅkaradeva, *Kīrttana-ghoṣa*, 3.23.
18 Śaṅkaradeva, *Bhakti-ratnakāra*, Maheswar Neog (ed.) (Patiala: Publication Bureau, Punjabi University, 1982), 21.17.
19 Cantlie, *The Assamese*, 260.
20 Śaṅkaradeva, *Kīrtana-ghoṣa*, 3.47. See *Bhakti-ratnakāra*, 7.6, 23.21–2.
21 Śaṅkaradeva, *Kīrtana-ghoṣa*, 3.40–1.
22 Śaṅkaradeva, *Kīrtana-ghoṣa*, 3.58.
23 Śaṅkaradeva, *Bhakti-ratnakāra*, 23.35.
24 Barua, *Temples and Legends of Assam* (Bombay: Bharatiya Vidya Bhavan, 1965), pp.121–2. See Biernacki, *Renowned Goddess of Desire: Women, Sex and Speech in Tantra* (New York: Oxford University Press, 2007), p.188.
25 H.V. Sreenivasa Murthy, *Vaiṣṇavism of Śaṅkaradeva and Rāmānuja* (Delhi: Motilal Banarsidass, 1973), pp.201–2.
26 Śaṅkaradeva, in B.K. Kakati (ed.), *Aspects of Early Assamese Literature* (Gauhati: Gauhati University Press, 1959), p.79.
27 Cantlie, *The Assamese*, p.116.
28 Mishra, *Kamakhya: A Socio-Cultural Study* (New Delhi: D.K. Printworld, 2004), p.73n.3
29 F. Kingdon Ward, *Plant Hunting at the Edge of the World: Travels of a Naturalist in Assam and Upper Burma* (Little Compton, RI: Theophrastus Reprints, 1974 [1930]), p.4.
30 T.T. Cooper, *The Mishmee Hills: An Account of a Journey Made in Attempt to Penetrate Thibet from Assam to Open New Routes for Commerce* (London: Henry S. King and Co., 1873), p.14.
31 Cooper, *The Mishmee Hills*, p.65.
32 Cooper, *The Mishmee Hills*, p.102.
33 Gait, *A History of Assam* (Calcutta: Thacker Spink and Co., 1933 [1905]), pp.9, 7.
34 Cooper, *The Mishmee Hills*, p.234. See Endle's discussion of sacrifice among Kacharis, pp.40–1.

35 Eliot, *Hinduism and Buddhism*, volume II, p.290.
36 Lyall, "The province of Assam," *Journal of the Society of Arts* (June 5, 1903), p.619.
37 A.C. Banerjee, "Resumptions and annexations, 1838–58," in H.K. Barpujari (ed.), *The Comprehensive History of Assam* (Guwahati: Publicaiton Board Assam, 1990), v.4, pp.107–8.
38 Lyall, "The province of Assam," p.625.
39 Cooper, *The Mishmee Hills*, p.106.
40 Gait, *A History of Assam*, p.8.
41 Jayeeta Sarma, "Missionaries and print culture in nineteenth-century Assam: The *Orunodoi* periodical of the American baptist mission," in Robert Frykenberg (ed.), *Christians and Missionaries in India: Cross-Cultural Communication Since 1500* (London: RoutledgeCurzon, 2003), p.257.
42 Sarma, "Missionaries," p.257.
43 Sarma, "Missionaries," p.272.
44 Barpujari (ed.), *American Missionaries and North-East India, 1836–1900: A Documentary Study* (Guwahati: Spectrum Publications 1986), p.xxx.
45 Baruah, *India Against Itself*, p.37.
46 Barpujari, *American Missionaries,* pp.xxxix, xiv.
47 *Jubilee Papers,* in Barpujari, *American Missionaries,* pp.178–9. As Rev. Miles Bronson commented in a letter of 1843, "The present race of Assamese seem to have set their faces like flint against all innovation, while their ignorance and indolent habits unite to oppose our efforts of their good" (Barpujari, *American Missionaries*, p.206).
48 Endle, *The Kacharis* (Delhi: Cosmo Publications, 1975), p.33.
49 Endle, *The Kacharis,* p.53.
50 Barpujari, *American Missionaries,* pp.xiii, li.
51 Swain, *Youth Unafraid: A Century of Christian Adventure in South China, Assam, Bengal-Orissa, South India* (New York: Baptist Board of Education, 1935), p.40.
52 Barpujari, *American Missionaries*, p.xlix.
53 J.P. Mills in Barpujari, *American Missionaries*, p.xlviii.
54 Barpujari, *American Missionaries*, p.xlviii. In Mizoram, the Baptist missionaries imposed a complete ban on beer, participation in festivals, native songs, and any other connections with the old religion. See Lalsangkima Pachuau, *Ethnic Identity and Christianity: A Socio-Historical and Missiological Study of Christianity in Northeast India* (New York: Peter Lang, 2002), p.100. The Welsh missionaries in the region likewise rejected any element within Khasi–Jaintia culture that they believed had religious implication, including sacrifice, belief in spirits, dances, cremation of the dead, and ancestor worship. See O.L. Snaitag, *Christianity And Social Change in Northeast India* (Calcutta: Firma KLM, 1993), pp.126–7.
55 Letter of Rev. Miles Bronson, June 28, 1852, in Barpujari, *American Missionaries,* p.209.
56 Wedgewood, cited in Baruah, *India Against Itself*, p.38.
57 This was an actual conversation on the Brahmaputra Express, 20 January 2001.
58 Baruah, *India Against Itself*, p.37.
59 Murthy, *Vaiṣṇavism*, p.41.

60 Neog, *Sankaradeva*, p.5.
61 White, *Kiss*, p.262.

Chapter Seven

1 Interviewed by Tracy Wares, director, "Shakti: The Performance of Gender Roles at Kamakhya, Assam," video documentary for a Senior Honors Thesis, Department of Anthropology, University of California, Berkeley, 2001.
2 Saraswati, *Shree Maa: The Life of a Saint* (Napa, CA: Devi Mandir Publications, 1997), p.122.
3 Barbara Carrellas, *Urban Tantra: Sacred Sex for the Twenty-first Century* (Berkeley, CA: Celestial Arts, 2007), back cover advertisement.
4 KRT 41–53.
5 Cassandra Lorius, *Tantric Secrets: 7 Steps to the Best Sex of Your Life* (London: Thorsons, 2003).
6 Altman, *Global Sex* (Chicago: University of Chicago Press, 2001), pp.106–21. See also Paul Heelas (ed.), *Religion, Modernity and Postmodernity* (London: Blackwell, 1998), pp.5–6.
7 McDermott, *Mother of My Heart, Daughter of My Dreams: Kālī and Umā in the Devotional Poetry of Bengal* (New York: Oxford University Press, 2001), p.3.
8 Urban, *The Economics of Ecstasy: Tantra, Secrecy, and Power in Colonial Bengal* (New York: Oxford University Press, 2001), chapters 3, 7; *Tantra: Sex, Secrecy, Politics and Power in the Study of Religion* (Berkeley, CA: University of California Press, 2003), chapter 4.
9 Mishra, *Kamakhya: A Socio-Cultural Study* (New Delhi: D.K. Printworld, 2004), pp.47–8. See p.73n.3.
10 Interview with a priest at the Bhairavī temple, January 15, 2008.
11 Interview at Sibsagar, Assam, March 5, 2006.
12 Mishra, *Kamakhya*, pp.48–9.
13 Mishra, *Kamakhya*, p.49.
14 Mishra, *Kamakhya*, p.54. On snake worship in Assam, see Harināth Sarma Doloi, *Asamat Śakti-Sādhanā āru Śākta-Sāhitya* (Nalbari, India: Padmapriya Library, 1999), pp.199–208. On the worship of Manasā in Bengal, see Manasi Dasgupta and Mandakranta Bose, "The goddess–woman nexus in popular religious practice," in Mandakranta Bose (ed.), *Faces of the Feminine in Ancient, Medieval and Modern India* (New York: Oxford University Press, 2000), pp.148–61.
15 B.K. Barua, *Temples and Legends of Assam* (Bombay: Bharatiya Vidya Bhavan, 1965), pp.39–40. The Rabhas, who worshiped the snake deity with animal sacrifices, are claimed by some to be the originators of Manasā worship in Kamrup district. See R. Rabha, *Rabha Jana Jāti* (Jorhat: Assam Sahitya Sabha, 1974), p.101.
16 Praphulladatta Goswami, "Hindu and tribal folklore in Assam," *Asian Folklore Studies* 26, no.1 (1967), p.21; Barua, *Temples and Legends*, pp.40–1.
17 Doloi, *Asamat Śakti Sādhanā*, p.208.
18 Mishra, *Kamakhya*, pp.56–8. See Subhendugopal Bagchi, *Eminent Indian Śākta Centres in Eastern India* (Calcutta: Punthi Pustak, 1980), pp.166–7.
19 "Twelve lakh turnout as Ambubachi ends," *The Telegraph*, June 26, 2008, http://www.telegraphindia.com/1080626/jsp/guwahati/story_9463608.jsp (accessed April 19, 2009).

20 "Hundreds of sadhus descend, Ambubachi mela starts," *OneIndia*, June 21, 2008, http://news.oneindia.in/2008/06/21/hundreds-of-sadhus-descend-ambubachi-mela-starts-1214053377.html (accessed April 19, 2009).
21 Mishra, *Kamakhya*, pp.52–4.
22 The priests claim that during the monsoon the iron-rich soil naturally turns the water in the shrine red; however, many skeptics believe the priests actually pour vermillion powder into the water. See "In Guwahati, the goddess has her periods," *India Travel Times*, April 24, 2004, http://www.indiatraveltimes.com/legend/kamakhya.html (accessed April 19, 2009).
23 Interview, Kāmākhyā temple, February 20, 2006.
24 Wares, "Shakti."
25 Interviews, Kāmākhyā temple, June 20–25, 2006; see Mishra, *Kamakhya*, p.53.
26 Interview, Kāmākhyā temple, February 18, 2005.
27 Barua, *Temples and Legends*, p.38; Dold, "Mahavidyas at Kamarupa: Dynamics of transformation in Hinduism." *Religious Studies and Theology* 23, no.1 (2004), p.102.
28 Interviewed by Wares, "Shakti."
29 Janet Chawla, "Celebrating the divine female principle," *Boloji.com*, September 16, 2002, http://www.boloji.com/wfs/wfs082.htm (accessed April 19, 2009).
30 Tāntrika Śrī Kāmadeu Pūjārī, *Sarva Manokāmanā Siddhi Tantra Mantra* (Guwahati: Amar Prakāśa, 2007), p.iii.
31 Tāntrikācārya Śrī Bhairava Śāstrī, *Kāmākhyā Tantrasāra* (Calcutta: Rajendra Library, 1987); Śāstrī, *Kāmarūpī Tantrasāra* (Calcutta: Rajendra Library, n.d.); *Kāmarūpīyā Tantramantra āru Ouṣadh* (Guwahati: Duttabaruwa Publishing, 2004).
32 Dehejia, *Yoginī*, p.60.
33 S.C. Banerji, *Companion to Tantra* (New Delhi: Abhinav Publications, 1990), p.139.
34 K.N. Sarma (ed.), *Kāmaratna Tantra* (Guwahati: Lawyer's Book Stall, 1998), p.i.
35 KRT 9–14.
36 KRT 24–5, 34, 53, 92, 118, 120, 123–29.
37 KRT 69, 75, 67, 76–7.
38 KRT 55, 61.
39 KRT 56.
40 KRT 59.
41 KRT 60.
42 KRT 65.
43 KRT 68.
44 Tāntrika Śrīkāmadeva Pujāri, *Sarva Manokāmana Siddhi Tantramantra* (Guwahati: Āmār Prakāśa, 2003); Tāntrikācārya Śrī Bhairava Śāstrī, *Sāontālī Vaśīkaraṇa Tantra* (Calcutta: Rejendra Library, n.d.); Tāntrikācārya Śrī Bhairava Śāstrī, *Bṛhat Yantra-Mantra Vidhāna Rahashya* (Calcutta: General Library and Press, n.d.).
45 See Johnson, *Sorrows of Empire: Militarism, Secrecy and the End of the Republic* (New York: Metropolitan Books, 2004), pp.283–311.
46 Maa, *Living with the Soul* (Napa, CA: Devi Mandir Publications, 2007), pp.51–2.

47 Maa, *Living*, pp.140–1.
48 Saraswati, *Shree Maa*, p.47.
49 Maa, *Living*, p.29.
50 Saraswati, *Shree Maa*, p. 38.
51 "Meet Swamiji," ShreeMaa.org, June 6, 2006, http://www.shreemaa.org/drupal/taxonomy_menu/54/87 (accessed April 19, 2009).
52 Loriliai Biernacki, "Shree Maa of Kamakhya," in Karen Pechelis (ed.), *The Graceful Guru: Hindu Female Gurus in India and the United States* (New York: Oxford University Press, 2004), p.196.
53 Saraswati, *Shree Maa*, p.114.
54 Maa, *Living*, pp.175–6.
55 Biernacki, "Shree Maa," p.187. See Johnsen, *Daughters of the Goddess: The Women Saints of India* (St. Paul, MN: Yes International, 1994).
56 Saraswati, *Shree Maa*, p.136.
57 Shree Maa, "There are no 'Alien Hindus,'" *Hinduism Today* 12, no.4 (1990), reproduced on the ShreeMaa.org Web site: http://www.shreemaa.org/drupal/blog/webdev (accessed December 1, 2008).
58 "Cosmic puja," ShreeMaa.org, December 12, 2006, http://www.shreemaa.org/drupal/node/831 (accessed April 19, 2009).
59 Maa, *Living*, pp.28–9. See also Biernacki, "Shree Maa," p.197.
60 Saraswati, *Shree Maa*, p.120.
61 Saraswati, *Shree Maa*, p.46.
62 Biernacki, "Shree Maa," p.193.
63 Interview with Swami Satyananda, August 7, 2007.
64 "Cosmic altar and puja," Shreemaa.org Web site, 1997, http://www.shreemaa.org/drupal-4.7.3/cosmic_altar_and_puja_2 (accessed July 1, 2008). See also Satyananda, "Mantra, yantra and tantra," Shreemaa.org Web site, 2007, http://www.shreemaa.org/drupal/yantra_mantra_and_tantra (accessed April 19, 2009).
65 Interview with Swami Satyananda, August 6, 2007.
66 Interview with Swami Satyananda, August 7, 2007.
67 Interview with Swami Satyananda, August 7, 2007.
68 "Ambuvaci," Shreemaa.org, June 22, 2006, http://www.shreemaa.org/drupal/node/485 (accessed April 19, 2009).
69 KAT 2.4–9.
70 "What we do," Shreemaa.org, May 30, 2006, http://www.shreemaa.org/drupal-4.7.3/taxonomy_menu/46/60 (accessed April 19, 2009).
71 Biernacki, "Shree Maa," pp.180–1.
72 E-mail interview, December 3, 2008. In fact, their response emphasized quite traditional notions of femininity: "Shree Maa certainly promotes feminine values and attributes, like nourishment and compassion. She also says that women . . . can make every home a divine place of worship."
73 Maa, *Living*, p.180.
74 Gross, *Feminism and Religion: An Introduction* (Boston, MA: Beacon Press, 1990), pp.26–7.
75 Halbfass, *India and Europe: An Essay in Understanding* (Albany, NY: SUNY Press, 1988), pp.339–40, 441–2.
76 Heelas, *Religion, Modernity and Postmodernity* (London: Blackwell, 1998), p.5.
77 Altman, *Global Sex*, pp.106, 117, 121.

78 Garrison, *Tantra: The Yoga of Sex* (New York: Julian Press, 1964). On Rajneesh and other neo-Tantric gurus, see Urban, *Tantra*, chapter 6.
79 Val Sampson, *Tantra between the Sheets: The Easy and Fun Guide to Mind-Blowing Sex* (Berkeley, CA: Amorata Press, 2003), back cover.
80 Tantra.com Web site, August 9, 2008, http://www.tantra.com/tantra/ (accessed April 19, 2009).
81 Carrellas, *Urban Tantra*, pp.xv, xiv.
82 Sprinkle, forward, to *Urban Tantra*, p.xv.
83 David Ramsdale, *Red Hot Tantra: Erotic Secrets of Red Tantra for Intimate, Soul-to-Soul Sex and Ecstatic, Enlightened Orgasms* (Beverly, MA: Quiver, 2004), p.12.
84 Zygmunt Bauman, *Modernity and Ambivalence* (Cambridge, MA: Polity, 1991), p.278.
85 Heelas, *Religion*, p.5
86 Heelas, *Religion*, p.6. See also Bryan Wilson, *Contemporary Transformations of Religion* (New York: Oxford University Press, 1976), p,277; Bryan S. Turner, *Orientalism, Postmodernism and Globalism* (New York: Routledge, 1994), p.9.
87 On the empire of the market, see Drury, "There can be life beyond politics," *Calgary Herald*, May 16, 1998, http://www.uregina.ca/arts/CRC/herald_belife.html. As Altman suggests, one way of defining globalization is simply "a further stage of capitalism and the incorporation. . . of larger parts of the world than ever before into the capitalist system" (*Global Sex*, p.21).

Conclusion

1 Foucault, *Religion and Culture* (New York: Routledge, 1999), p.113.
2 On contemporary imperialism "in its death-throes," see Michael Hardt, "From Imperialism to Empire," *The Nation*, July 13, 2006. http://www.thenation.com/doc/20060731/hardt/1.
3 See Jeremy R. Carrette, *Foucault and Religion: Spiritual Corporeality and Political Spirituality* (New York: Routledge, 2000); Rita Grosz, *Volatile Bodies: Toward a Corporeal Feminism* (Bloomington: Indiana University Press, 1994).
4 Pollock, "Deep Orientalism? Notes on Sanskrit and power beyond the raj," in Carol A. Breckenridge and Peter van der Veer (eds), *Orientalism and the Postcolonial Predicament* (Philadelphia, PA: University of Pennsylvania Press, 1993)," pp.79–80.
5 Marcus and Fischer, *Anthropology as Cultural Critique: An Experimental Moment in the Human Sciences* (Chicago: University of Chicago Press, 1986), p.138.
6 Turner, *Orientalism, Postmodernism, Globalism* (New York: Routledge, 1994), p.103. See King, *Orientalism and Religion: Postcolonial Theory, India and "The Mystic East"* (New York: Routledge, 1999), pp.217–18; Fred Dallmayr, *Beyond Orientalism: Essays on Cross-Cultural Encounter* (Albany, NY: SUNY Press, 1996).
7 Alameddine, *Koolaids: The Art of War* (New York: Picador, 1999), p.94. See Dennis Altman, *Global Sex* (Chicago: University of Chicago Press, 2001), pp.148–49.
8 McNair, *Striptease Culture: Sex, Media and the Democratization of Desire* (New York: Routledge, 2002), pp.7, 38.

9 Pollock, "Deep Orientalism," p.117.
10 Drury, "There can be life beyond economics and politics," *Calgary Herald,* May 16, 1998, http://www.uregina.ca/arts/CRC/herald_belife.html. This is what Bryan S. Turner likewise calls "the everyday nature of imperial penetration of cultures via the materiality of commodity exchanges" (*Orientalism,* p.18).
11 Dipesh Chakrabarty, *Provincializing Europe: Postcolonial Thought and Historical Difference* (Princeton: Princeton University Press, 2000).
12 See Johnson, *Sorrows of Empire: Militarism, Secrecy and the End of the Republic* (New York: Metropolitan Books, 2004) pp.283–312; Ferguson, *Colossus: The Price of America's Empire* (New York: Penguin, 2004); Hardt, "From Imperialism to Empire", and many other critiques of waning US imperial power.
13 McClintock, *Imperial Leather: Gender and Sexuality in the Imperial Contest* (New York: Routledge, 1997), p.15.
14 Lawrence, "From fundamentalism to fundamentalisms: A religious ideology in multiple forms," in Paul Heelas (ed.), *Religion, Modernity and Postmodernity* (Oxford: Blackwell, 1998), p.99.
15 See Urban, *Tantra: Sex, Secrecy, Politics and Power in the Study of Religion* (Berkeley, CA: University of California Press, 2003), chapter 6.
16 Campbell, *Traveller in Space: In Search of Female Identity in Tibetan Buddhism* (New York: George Braziller, 1996), p.171.
17 Prashad, "Letter to a young American Hindu," *Passtheroti.com,* May 17, 2007, http://www.passtheroti.com/?p=487.
18 Pollock, "Deep Orientalism?" p.115.
19 Pollock, "Deep Orientalism?" p.116.
20 King, *Orientalism,* p.190.
21 King, *Orientalism,* p.95.
22 Carrette, *Foucault,* p.146.
23 Foucault, "Le clef mythique de la révolte de l'Iran," in *Dits et écrits, 1948–1988* (Paris: Gallimard, 1994), v.3, p.716. See Foucault, "Questions of Method," in Graham Burchell, Colin Gordon, and Peter Miller (eds.), *The Foucault Effect: Studies in Governmentality* (Hemel Hempstead: Harvester Wheatsheaf, 1991), pp.73–86.
24 Carrette, *Foucault,* p.140. See Grosz, *Volatile Bodies,* pp.164 65.
25 Deleuze, *Essays Critical and Clinical* (Minneapolis: University of Minnesota Press, 1997), p.131.
26 Grosz, *Volatile Bodies,* p.23
27 Hollywood, *Sensible Ecstasy,* p.278. See also Kripal's discussion of the "enlightenment of the body" in *Esalen: American and the Religion of No Religion* (Chicago: University of Chicago Press, 2007), pp.456–59.

SELECT BIBLIOGRAPHY

Abbreviations

AVT *Akulavīra Tantra*. In Prabodh Chandra Bagchi (ed.), *Kaulajñānanirṇaya and Some Minor Texts of the School of Matsyendranātha*. Calcutta: Metropolitan Printing and Publishing House, 1934.

BNT *Bṛhannīla Tantra*. Madhusudhan Kaul (ed.). Delhi: Butala and Company, 1984.

BTS *Bṛhat-Tantrasāra* of Kṛṣṇānanda Āgamavāgīśa. Śrīrasikamohana Caṭṭopādhyāya (ed.). Calcutta: Navabhārata Publishers, 1996.

BVT *Brahmavaivarta Purāṇa*. Shanti Lal Nagar (ed.). New Delhi: Parmal Publications, 2001.

DBP *Devībhāgavata Purāṇa* of Kṣemarāja Śrī Kṛṣṇdāsa. Delhi: Nag Publishers, 1986.

HT *Hevajra Tantra: A Critical Study*. David Snellgrove (ed.). London: Oxford University Press, 1959.

KAN *Kaulāvalīnirṇayah* of Paramahamsa Śrī Majjñānānanda. Varanasi: Chowkhamba Sanskrit Series, 2005.

KAT *Kulārṇava Tantra*. Taranatha Vidyaratna (ed.). Delhi: Motilal Banarsidass, 1975.

KCT *Kulacūḍāmaṇi Tantra*. Arthur Avalon (ed.). Madras: Ganesh and Co., 1956.

KJN *Kaulajñānanirṇaya and Some Minor Texts of the School of Matsyendranātha*. Prabodh Chandra Bagchi (ed.). Calcutta: Metropolitan Printing and Publishing House, 1934.

KKV *Kāmakalāvilāsa* of Puṇyānandanātha. Arthur Avalon (ed.). Madras: Ganesh and Co., 1961.

KP *Kālikā Purāṇa*. B.N. Shastri (ed.). Delhi: Nag Publishers, 1991.

KRT *Kāmaratna Tantra*. K.N. Sarma (ed.). Guwahati: Lawyer's Book Stall, 1998.

KT *Kāmākhyā Tantra*. Viśvanārāyaṇa Śāstrī (ed.). Varanasi: Bhāratīya Vidyā Prakāśana, 1990.

MB *The Mahābhārata, volume II.* J.A.B. van Buitenen (ed.). Chicago: University of Chicago Press, 1975.

MBP *The Mahābhāgavata Purāṇa: An Ancient Treatise on Śakti Cult.* Pushpendra Kumar (ed.). Delhi: Eastern Book Linkers, 1983.

MMT *Muṇḍamālatantram.* Śrī Pañcānana Śāstrī (ed.). Calcutta: Navabhārata Publishers, 1980.

PTT *Prāṇatoṣinī Tantra* of Rāmatoṣaṇa. Soumyānanda Nāth (ed.). Calcutta: Navabhārata Publishers, 1991.

SB *Śatapatha Brāhmaṇa.* Julius Eggeling (ed.). Delhi: Motilal Banarsidas, 1963.

TA *Tantrāloka* of Abhinavagupta with the commentary of Jayaratha. M.K. Śāstrī (ed.). Śrīnagar: Kashmir Series of Texts and Studies, 1921–38.

YogT *Yoginī Tantra.* B.N. Shastri (ed.). Delhi: Bhāratīya Vidyā Prakāśana, 1982.

YT *Yoni Tantra.* J.A. Schoterman (ed.). Delhi: Manohar, 1980.

Other works in Assamese, Bangla, and Sanskrit

Āśrama, Daṇḍīsvāmī Damodara (ed.). *Jñānārṇava Tantra.* Calcutta: Navabhārata, 1982.

Baragohāiṅ, Gaṅgāprasād. "Tāi āhomer hindudharma grahaṇ āru paravatī asamar rājnītit iyār prabhāv." In Praphulla Dās and Candan Phukan (eds). *Mahādev.* Śivasāgar, India: Śivarātri Udyāpan Samiti, 2006.

Barua, Golap Chandra (ed.). *Ahom Buranji: From the Earliest Time to the End of Ahom Rule.* Guwahati: Spectrum Publications, 1985.

Baruwā, Guṇābhirām. *Āsām Burañjī.* Guwahati: Asam Prakāśana Pariṣad, 1972.

Baruwa, Harakanta (ed.). *Assam Buranji: A History of Assam from the Commencement of Ahom Rule to the British Occupation of Assam.* Guwahati: Dept. of Historical and Antiquarian Studies, 1962.

Baruwa, Śrī Rudreśvara. *Mahātīrtha Kāmākhyā.* Calcutta: Rajendra Library, n.d.

Bhattcharyya, Benyotosh (ed.). *Śaktisaṅgama Tantra.* Baroda: Oriental Institute, 1932–78.

Bhaṭṭācārya, Debendranāth. *Asamat Śaktipūjā.* Guwahati: Bāṇī Prakāśa, 1977.

Bhaṭṭācāryya, Mahendra Nāth. *Śrī Śrī Kāmākhyā-Tīrtha.* Guwahati: D. Bhaṭṭācāryya Press, 2000.

Bhuyan, Suryya Kumar (ed.). *Deodhāi Asam Burañjī.* Gauhati: Department of Historical and Antiquarian Studies, 1962.

—. *Kachārī Burañjī.* Gauhati: Department of Historical and Antiquarian Studies, 1984.

Brahmānandagiri. *Śāktānandataraṅginī.* Rājanātha Tripāṭhī (ed.). Varanasi: Sampurnanand Sanskrit University, 1987.

Cakravartī, Ābhārāṇī. *Puṇyatīrtha Kāmākhyā.* Guwahati: Savitā Prakāśa, 2005.

Dāsa, Jyotirlāla (ed.). *Māyātantram: Mūla Saṃskṛta o Bāṅgānuvada Sameta.* Calcutta: Navabhārata, 1978.

Devaśarmā, Dharaṇīkānta. *Kāmākhyā Darśan*. Guwahati: Kāmākhyā Pradarśanī, n.d.

Doloi, Harināth Sarma. *Asamat Śakti-Sādhanā āru Śākta-Sāhitya*. Nalbari, Assam: Padmapriya Library, 1998.

Khan, Amantullah. *Cooch Behārer Itihās*. Cooch Behar: Cooch Behar State Press, 1936.

Kuvalayānanda, Swāmī and S.A. Shukla (eds). *Gorakṣaśatakam*. Bombay: Kaivalyadhāma S.M.Y.M Samiti, 1974.

Nigamānanda, Svāmī. *Tāntrik Guru, vā Tantra o Sādhana Padhati*. Calcutta: Sāradā Press, 1991 (1911).

Phukan, Kashinath Tamuli. *Assam Buranji*. Calcutta, 1906.

Śaṅkaradeva. *The Bhakti-ratnakāra*. Maheswar Neog (ed.). Patiala: Publication Bureau, Punjab University, 1982.

—. *Kīrttana-ghoṣa*. Maheswar Neog (ed.). Guwahati: Lawyer's Book Stall, 1962.

Sarasvatī, Nigamānanda. *Tāntrik-Guru, vā Tantra o Sādhana Padhati*. Jorhat, Assam: Āsām-Bāṅgīya Sārasvata Maṭh, 1981.

Sarma, Gaṅgā. *Kāmākhyāy Tāntrik Pūjā o Paddhati*. Guwahati: Viṣṇu Prakāśa, 2001.

—. *Kāmarūpa Kāmākhyā: Itihāsa o Dharmmamūlaka*. Guwahati: Viṣṇu Prakāśa, 2003.

Sarma, N.C. (ed.). *Daraṅga Rājavaṃśāvalī*. Guwahati: Bāṇī Prakāśa, 1973.

Śāstrī, M. "Dharma āru darśan." In G. Sarma (ed.). *Asamīya Jātir Itivṛtta*. Jorhat, Assam: Assam Sāhitya Sabhā, 1977.

Śāstrī, Tāntrikācārya Śrī Bhairava. *Kāmākhyā Tantrasāra*. Calcutta: Rajendra Library, 1987.

—. *Kāmarūpī Tantrasāra*. Calcutta: Rajendra Library, n.d.

Tarkaratna, P. (ed.). *Kālikāpurāṇam: Mūla Saṃskṛta o Bāṅgānuvāda sameta*. Calcutta: Navabhārata, 1977.

Tarkatīrtha, Hemantakumāra (ed.). *Mātṛkābhedatantram*. Calcutta: Navabhārata Publishers, 1978.

Upādhyāya, Śītalā Prasāda (ed.). *Tripurārṇava Tantram*. Varanasi: Sampurnanand Sanskrit University, 1992.

Works in English and European languages

Acharyya, N.N. *The History of Medieval Assam: From the Thirteenth to the Seventeenth Centuries*. Gauhati: Dutta, Baruah and Company, 1966.

Adhikary, Gajendra. *A History of the Temples of Kamrup and Their Management*. Guwahati: Chandra Prakash, 2001.

Armour, Ellen T. and Susan M. St. Ville (eds). *Bodily Citations: Religion and Judith Butler*. New York: Columbia University Press, 2006.

Bahadur, K.P. *Caste, Tribes and Culture of India: Assam*. Delhi: Ess Ess Publications, 1977.

Barkataki, S. *Tribes of Assam*. New Delhi: National Book Trust, 1969.

Barpujari, H.K. *The Comprehensive History of Assam: Ancient Period.* Publication Board of Assam, 1990.

—. *The American Missionaries and North-east India (1836–1900 AD): A Documentary Study.* Guwahati: Spectrum Publications, 1986.

Barua, B.K., *Temples and Legends of Assam.* Bombay: Bharatiya Vidya Bhavan, 1965.

—. *A Cultural History of Assam (Early Period).* Gauhati: Bina Library, 1986.

Barua, K.L. *Early History of Kamarupa.* Guwahati: Lawyer's Book Stall, 1966.

Basu, Nirmal Kumar. *Assam in the Ahom Age.* Calcutta: Sanskrit Pustak Bandhar, 1970.

Bataille, Georges. *Erotism: Death and Sensuality.* San Francisco: City Lights, 1986.

—. *The Accursed Share, volumes II and III.* New York: Zone Books, 1999.

Beane, Wendell C. *Myth, Cult and Symbols in Śākta Hinduism: A Study of the Indian Mother Goddess.* Leiden: E.J. Brill, 1977.

Beck, Brenda. "The goddess and the demon: A local south Indian festival and its wider context," *Puruṣārtha* 5 (1981), pp.83–136.

Best, Steven and Douglas Kellner. *Postmodern Theory: Critical Interrogations.* New York: Guilford Publications, 1991.

Bharati, Agehananda. *The Tantric Tradition.* New York: Anchor Books, 1970.

Bhattacharyya, Narendranath. *History of the Śākta Religion.* New Delhi: Munshiram Manoharlal, 1974.

Biardeau, Madeleine and Charles Malamoud. *Le sacrifice dans l'Inde ancienne.* Paris: Presses universitaires de France, 1976.

—. *Hinduism: The Anthropology of a Civilization.* Paris: Flammarion, 1981.

—. "Devi: The goddess in India." In Yves Bonnefoy (ed.). *Asian Mythologies.* Chicago: University of Chicago Press, 1993, pp.95-98.

—. *Stories about Posts: Vedic Variations around the Hindu Goddess.* Chicago: University of Chicago Press, 2004.

Biernacki, Loriliai. "Shree Maa of Kamakhya." In Karen Pechilis (ed.). *The Graceful Guru: Female Gurus in India and the United States.* New York: Oxford University Press, 2004.

—. *Renowned Goddess of Desire: Women, Sex and Speech in Tantra.* New York: Oxford University Press, 2007.

Bose, Samaresh. "The Tantrik quest," *Sunday*, January 25, 1981. http://www.shrikali.org/tantricquest.php (accessed April 19, 2009).

Braverman, M. Amy. "The interpretation of Gods." *University of Chicago Magazine* 97, no.2 (2004). http://magazine.uchicago.edu/0412/features/index.shtml (accessed April 19, 2009).

Briggs, George Weston. *Gorakhnāth and the Kānphata Yogīs.* Delhi: Motilal Banarsidass, 1938.

Brooks, Douglas R. *The Secret of the Three Cities: An Introduction to Hindu Śākta Tantra.* Chicago: University of Chicago Press, 1990.

Brown, W.B. *An Outline of the Deori Chutiya Grammar.* Shillong: Assam Secretariat Printing Office, 1895.

Brunner, H., G. Oberhammer, and A. Padoux (eds). *Tāntrikābhidhānakośa: Dictionairre des termes techniques de la littérature hindoue tantrique II.* Wien: Verlag der Österreichischen Akademie der Wissenschaften, 2004.

Butler, Judith. *Subjects of Desire: Hegelian Reflections in Twentieth Century France.* New York: Columbia University Press, 1987.

—. *Bodies that Matter: On the Discursive Limits of "Sex."* New York: Routledge, 1993.

—. "Afterward." In Ellen T. Armour and Susan M. St. Ville (eds).*Bodily Citations: Religion and Judith Butler.* New York: Columbia University Press, 2006.

—. *Gender Trouble: Feminism and the Subversion of Identity.* New York: Routledge, 1989.

Caldwell, Sarah and Brian K. Smith. "Introduction: Who Speaks for Hinduism?" *Journal of the American Academy of Religion* 68, no.4 (2000): 705-710.

Cantlie, Aubrey. *The Assamese: Religion, Caste and Sect in an Indian Village.* London: Curzon, 1984.

Carrette, Jeremy R., *Foucault and Religion: Spiritual Corporality and Political Spirituality.* New York: Routledge, 2000.

Choudhury, P.C. *The History of the People of Assam to the Twelfth Century AD.* Gauhati: Department of Historical in Assam, 1966.

Coburn, Thomas B. *Encountering the Goddess: A Translation of the Devī-Māhātmya and a Study of its Interpretation.* Albany, NY: SUNY Press, 1991.

Courtright, Paul. "Silenced for hinting at an Indian oedipus," *Times Higher Education,* November 28, 2003. http://www.timeshighereducation.co.uk/story.asp?storyCode=181462şectioncode=26 (accessed April 19, 2009).

—. "Studying religion in an age of terror: Internet death threats and scholarship as a moral practice," *The Academic Exchange,* April–May 2004. http://www.emory.edu/ACAD_EXCHANGE/2004/aprmay/courtright.html (accessed April 19, 2009).

Davidson, Ronald M. *Indian Esoteric Buddhism: A Social History of the Tantric Movement.* New York: Columbia University Press, 2002.

Dehejia, Vidya. *Yoginī Cult and Temples: A Tantric Tradition.* Delhi: National Museum, 1986.

Deka, Pranav. *Nīlācala Kāmākhyā: Her History and Tantra.* Guwahati: Lawyer's Book Stall, 2004.

Deleuze, Gilles. "Désir et plaisir." *Magazine littéraire* 325 (October 1994), pp.59–65.

Deleuze, Gilles and Félix Guattari, *Anti-Oedipus: Capitalism and Schizophrenia.* Minneapolis, MN: University of Minnesota Press, 1983.

Devsharma, Sree Dharanikanta. *The Holy Shrine of Kamakhya.* Guwahati: The Author, 1999.

Dold, Patricia. "The mahavidyas at Kamarupa: Dynamics of transformation in Hinduism." *Religious Studies and Theology* 23, no.1 (2004), pp.89–122.

Doniger, Wendy. "Tantric bodies." *Times Literary Supplement,* May 2004. http://www.indology.net/printout30.html (accessed April 19, 2009).

Doniger, Wendy and Sudhir Kakar, trans. *The Kamasutra: A New Complete English Translation of the Sanskrit Text.* New York: Oxford University Press, 2002.

Douglas, Mary. *Purity and Danger: An Analysis of Concepts of Pollution and Taboo.* London: Routledge, 1966.

Dupuche, John R. *Abhinavagupta: The Kula Ritual, as Elaborated in Chapter 29 of the Tantrāloka.* Delhi: Motilal Banarsidass, 2003.

Eliade, Mircea. *Yoga: Immortality and Freedom.* Princeton: Princeton University Press, 1971.

Eliot, Sir Charles. *Hinduism and Buddhism: An Historical Sketch.* London: Routledge and Kegan Paul, 1921.

Endle, S. *The Kacharis.* Delhi: Cosmo Publications, 1975.

Erndl, Kathleen M. "The goddess and women's power: A Hindu case study." In Karen L. King (ed.). *Women and Goddess Traditions.* Minneapolis, MN: Fortress Press, 1997, pp.17–38.

Ferguson, Niall. *Colossus: The Price of America's Empire.* New York: Penguin, 2004.

Finn, Louise M., trans. *The Kulacūḍāmaṇi Tantra and the Vāmakeśvara Tantra.* Wiesbaden: Otto Harrassowitz, 1986.

Flood, Gavin. *The Tantric Body: The Secret Tradition of Hindu Religion.* London: I.B. Tauris, 2006.

Foucault, Michel. *Language, Counter-Memory, Practice: Selected Essays and Interviews.* Ithaca, NY: Cornell University Press, 1977.

—. *The History of Sexuality, Volume I: An Introduction.* New York: Vintage, 1978.

—. *Power/Knowledge: Selected Interviews and Other Writings.* New York: Pantheon, 1980.

Gait, Edward Albert. "Human sacrifice in ancient Assam," *Journal of the Royal Asiatic Society of Bengal* 67 (1898), pp.56–65.

—. *A History of Assam.* Calcutta: Thacker, Spink and Co., 1963.

Gohain, Bikash Chandra. *Human Sacrifice and Head-Hunting in Northeastern India.* Gauhati: Lawyer's Book Stall, 1977.

Goswami, Kali Prasad, *Kamakhya Temple: Past and Present.* New Delhi: A.P.H. Publishing Corporation, 1998.

Government of Assam. *Assam District Gazetteer.* Shillong: Govt. of Assam, 1967.

Gupta, Sanjukta, Teun Goudriaan, and Dirk Jan Hoens. *Hindu Tantrism.* Leiden: E.J. Brill, 1979.

Halbfass, Wilhelm. *India and Europe: An Essay in Understanding.* Albany, NY: SUNY Press, 1988.

Harper, Katherine Anne and Robert L. Brown (eds). *The Roots of Tantra.* Albany, NY: SUNY Press, 2002.

Heesterman, J.C. *The Inner Conflict of Tradition: Essays in Indian Ritual, Kingship and* Society. Chicago: University of Chicago Press, 1985.

—. The *Broken World of Sacrifice: An Essay in Ancient Indian Ritual.* Chicago: University of Chicago Press, 1993.

Hiltebeitel, Alf. *The Cult of Draupadī, vol. 2: On Hindu Ritual and the Goddess.* Chicago: University of Chicago Press, 1991.

Holland, Eugene. *Deleuze and Guattari's Anti-Oedipus: Introduction to Schizoanalysis.* New York: Routledge, 1999.

Hollywood, Amy. *Sensible Ecstasy: Mysticism, Sexual Difference and the Demands of History.* Chicago: University of Chicago Press, 2002.

Hoy, David Cousins (ed.) *Foucault: A Critical Reader.* New York: Basil Blackwell, 1986.

Inden, Ronald. *Imagining India.* Cambridge, MA: Blackwell, 1990.

Johnsen, Linda. *Daughters of the Goddess: The Women Saints of India.* St. Paul, MN: Yes International, 1994.

Kakati, Banikanta. *The Mother Goddess Kamakhya.* Guwahati: Publication Board, Assam, 1989.

—(ed.). *Aspects of Early Assamese Literature.* Gauhati: Gauhati University Press, 1959.

Karmakar, Rahul. "The temple revives human sacrifice," *BBC News*, April 2, 2002.

Khanna, Madhu. "The goddess–woman equation in the Tantras." In Durre S. Ahmed (ed.). *Gendering the Spirit; Women, Religion and the Post-Colonial Response.* New York: Zed Books, 2002, pp.35–69.

King, Richard. *Orientalism and Religion: Postcolonial Theory, India and 'The Mystic East.'* New York: Routledge, 1999.

Kooij, K.R. van. *Worship of the Goddess according to the Kālikāpurāṇa.* Leiden: E.J. Brill, 1972.

Kripal, Jeffrey J. *Kālīs' Child: The Mystical and the Erotic in the Life and Teachings of Ramakrishna.* Chicago: University of Chicago Press, 1998.

—. *The Serpent's Gift: Gnostic Reflections on the Study of Religion.* Chicago: University of Chicago Press, 2007.

Kristeva, Julia. *Powers of Horror: An Essay on Abjection.* New York: Columbia University Press, 1982.

Lincoln, Bruce. *Discourse and the Construction of Society: Comparative Studies in Myth, Ritual and Classification.* New York: Oxford University Press, 1989.

Malamoud, Charles. *Cooking the World: Ritual and Thought in Ancient India.* Delhi: Oxford University Press, 1996.

Malhotra, Rajiv. "Wendy's child syndrome," *Sulekha.com*, September 2002. http://rajivmalhotra.sulekha.com/blog/post/2002/09/risa-lila-1-wendy-s-child-syndrome.htm (accessed April 19, 2009).

—. "What is the political agenda behind American studies of South Asian Tantra?"*Svabhinava.org*, May 27, 2004. http://www.svabhinava.org/friends/RajivMalhotra/WendyWhite-frame.html (accessed April 19, 2009).

Marcus, George E. and Michael M. Fischer. *Anthropology as Cultural Critique: An Experimental Moment in the Human Sciences.* Chicago: University of Chicago Press, 1986.

Marglin, Frédérique Apffel. *Wives of the God-King: The Rituals of the Devadasis of Puri.* New York: Oxford University Press, 1985.

—. "Female sexuality in the Hindu world." In Clarissa W. Atkinson (ed.). *Immaculate and Powerful: The Female in Sacred Image and Social Reality*. Boston, MA: Beacon Press, 1985, pp.39–60.

McClintock, Anne. *Imperial Leather: Gender and Sexuality in the Imperial Contest*. New York: Routledge, 1997.

McDaniel, June. "Does Tantric ritual empower women?" In Tracy Pintchman (ed.). *Women's Lives, Women's Rituals in the Hindu Tradition*. New York: Oxford University Press, 2007, pp.159–75.

McNay, Lois. *Foucault: A Critical Introduction*. New York: Continuum, 1994.

Mishra, Nihar Ranjan. *Kamakhya: A Socio-Cultural Study*. New Delhi: D.K. Printworld, 2004.

Nath, D. *History of the Koch Kingdom, 1515–1615*. Delhi: Mittal Publications, 1989.

Neog, Maheshwar. *Early History of the Vaiṣṇava Faith and Movement in Assam*. Delhi: Motilal Banarsidass, 1980.

O'Flaherty, Wendy Doniger. *The Origins of Evil in Hindu Mythology*. Berkeley, CA: University of California Press, 1976.

—, trans. *The Rig Veda*. New York: Penguin, 1984.

—. *Other Peoples' Myths*. New York: MacMillan, 1988.

Olivelle, Patrick, trans. *The Early Upaniṣads: Annotated Text and Translation*. New York: Oxford University Press, 1998.

—. *Dharmasūtras: The Law Codes of Ancient India*. New York: Oxford University Press, 1999.

Orzech, Charles. *Politics and Transcendent Wisdom: The Scripture for Humane Kings in the Creation of Chinese Buddhism*. University Park, PA: Pennsylvania State University Press, 1998.

Padoux, André. "What do we mean by Tantrism?" In Katherine Anne Harper and Robert L. Brown (eds). *The Roots of Tantra*. Albany, NY: SUNY Press, 2002, pp.17–24.

—. "Tantrism, an overview." In Mircea Eliade (ed.). *Encyclopedia of Religion*, vol.14. New York: MacMillan, 1986, pp.272–4.

Pollock, Sheldon. "Deep Orientalism? Notes on Sanskrit and power beyond the raj." In Carol A. Breckenridge and Peter van der Veer (eds). *Orientalism and the Postcolonial Predicament*. Philadelphia, PA: University of Pennsylvania Press, 1993, pp.76–133.

Rawson, Philip. *The Art of Tantra*. London: Routledge, 1973.

Said, Edward. "Representing the colonized: Anthropology's interlocutors." *Critical Inquiry* 15 (Winter, 1989), pp.217–24.

Sanderson, Alexis. "Purity and power among the brahmins of Kashmir." In Michael Carrithers, Steven Collins and Steven Lukes (eds). *The Category of the Person: Anthropology, Philosophy, History*. Cambridge: Cambridge University Press, 1985, pp. 190–216.

Saraswati, Swami Satyananda. *Shree Maa: The Life of a Saint*. Napa: Devi Mandir Publications, 1997.

Sarma, Chandra Kanta. *An Early History of Kamarup Kamakhya*. Gauhati: Kalita Art Press, 1998.

Sarma, P.C. *Architecture of Assam*. Delhi: Agam Kala Prakashan, 1988.

Sarma, Satyendranath. *Assamese Literature*. Wiesbaden: Harrassowitz, 1976.

Sastri, B.N. "Destruction of the Kamakhya temple as referred to in Yogini Tantra." *Journal of the Assam Research Society* 14 (1979–80), pp.6–7.

Shapiro, Lily. "Discourse for whom? Knowledge, power, complicity and irony in the debate between American academics and Hindus," Honors Thesis, Department of Anthropology, Amherst College, 2008.

Sharma, M. "Religion." In H.P. Barpujari (ed.).*The Comprehensive History of Assam: Ancient Period*. Guwahati: Publication Board, Assam, 1990.

Sharma, Mukunda Madhava. *Inscriptions of Ancient Assam*. Gauhati: Gauhati University, 1978.

Shaw, Miranda. *Passionate Enlightenment: Women in Tantric Buddhism*. Princeton, NJ: Princeton University Press, 1994.

Shulman, David. *Tamil Temple Myths: Sacrifice and Divine Marriage in South Indian Śaiva Tradition*. Princeton, NJ: Princeton University Press, 1980.

Silburn, Lilian. *Kuṇḍalinī: Energy of the Depths*. New York: SUNY Press, 1988.

Sircar, D.C., *The Śākta Pīṭhas*. Delhi: Motilal Banarsidas, 1973.

Smith, Brian K. *Reflections on Ritual, Resemblance and Religion*. New York: Oxford University Press,1989.

—. *Classifying the Universe: The Ancient Indian Varna System and the Origins of Caste*. New York: Oxford University Press, 1994.

Urban, Hugh B. "The extreme Orient: The construction of 'Tantrism' as a category in the Orientalist imagination." *Religion* 29 (1999), pp.123–46.

—. "The path of power: Impurity, kingship and sacrifice in Assamese Tantra." *Journal of the American Academy of Religion* 69, no.4 (2001), pp.777–816.

—. *The Economics of Ecstasy: Tantra, Secrecy, and Power in Colonial Bengal*. New York: Oxford University Press, 2001.

—. *Tantra: Sex, Secrecy, Politics and Power in the Study of Religion*. Berkeley, CA: University of California Press, 2003.

—. "The power of the impure: Transgression, violence and secrecy in Bengali Śākta Tantra and modern western magic." *Numen* 50, no.3 (2003), pp.269–308.

—. "Matrix of power: Tantra, kingship and sacrifice in the worship of mother goddess Kāmākhyā." *South Asia* 31, no.3 (2008), pp.500–34.

—. "Hinduism in Assam." In Knut A. Jacobsen (ed.). *The Encyclopedia of Hinduism*. Leiden: Brill, forthcoming.

Wares, Tracy, director. "Shakti: The Performance of Gender Roles at Kamakhya, Assam." Video documentary for a Senior Honors Thesis, Department of Anthropology, University of California, Berkeley, 2001.

White, David Gordon (ed.). *Tantra in Practice*. Princeton, NJ: Princeton University Press, 2000.

—. *Kiss of the Yoginī: Tantric Sex in its South Asian Contexts*. Chicago: University of Chicago Press, 2003.

—. "Tantrism: An overview." In Lindsay Jones (ed.). *Encyclopedia of Religion.* New York: MacMillan, 2005, pp.8984–7.

Wilson, H.H., trans. *The Vishnu Purana, a System of Hindu Mythology and Tradition.* Calcutta: Punthi Pustak, 1972.

Woodroffe, Sir John. *The World as Power.* Madras: Ganesh and Co., 1974.

Woodward. Mark R. "Economy, polity and cosmology in the Ao Naga Mithan Feast." In Susan D. Russell (ed.). *Ritual, Power and Economy: Upland-Lowland Contrasts in Mainland Southeast Asia,.* Northwestern Illinois University Center for Southeast Asian Studies, 1989, pp.121–42.

—. "Gifts for the sky: Animal sacrifice, head hunting and power among the Naga of Burma and Assam," In Graham Harvey (ed.). *Indigenous Religions: A Companion.* New York: Cassell, 2000, pp.219–29.

Zimmer, Heinrich. "On the significance of the Tantric yoga." In Joseph Campbell (ed.). *Spiritual Disciplines: Papers from the Eranos Yearbooks.* New York: Pantheon, 1960, pp.3–58.

INDEX

Abhinavagupta 10
abhiṣeka 105
Ahoms 27, 47, 74, 77–78, 82–86, 90, 96, 101, 147, 158, 170, 214n49
Akulavīra Tantra 40, 121
Ambuvācī Melā 53–55, 71, 91, 97, 170–2, 176, 181
Assam 2–4, 8–10, 28–29, 32, 36–40, 42, 44, 46, 52, 56, 61, 63, 65, 70, 72, 75, 81, 87, 91, 97–98, 100–102, 105, 109, 111, 118, 121–2, 130, 132, 137, 147–64, 168, 173–6, 222n13, 224n41, 228n47
  as birthplace of Tantra 2, 8–9, 32, 39–40, 100, 156, 198n27, 212n6
  as "extreme Orient" 155, 158

Bengal 34, 38, 44, 57, 63, 81, 84, 139, 148–9, 151, 162, 167, 170, 176–7, 222n13, 224n41
Bataille, Georges 53, 68, 99, 119
bhaga 48, 110–11, 133, 219n51
Bhāgavad Gīta 51
Bhairava 41, 58–59, 63, 70, 93, 103, 209n21
Bhairavī 41, 54, 59, 63, 103, 130, 168
bhairavī cakra 105
Biardeau, Madeleine 19, 51–52, 87
blood 9, 24, 26–28, 31, 43, 48, 50, 52, 57, 60–62, 65–69, 71, 74, 78, 87, 90, 93–94, 98–102, 110, 115, 119, 121, 130–1, 135, 171–2, 175, 180, 189, 208n3
Bodos 8, 44, 46, 170
body 3, 10, 19–20, 24–26, 37, 49, 55–56, 67, 69, 73, 101, 103, 106–7, 115, 117, 121, 172, 188, 194–6, 233n27
Brahman 31, 114, 117
Brāhmaṇas 51, 62, 92
Brahmaputra 38, 84, 158
Bṛhannīla Tantra 199n32
Bṛhat Tantrasāra 100, 109
Buddha 121
Buddhist Tantra 37–38, 40, 42–43, 73, 127, 137–8
buffaloes 27, 52, 62–65, 75, 84, 90–91, 102, 110–11, 118, 130, 169, 172, 210n48–9, 212n4, 219n49
burañjīs 10, 96
Butler, Judith 23–24, 128, 134–6, 140–1, 144, 202n93, 207n87, 224n59–60

cakra pūjā 104–5, 122, 137
cakras 108, 114, 139, 185, 218n36
Cāmuṇḍā 41, 48, 95–96
capitalism 16, 26–7, 167, 183, 185–6, 191, 232n87
Caryāpadas 42
Christianity 1, 9, 28, 125, 136, 141, 147–9, 158–63, 179, 184, 186
  missionaries 1, 19, 28, 99, 125, 147–9, 158–63, 165, 228n47, 228n54
Chutiyas 46, 92, 97, 101, 147, 170
colonialism 2, 10–12, 16, 18, 28–29, 74, 140, 147–9, 154–63, 165, 183, 186, 192, 199n38

colonialism (*cont*).
cultural 16
neo- 140, 186, 199n38
Cooch Behar 10, 81, 111, 132, 150, 199n32, 217n10
consumerism 6, 11–12, 167, 183, 185–6, 191
Courtright, Paul xi, 2, 14, 200n59

ḍākinī 8, 48
dakṣiṇācāra 102, 168, 181
Deleuze, Gilles 3, 10, 22–23, 49–50, 101, 128, 140–1, 188, 195, 202n92–3
desire 3–4, 9, 19–25, 48, 69, 82, 101, 103, 105, 108, 123, 129, 135, 175, 202n92–3, 203n94
Devī Bhāgavata Purāṇa 53–54
Dharmapāla 38, 77–78
Doniger, Wendy xi, 2, 12–15, 20, 200n59
Durgā 45–47, 63, 84, 89, 96, 120, 133, 169, 178, 212n11, 215n69

Earth 45, 54, 80, 116, 208n6
essentialism 28, 134–6, 143, 224n52–3

feminism 125–45, 172, 182, 203n100, 224n52–3
"Five M's" 102–3, 105, 109
Foucault, Michel 1, 3, 10, 22–25, 32, 49–50, 119, 143, 187–8, 194–5, 203n100, 207n84

Garos 8, 46–47, 161, 206n69, 207n72
gender 25, 32, 125–145, 182, 188, 224n60

Hevajra Tantra 37–38
Hindu nationalism 7, 17–18, 26
Hinduism 7, 14–15, 17–18, 44, 51–52, 67, 71–72, 79, 81, 149, 151, 157, 160–2, 192–3, 201n70
Hirapur 33, 41, 52, 57

imperialism 7, 10–11, 13, 15–17, 26, 158, 186–95, 199n38, 201n66
American 12–13, 15–17
market 16, 186, 191, 201n66, 232n87
neo-imperialism 29, 199n38
impurity 19, 26–27, 51, 53, 55, 67, 72, 74, 78, 87, 92–95, 97–98, 112–13, 115–21, 130, 181, 221n86, 226n85
Indrapāla 42, 77–78, 213n21–2, 213n33
Invading the Sacred 1, 13, 16–17, 193
Islam 36, 96, 147–8, 151, 165, 212n6

Jaintias 8, 46, 83, 85, 92, 96, 157–8, 216n97, 228n54
Jālandhara 34–35, 38, 107
Jñānārṇava Tantra 221n86

Ka Meikha 46
Kālī 47–48, 95–96, 147, 157–8, 167, 177, 209n11, 219n54
Kālīghāṭ 33, 36
Kālikā Purāṇa 5, 10, 20–21, 27, 34, 38, 40–41, 44–45, 48, 51–52, 57–60, 62–63, 73–74, 78, 80, 88–96, 98, 100–103, 121–2, 130, 169, 199n32
kāma 2–3, 10, 19–25, 47, 82, 101, 166, 188, 190, 194, 218n36
defined 20
Kāma (deity) 21, 40, 69, 77–78, 98, 103, 118, 219n53
Kāma Sūtra 20, 73
Kāmakalāvilāsa 1
Kāmākhyā 2–3, 5–6, 27–29, 31–32, 38–41, 44, 46–49, 52, 54, 57, 61–62, 68–71, 74, 77, 80–84, 86, 96–98, 100, 103, 106, 118, 122–3, 144–5, 148, 153, 157, 163, 166–73, 176–84, 187, 204n23, 207n72, 211n63, 213n33, 217n10
composite goddess 46–48
identified with the female *yoni* 106
possibly a tribal deity 46, 207n72

Kāmākhyā Tantra 10, 47–48, 71, 101, 109–12, 116, 122, 132–3, 135, 199n32, 217n10, 218n31, 219n50–1
Kāmaratna Tantra 172–5
Kāmarūpa 9, 31, 34–35, 37–40, 54, 76–78, 81–82, 86, 100–1, 103–4, 106–8, 114, 143, 204n27, 205n39, 205n46, 214n49, 218n36
identified with the *yoni* 105–8, 218n36
secret 106, 218n32
Kāmeśvara 38, 77, 98, 213n33
Kāmeśvarī 38, 47, 98
Kāpālikās 4, 43, 58–59, 131–2
Kashmir 32, 36
Kashmir Śaivism 10, 13, 101
Kaula 4, 39–40, 57, 132, 177
Kaulajñāna Nirṇaya 10, 40, 70–71, 101, 120–1, 199n32, 210n49, 219n49, 221n87
Kaulāvalī Nirṇaya 57, 106, 130
Kecāi Khātī 46, 97, 216n102
Khajuraho 33, 76, 118
Khasis 8, 46–47, 92, 158, 169, 210n50, 228n54
kingship 4, 25, 27–28, 38–39, 69–71, 73–98, 144, 161–2, 188, 193, 212n4, 213n22, 213n26, 213n28, 214n66, 215n69
impurity of 78–88
kirātas 44–45, 59, 104
Koch dynasty 27, 74, 77–78, 81–84, 101, 139, 147, 150, 212n6, 214n45
Kolkata 16, 162, 173, 195
Krama 4
Kripal, Jeffrey J. xi, 2, 12–14, 26, 200n41, 200n59, 233n27
Kṛṣṇa 149–52, 178
Kubjikā 35, 114, 204n13
Kubjikā Tantra 54
kula 105–6, 110, 112–13, 120, 130, 181, 218n31–2
kula cakra 219n51
kula dravya 111–13
Kulacūḍāmaṇi Tantra 31, 37, 107, 219n53, 223n36
Kulārṇava Tantra 109, 181, 219n55
kulayāga 100, 108–9
kumārī 128–9, 169, 222n23
kumārī pūjā 129, 169, 222n23, 223n24
kuṇḍalinī 113–15, 122, 204n13

"left-hand" Tantra 102–4
liṅgam 35, 48, 109, 111, 128, 135, 218n36, 219n51
liquor 9, 115, 130

magic 4, 8–10, 59, 148, 157, 163, 166, 172–5
Mahābhārata 44, 61–62, 78, 100, 203n7
Mahiṣamardinī 31, 130
maithuna 102, 114, 116, 119, 137
Malhotra, Rajiv 12–13, 15–18, 200n59
Manasā 169–70, 229n14
Mātṛkābheda Tantra 139
Matsyendranātha 39–42, 120–1, 139, 205n39
Māyā Tantra 218n47
meat 57–59, 102–3, 114, 117, 130, 147, 151
menstrual blood 23, 53–56, 110, 128–30, 132, 171–2, 209n11, 218n47, 219n49–50, 221n86, 223n36
menstruation 2, 23, 50, 52–57, 71, 80, 110, 116, 170–2, 174–7, 181, 187, 208n6, 218n47
mlecchas 59, 76, 81–82, 86, 103–4, 116, 121
Mughals 74, 85, 96, 101

Nagas 8, 64–65, 92, 161–2
Nātha 4, 171
Naraka 27, 45, 74, 76–77, 80–82, 85–86, 98, 116
Naranārāyaṇa Siṅgha 74, 78, 83–86, 214n45
New Age 1–2, 99, 126

Orientalism 1–2, 4, 7 ,11, 15–16, 18–19, 26, 99, 122, 125, 148, 155, 184, 187, 189–93, 198n14
  neo–Orientalism 2–3
  "recovering Orientalist" 14–15, 19
orgasm 22, 114, 184–5

Pāla dynasty 27, 38–39, 41, 64, 77–78, 81, 87–88, 96, 101, 147, 204n27
pañcamakāra 102, 221n90
parakīyā 116, 167, 220n71, 224n41
postcolonial studies 193
power 1, 3, 11, 15, 19, 21–28, 39, 46, 48–50, 53, 56, 59–60, 66–71, 73, 78, 85, 88, 94, 97–98, 101–2, 113, 117, 119, 121, 127–8, 130–1, 138, 144–5, 175, 187–9, 192, 207n86, 209n11, 226n85, 226n89
Prāgjyotiṣapura 9, 44, 80
Prāṇatoṣiṇī Tantra 100, 109, 223n37
prostitutes 45, 105, 116–17, 128–9, 132, 219n51
Purāṇas 9, 75, 203n7
Pūrṇagiri 31, 33–35, 38, 107
Puruṣa 35, 58–59, 63, 88–90, 93–94, 107

Ramakrishna 12–14, 139, 177–80
Ratnapāla 38, 42, 77, 88
Rudra Siṅgha 78, 85–86, 98

sacrifice 3–4, 8–9, 19, 27–28, 31, 34–36, 43, 48, 50–72, 74, 79, 84, 87–123, 148, 151, 156–8, 161, 168–70, 180, 182, 187, 206n69, 207n72, 210n39, 210n49–50, 211n63
  buffalo 62–65, 84, 90–1, 168–9, 210n48–9, 215n76, 220n57, 220n79
  horse 63, 87, 89
  human 3, 8–9, 43, 57, 62, 74, 91–97, 157–9, 215n76, 215n78
  of battle 28, 51, 61, 88, 981, 00
  of desire 28, 98–123
  Tantric 59–61, 94–95, 112, 122, 208n3, 211n63
  Vedic 58–61, 66, 94–95, 100, 112, 215n78
śākta pīṭhas 2, 9, 27, 31–50, 58, 104, 106–8, 195
  in the human body 37, 101, 104, 107–8
Śākta Tantra 3–4, 9, 12, 18, 20, 36, 38, 52, 61, 69, 73, 75, 77, 88, 91, 95, 97–98, 101, 104, 130, 137–8, 143, 149, 152, 157, 159–60, 179, 182–3, 187–8
śakti 3, 10, 19, 21–26, 31–32, 36–37, 49–50, 69, 77–78, 85, 95, 98, 104, 107–8, 111–14, 121, 129, 135–6, 143, 166, 168, 171, 182, 188, 190, 194, 219n54–5
  defined 21–22
Śaṅkaradeva 122, 147–54
Śatapatha Brāhmaṇa 62, 203n7, 210n39
Satī 27, 31, 34–36, 58–59, 107
secrecy 28, 137–8, 168
semen 23, 108–9, 111, 114, 135, 219n50
sex 1, 3, 6, 8, 12–13, 16, 19–20, 22, 24–25, 45, 49, 51, 66, 98–145, 152, 174–5, 180, 184–5, 188, 190, 194, 217n15, 219n50, 223n41, 224n59, 226n78
sexual fluids 4, 23, 28, 55, 100, 111–12, 115, 131, 135, 189, 219n50
sexual rituals 8, 28, 98–145. *See also* maithuna
  as sacrifice 99–123
Shree Maa of Kāmākhyā xi, 4, 29, 140, 166, 176–84, 195
siddhas 36, 39–43, 54, 177, 205n46, 206n48
siddhis 69–71, 166
Śiva 20, 31, 34–35, 37, 39, 47, 57–59, 65, 77, 82, 84, 93–96, 98, 103–5,

108–9, 113–14, 120–1,129, 135–6, 157, 169, 213n33, 223n36
Soma 108–9, 111–12
South Asian Studies 1–29, 187–96
Śrīvidyā 4
Swami Satyananda Saraswati xi, 165, 177–83

Tāmreśvārī 97, 159
Tantra *passim*
as "cult of ecstasy" 1
as "cult of the feminie" 126
as "extreme Orient" 4, 7–8, 148
as "path of desire" 21
as "path of power" 21, 25, 69
as "yoga of sex" 1
definitions of 4–6, 19–22, 25–26, 201n73
"left-hand" 102–104
neo-Tantra 20, 183
origins of 32, 103, 203n3
tribal elements in 42–46, 52, 57–58, 71–72, 74, 206n51
Urban 165, 185
tantras 18, 32, 61, 73, 99, 125, 131–3, 138, 181, 203n3
tāntrika 12, 18, 50, 66, 113, 133–4, 168, 171, 173, 188
Tārāpīṭha 33, 36
transgression 19, 28, 51, 53, 57, 67–69, 102–4, 118–21, 153, 181–2, 189, 208n5
tribals 8–10, 26, 42–47, 49, 52, 57–59, 61, 63–65, 67, 74–86, 91–92, 103, 160, 169–70, 175, 187, 206n51, 206n66, 211n63, 228n54
Trika 4
Tripurārṇava Tantra 138

ucchiṣṭa 112–13, 118, 219n54–5
Uḍḍiyāna 31–35, 38, 107
Ugratārā 59, 65, 103–4
United States 10–12, 16–17
Upaniṣads 51, 59–60, 108–9, 115, 122

vāmācāra 102–4, 150, 153, 168, 181
Varman dynasty 38, 75–76, 81, 87
Vasiṣṭha 80, 104
Vedas 9, 35, 42–43, 49, 51, 57–61, 67, 75, 79, 88–89, 92–93, 104, 139, 152, 215n78
veśyās 105, 116, 128–9
Victorian era 1, 20
viparīta 111, 117–18
Viṣṇu 39, 45, 47, 54, 58–59, 76, 80, 93, 103–4, 129, 139, 149–50, 223n36
Viśva Siṅgha 74, 78, 139, 212n6, 213n38

White, David Gordon xi, 2, 13, 16, 100–101, 122, 201n73, 217n15
wine 43, 54, 58–59, 102, 114, 147, 151
womb 3, 8.
women 25, 28, 55, 101, 104, 110–11, 116, 125–45, 147, 151–52, 165, 172, 188, 193, 208n6, 221n86, 222n19–20, 223n28, 224n52–3, 226n85, 231n72
as gods 131, 139, 143, 222n19, 223n36
as gurus 28, 127, 138–45, 175, 188, 222n19
as *yoginīs* 205n39
as *yonis* 133–4
identified with sacrificial altar 108–9, 112
in sexual rituals 28, 101, 104, 110–11, 125–45, 218n47

yoginī cakra 105
yoginī kaula 39–40, 42–43, 139
yoginī-pīṭha 45
yoginīs 36, 38–42, 47–48, 57–58, 76, 81–82, 82, 126, 128, 139, 168, 188, 205n39, 205n46, 219n49
yoginī temples 33, 38, 40–42, 52, 57, 76

Yoginī Tantra 10, 44, 60, 62, 74, 91–92, 98, 114–15, 117, 122, 129, 139, 187, 196, 210n49, 212n6, 218n32

yoni 2, 9, 28, 35, 37, 40–41, 47, 54, 82, 98, 105–12, 114, 117, 128, 131–6, 152, 168, 174, 218n31, 218n36

yoni pīṭha 37, 41, 48–49, 54, 104–8, 129, 168, 170

yoni pūjā 104–5, 119, 132, 137

Yoni Tantra 10, 99–101, 104–6, 109–112, 114–16, 120, 122, 125, 131–3, 135, 199n32, 199n34, 217n10

yonitattva 110–12, 118, 120

1. Kāmākhyā temple today

2. Possible Yoginī, Kāmākhyā temple grounds, ca. twelfth century

3. Bala Bhairavī, ruins behind the Bhairavī temple, ca. twelfth century

4. Siddha with female consort or disciple, Assam State Museum, twelfth to fourteenth centuries

5. Contemporary popular poster of Kāmākhyā

6. Kāmeśvarī, Kāmākhyā temple

7. Cāmuṇḍā, Kāmākhyā temple ruins, ca. twelfth century

8. Female figure with severed head, Sixty-Four Yoginī temple, Hirapur, Orissa

9. Menstruating figure, Kāmākhyā temple outer wall

10. Śākta Tantric guru, Kāmākhyā temple

11. Bhairava, Deopahar ruins, central Assam, tenth to eleventh centuries

12. Sacrificial post for goats, pigeons, and fish, Kāmākhyā temple

13. Sacrificial post for buffaloes, Kāmākhyā temple

14. Mahiṣamardinī with severed head, Kalipahara, Guwahati, tenth to eleventh centuries

15. Buffalo skull, Ugratārā temple, Guwahati

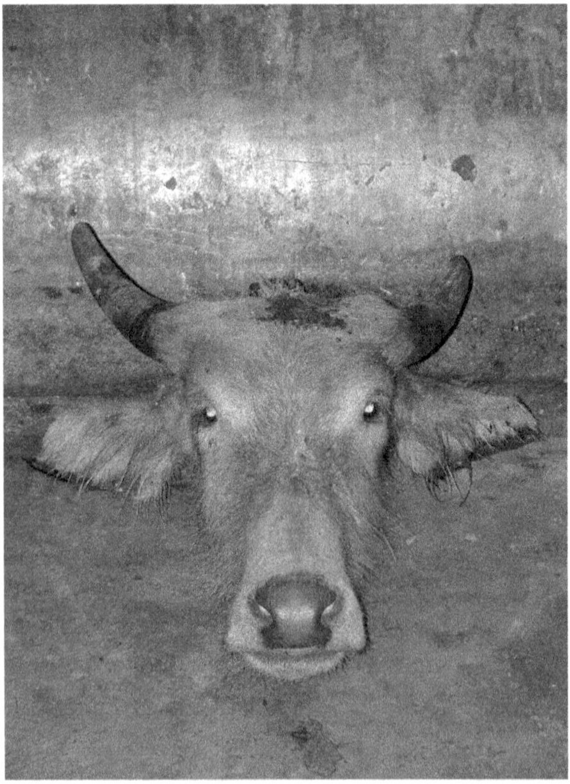

16. Severed buffalo head, Kāmākhyā temple

17. Mask worn by sacrificial victims, Jaintia Durgā temple

18. Śākta priest ladling offerings into the fire, Tārāpīṭh, West Bengal

19. Couple in *viparīta-rati*, Madana Kāmadeva temple, Assam, tenth to twelfth centuries

20. Female Śākta, Kāmākhyā temple

21. Female Śaivite, Kāmākhyā temple

22. Cover image for Kāmākhyā Tantrasāra

23. Shree Maa of Kāmākhyā

24. The "White Sadhu" and Shree Maa

www.ingramcontent.com/pod-product-compliance
Lightning Source LLC
Chambersburg PA
CBHW071248230426
43668CB00011B/1633
9781845118747